To Hugh

With best wishes
for your future
happiness
in your new home
~in Maybole

Sandra

12th October 1995.

£12.50

MAYBOLE

Carrick's Capital

Facts, Fiction & Folks

by

JAMES T. GRAY

ALLOWAY PUBLISHING,
AYR.

Copyright ©

First Puplished 1972
Reprinted 1973

This edition published
by Alloway Publishing Ltd.
1982

I.S.B.N. No. 0-907526-09-8

Printed and bound in Great Britain by
Redwood Burn Ltd, Trowbridge and Esher

CONTENTS

Chapter		Page
1.	First Facts	1
2.	Meibothelbeg and Bethoc	6
3.	Town Charter	11
4.	Seventeenth Century	14
5.	Eighteenth Century	20
6.	Nineteenth Century	24
7.	Twentieth Century	35
8.	Council Records	44
9.	Burgesses	71
10.	Industry	75
11.	Street Names	89
12.	Buildings, Past and Present	113
13.	Crossraguel Abbey	140
14.	"Adam's Ale"	143
15.	Martial Minniebolers	151
16.	Social Activities	161
17.	Sport	176
18.	Famous Folks	192
19.	Personalities	198
20.	Johnnie Stuffie	220
21.	Humour in Court and Council	225
22.	Maybole Minstrelsy	234
23.	Freemasonry in Maybole	279
24.	Robert Burns' Association with Maybole	288
25.	Abbot of Crossraguel and John Knox	297
26.	The Countess and The Gypsy	304
27.	Miscellany	310

FOREWORD

It is some 10 years since the first edition of my late father's book on Maybole was published. In the time that has elapsed, and in particular, since the book itself went out of print, many people in Maybole have felt that a further edition would be beneficial to the town.

My father was a man who had immense pride in his hometown, a pride which prompted him, after a lifetime of public involvement, to culminate his enthusiasm, by writing an authoritative account on 'Maybole', Carricks Capital, its facts, fiction and folks.

It is to be hoped that this further edition proves to be as interesting to the new generation of Minnibolers whether born or adopted, as has been evident in the past.

James F. Gray,

Craigengillan,
    Maybole.   December, 1982.

PREFACE

No book on Maybole has been published for over sixty years and it is almost impossible to get any copies of the Rev. Roderick Lawson's works or the earlier book on Carrick by the Rev. Abercrumbie. While the various Statistical Accounts may be got on loan from any Public Library these accounts, although giving vital information, must of necessity leave out many interesting sidelights in the history of the old town and I feel that a new book on Maybole is long overdue.

In this book on "Carrick's Capital" I do not intend to rival either of the two clergymen who wrote so interestingly on the town, nor do I look to providing a sequel to their books. My endeavour is to gather together in a convenient form the many factual and fictional matters of interest to Minniebolers who have a love for their birthplace and to give a picture of the town and its inhabitants over the centuries to those strangers who are wise enough to come and dwell among us.

Much of the matter has been gleaned from the town's records, old books and newspaper articles, but many of the stories have been told me by old residenters who are ever happy to crack about the days gone past to anyone really interested in them and my thanks go especially to these people who have passed on to me many of their personal recollections or stories handed down to them by their forefathers.

If the following articles give pleasure to the readers, and the old lore of Maybole is preserved for future generations, I shall be happy in the knowledge that the years I have spent in gleaning information about my beloved hometown have been fruitful and well worth while.

JAMES T. GRAY.

The Castle,
  Maybole.
May, 1972.

Chapter 1

FIRST FACTS

For many centuries the district around Maybole has been inhabited and there is evidence of this in the number of old forts sited throughout the parish, the numerous standing stones and memorial mounds and the many old relics and antiquarian finds which have been turned up from time to time. Indeed John Smith in his book *Prehistoric Man in Ayrshire* states that Maybole might well be called "the antiquarian district of Ayrshire."

There are prehistoric forts at Bowerhill in the north part of the parish near the Heads of Ayr, at Dunduff, (or Danes Hill as it was called from a tradition that a battle with the Danes was fought there) and on Trees Farm, below the quarry on How Muir, there is an excellent example of a fort which went by the name of Dun Ean and which is preserved as an ancient monument. On Kildoon Hill there is a fine example of another prehistoric fort and the monument to Sir Charles Fergusson of Kilkerran, who died in 1849 stands within its ramparts, while there are numerous other examples throughout the district.

There are several old standing stones and memorial mounds in Maybole Parish and perhaps the best known local one is in a field on Lyonstone Farm on the south side of the low road to Ayr. This stone, which is of grey granite, was probably erected to commemorate some long forgotten important event in the history of the district. There is another well known Standing Stone on Blairstone Farm near Alloway on which there is roughly engraved a cross. Local tradition has it that the cross represents Wallace's sword, which he is supposed to have laid down on the stone, but even a cursory glance shows the incised figure is not meant to represent a sword but a cross, and this stone is believed to mark the spot where a treaty was formed between the Picts and the Scots. Near the mouth of the River Doon in a field known as Stone Park there is another Standing Stone which is again believed to commemorate a treaty between Picts and Scots who seem to have been as adept at making and breaking treaties as the nations of the twentieth century.

It was a common custom to erect standing stones or memorial mounds in bygone days and on Newarkhill there used to be a flat stone set in the hillside which was said to mark the spot where the local people gathered to watch the ships of the Spanish Armada which had been blown up the firth and wrecked on the rocky headlands. Although this stone has long since disappeared and there are no local traditions about this event it is interesting to note that the records of Ayr Town Council for 1577-1578 show an entry for £4 expended for "meat and drink for the pure Spainyardis" who were shipwrecked sailors of the Spanish Armada.

For over two hundred and fifty years there was a memorial mound on the lands of West Enoch Farm which was erected to commemorate the skirmish between the Earl of Cassillis and the laird of Bargany on 11th December, 1601 when young Bargany was killed. This was erected a few years after the event but was unfortunately levelled by the tenant farmer in the latter part of the nineteenth century as undoubtedly it was the last memorial mound erected in Carrick.

In 1846 a collection of bronze celts (axes) was found on Lagg Farm, three of which are preserved in the National Museum in Edinburgh, while on Lochland Farm, just to the south of Maybole a fine Whinstone hammer axe was found in 1856. About the same period the farmer at Drumshang, when ploughing a field, turned up a bronze figure holding scales which is believed to represent "Justice", and many other stone and bronze implements have been unearthed around Maybole from time to time.

The most interesting find in the district was the discovery of crannog dwellings at Lochspouts when this loch was drained and cleaned to make the town reservoir in the 19th century. When the loch was drained the remains of a settlement of lake dwellers was found and this was one of the most important antiquarian finds in Ayrshire and indeed in Scotland. A circular wooden platform made of oak beams about 95 feet in diameter had been built on oak piles set in the loch and on this platform three stone hearths or fireplaces had been formed in stone and clay. Access to the little loch village or crannog was by a wooden gangway built just below the level of the water so that intruders would not easily find it and the inhabitants of the crannog dwelling were fairly safe from unexpected visits of not too friendly neighbours. Being sited in the loch the inhabitants of the settlements had a handy coup for their refuse and everything was thrown into the water when it was of no further use. To the antiquarians this coup proved invaluable and many interesting finds were made by carefully sifting the silt at the bottom of the loch. A large quantity of stone hammers and axes were found, also stone pestles and querns for grinding corn, nearly all made of granite, together with huge heaps of small pebbles, probably used as heating stones for the meat pots or for slingstones for hunting game. Some very fine ornaments were unearthed, many in bone in the shape of rings and pins, and a bronze ornament with a loop which probably fastened on to a hide thong to hang as a necklace, also a quantity of shaped and pierced beads. A great deal of broken pottery had been tipped into the loch and many of the shards found had decorative designs characteristic of ancient pottery of that period. One of the most interesting finds was a triangular shaped piece of rock crystal which had been carefully formed and highly polished and would be worn probably as a pendant. No doubt its owner would greatly prize it and bewail its loss over the side of the crannog platform into the loch, as it was too fine an object to have been discarded and thrown over into the natural and handy rubbish dump. A sandstone spindle whorl was also found and it would seem that the crannog dwellers of the first century were weavers as were also practically all the townspeople in the 18th and 19th centuries. Two hollowed out tree trunks (presumably used as boats) were found embedded in the silt and one was taken to a museum in Glasgow and the other given to the Marquess of Ailsa and it could be seen at the Pond Cottage at Culzean until a few years ago. There is no doubt that the discovery of the Lochspouts Crannogs was one of the most important discoveries in the country and it gives ample proof that the Maybole area has been inhabited for over two thousand years.

These small communities through the centuries no doubt gathered together to gain greater strength in numbers and probably chose the sheltered hillside on which the town now stands to form a small township long before the name of Maybole appears in the charter by Duncan dated 1193. It is rather interesting that the townspeople still draw much of their water supply from Lochspouts, which was the site of the earliest known dwellings in the district, and that two thousand years ago the town's forefathers were using water for washing and drinking from the same source as the present Minnieboler does today.

It is also of interest to learn from the antiquarian finds in the district that the people in these old days were not altogether the rude barbarians one is inclined to picture in one's mind. They lived in little communities well designed for protection against marauders and well laid out for the living needs of their day, with much thought evidently given to the choosing of suitable sites. The men of these times had spears and axes for hunting and for offence or defence as the occasion arose, their wives and daughters decorated themselves with rings, bangles and necklaces as do present day wives and daughters and their children supped from wooden porringers with bone spoons and had their unruly hair combed with bone combs just as many townspeople of this century had, in their childhood, a wooden bowl and a horn spoon. The crannog dwellers hunted animals, caught fish, and cooked their food in wood pots by throwing heated stones into the water when it was not roasted over the large fireplaces. Food and shelter were the main necessities of life then as now and if one discounts electric cookers, refrigerators, etc., there would be found to be little difference in the life of the Minnieboler over the centuries.

There are no written records or mention of the town and district until the twelfth century although this part of Scotland was mentioned by the Romans during their occupation of South Scotland. The inhabitants were then known as the Damnii, and were Druids, and there are many Druidical remains in the surrounding districts, although there are no traces of any left in Maybole Parish. In the fifth century the people of Carrick were converted to Christianity and since then it has been closely connected with religious houses and the place names give great evidence of this.

Chapter 2

MEIBOTHELBEG AND BETHOC

It is not until the 12th century that the first written reference can be found regarding Maybole as the district around the town which we know today. In the year 1193 Duncan, (son of Gilbert and grandson of Fergus) granted a charter to the Monks of Melrose of the "lands of Meibothelbeg and Bethoc in Carric" for the building of a church, and this is the first time mention is made of the original name which gradually throughout the centuries changed through various spellings to "Maybole" as it is today.

The original charter was written in Latin, and very carefully detailed the boundaries of the area and with a little study and local knowledge these boundaries are traceable to this day. The first place mentioned is "Crubder" or "Crumder" which is near the site of the old rifle range on the Howmuir on Trees Farm. A stream ran from there and marked the boundary to "Culelungford", which was near where Garryhorn Farm now stands, then followed a stream called "Poltiber" or "Polnetiber", (now known as Culroy Burn), to the River Doon at Auchendrane near Minishant. The boundary then followed the River Doon up stream to a burn called in the Charter the "Polnegarrah", (now Chapelton Burn) then followed the "Polnegarrah" up to "the little moss" between what is now Laigh Smithston and Laigh

Grange. The next traceable point in the description is "Duvah" between "Meibothelbeg" and "Meibothelmore" and it is thought this was where Slateford village was sited in later years. The boundary then continued to "Brocklaue" (now Brockloch) and by a wooded glen to the first point mentioned at "Crubder". All the area within the boundaries detailed in the old Charter was described as the lands of "Meibothelbeg".

The Charter, after detailing the lands of "Meibothelbeg", then continues with a description of the lands of "Bethoc" and once again the boundaries are easily followed by a native Minnieboler. The first point named is "Lemenelung" which is now locally called the "Spout of Lumling" on the Howmuir and is a well known spot in the district. From there the boundary followed east to "Tunregaith" on the "Polsalacharic" which is the Sauchrie Burn and follows this to the "Polnetiber" (Culroy Burn) linking up with the first area described and completing the area of "Meibothelbeg and Bethoc" gifted by Duncan to the Monks of Melrose.

The area comprised a large portion of what is now the Parish of Maybole but did not actually include the site of the present township. It is probable however that there was a clachan or small "toun" on the hillside facing south and sheltered from the north winds as it would seem to be the natural place for people to settle, having a plentiful supply of water from the many local springs and wells. Probably the site of the township was noted by the farseeing Duncan as a place of potential growth and, while he wished to make a gift to the Church, he was practical enough to give a large tract of what was then not of such value as the pleasant site of the present town and its immediate surroundings.

Meibothelbeg was the name first given to the district and as the small village grew, and became the most populous part, it would naturally assume the name. From then onwards the spelling was varied in many charters and records and was given as "Meybothel" (dropping the "beg" or "little part"), "Maybotel", "Minnyboil", "Minniebole", "Maiboil" and finally "Maybole".

Owing no doubt to such a diversity of spelling etymologists have given many derivations of the meaning of the name and even the ingenious George Chalmers seems to have been puzzled and tries to account for it by stating that "Maybottle" is from the Anglo-Saxon and means "the dwelling place of the Kinsman or cousin". Three factors however seem to discountenance Chalmers' derivation, the first being that at no time has the spelling of "Maybottle" ever been used in records except in the original charter; secondly the Celtic language was used in Carrick until a comparatively late date (some say as late as the sixteenth century) and the local people would not be likely to use Anglo-Saxon words for place names as it was then a foreign language, and thirdly there must have been many houses of kinsmen or cousins in the area and there seems no special reason why one in Maybole should be singular in any respect. The one and only time the spelling of "Maybottle" was used can be accounted for by the fact that the Monks of Melrose themselves wrote the original charter and were better acquainted with names in the South of Scotland where Anglo-Saxon was used at an early period and they probably spelled the name according to their own ideas of its meaning.

Another rather fanciful description of the name gives it as meaning "a little fold for milk cows, sometimes on the hill and sometimes on the plain". This comes from the Gaelic "Maigh" or "Mai", a plain, and "Buile" a fold for milk cows. While possibly correct it does not somehow fit or seem probable, as the "plain" below the town was, in early days, a large marsh running from what is now Allan's Hill down the valley past Myremill (the mill on the marsh) to the River Doon and it would be impossible to fold or graze cows on what was a large bog subject to continual flooding.

As Carrick was inhabited by Celtic speaking people it seems natural that the correct and most acceptable derivation should come from that language. If, however, the most common old spelling of "Minniebole" is taken it is easy to trace from it "Minnie" or "Minnyz", a moss or miry place, and "Botil', a dwelling place, giving a complete picture of Maybole as it was some centuries ago—"the town, or dwelling place, above the mire". Looking to the situation of the town on the sloping hillside above the flat ground below it, which was a large marsh until it was drained, (and is still referred to as "The Bog") this is the most acceptable and probably correct meaning of the name and is supported by the age old rhyme—

"Minniebole's a dirty Hole;
It site abune a mire",

which the youngsters of the town have chanted for generations but few of whom nowadays add the last couplet—

"But to me and hundreds like me,
It's the finest in the Shire."

It has also been said that the name means "the heath ground upon the marsh" and once again this gives an exact description, as the hillside on which the town is now built would probably be covered with heath or heather in early days. The difference between these last two derivations is so slight it can surely be accepted that the true meaning of the name is to be found in one of them. For many generations arguments have been put forward to support the various derivations given and many ingenious explanations only add to the trueness of the saying that "the manner in which etymologies have been sought from a distance, while they may be found at the very door is a satire on the researches of philological antiquaries".

Whatever the derivation may be, Maybole has meant "Home" to thousands of townspeople throughout the centuries and no "Minnieboler" ever forgets it, no matter how far he may stray, and it is not surprising so many come back to settle down in the old town to spend the last of their days at "Parliamentary Dyke" or the "Castle Corner" or to take a "daun'er" round the "Cross Roads" or the "Whinny Knowes".

Chapter 3

TOWN CHARTER

It has long been thought by many townspeople that Maybole is a Burgh of Regality and this idea was to a certain extent fostered by some earlier writers on the history of the town. There are no authoritative grounds however for such a belief and there is certainly no suggestion of it in the papers from Crossraguel Abbey, and the Abbot was the most likely person to issue such a document. The privileges granted in the Charter of 1516 are certainly more than those ordinarily granted to Burghs of Barony and are nearly equal to those of a Royal Burgh but it is wrong to class Maybole as a Burgh of Regality.

The Charter is one of Barony to "my Lord of Cassillis" and the Provost and Prebendaries of the Collegiate Church. It was confirmed on 14th November 1516 by King James V, or rather his guardian John, Duke of Albany, as the King was a young child at that time. It starts by clearly stating that the Charter was granted to "our beloved cousin and councillor, Gilbert, Earl of Cassillis, and our devout priests, the Provost and Prebendaries, of the Collegiate Church of Maybole". The magistrates and "those who sit in Counsil with them" were not to be appointed, as was customary *in a Burgh of Barony,* by the Earl, but were to be elected annually by the burgesses, and from a "leet" of seventeen the Earl was to appoint the Bailies, and this clause in the Charter gave rise to a bitter dispute between the councillors and the burgesses three hundred years later. The townspeople were granted full power and free faculty to buy and sell within the town "wine, wax, cloth and all other common merchandise", with the "power and liberty of having and holding in the said Burgh, bakers, brewers, fleshers and vendors of flesh and fish and all other tradesmen belonging *to a free Burgh of Barony*". The Charter also stated that "there be in the said Burgh free burgesses and that they have power, in all time to come, of electing annually Bailies and all other officers necessary for the government of the said Burgh". It also granted the right to the townspeople to hold a town market each Thursday and public fairs at Lammas and to have a Market Cross set up for ever. The old town cross, erected about this time, stood in the centre of the High Street until it was removed in 1773 as it was causing obstruction to traffic which had increased considerably in the second part of the eighteenth century.

From the granting of the Charter in 1516 the Burgh had the right to bear Ensigns Armorial and in 1672 an Act of Parliament was passed concerning the recordings of such armorial bearings in the Public Register of All Arms and Bearings but the town authorities did not make application to have the Arms recorded at that time. It was not until 4th January, 1931 that the Council petitioned the Lord Lyon King of Arms to have the bearings recorded and on 22nd January, 1931, the Arms were matriculated and recorded in accordance with the Act of 1672. The Heraldic description of the coat-of-arms is as follows:

"Argent, a chevron Gules between three lions rampant Azure, armed and langued of the second. Above the shield is placed a Burghal coronet and a helmet befitting their degree with mantling Gules double Argent and on a wreath of their Liveries is set for Crest a Dolphin naiant proper and in an escrol over the same the motto—"Ad Summa Virtus".

In layman's language the coat of arms can be described as a white shield with a red chevron and three blue rampant lions.

The helmet and coronet are common to burghs such as Maybole and the motto can be loosely translated as "To the highest point of valour".

In 1639 the town was made the site of the head-court of the bailiary of Carrick and the principal Carrick matters were disposed of in the town for many years afterwards. The magistrates met annually to "fix the stent", inspect the wells in the town and carry out other functions still common to this day when the local councillors fix the rates, have their annual trip to the local water works and deal diligently with the affairs of the town, to their own satisfaction and the continued dissatisfaction of the cronies at the Castle Corner, who, never having been in Council, always know best how things should be done.

The town continued quietly to run its own affairs until 1857 when the old Burgh of Barony became an ordinary police burgh and nearly all the old rights and privileges were swept away and much dignity and independence was lost through the march of time.

Chapter 4

SEVENTEENTH CENTURY

IT was not until the second part of the seventeenth century that a clear and full description of Maybole was written by a member of the community who had great local knowledge of the district. In 1683 the Rev. William Abercrummie became minister of the parish and remained so until his death in 1722. He wrote *A Description of Carrick* and although it is without date it is believed it was written around 1686. This article has been printed in full in Robertson's *Historic Ayrshire, 1891* and some other history books on Scotland and one historian speaks of the author as "the inimitable Abercrummie" and states "the description of the village of Maybole is mighty nicely written" which is complimentary to the writer but nowadays the townspeople take umbrage if the town is described as a "village".

In his lengthy article the Rev. Abercrummie deals very fully with all parishes in the old Kingdom of Carrick and gives a great deal of interesting information regarding the places and people of his time. He devotes quite a lengthy part of his book to the town itself and this is really the first definite description of the township of Maybole. Many of the places he mentions in and around it can still be traced to this day and indeed many are little changed after three hundred years.

He writes of the "Towne of Mayboll" and not "Minniebole" as some writers have suggested and it would seem that by the end of the seventeenth century the old spelling of "Minniebole" had changed to practically its present spelling. He describes the town as lying on sloping ground from East to West, open to the south and well sheltered by a ridge of hills on the north, with one principal street, built on both sides with houses and "beautified" with two castles, one at each end of the street, the one on the east, or bottom of the street, belonging to the Earl of Cassillis, beyond which was a great new building forming the granaries or yards of the Earl (hence New Yards, now Cassillis Road) and the other at the west end of the principal street, which formerly was the Castle of the Laird of Blairquhan, but by Abercrummie's time it had been converted into the Tolbooth and local jail. He describes the Tolbooth as being "adorned with a pyramide and a row of ballesters round it, raised upon the top of the staircase, into which they have mounted a fyne clock." (In the nineteenth century the "pyramide" was blown down and was replaced by a larger "pyramide" with a new clock in it, the former clock having been set into the stonework of the tower).

In the 17th century there were four lanes, or vennals, leading off the principal street (now High Street), one called the Back Vennal (now John Knox Street) leading down from the Tolbooth to a lower street running from the Kirklands to Welltrees (now Abbot Street and Ladywell road) and one (now School Vennal) leading up from the Tolbooth to the Green which was an open space where the townspeople played football, "gowffe" and "byasse bowles" and which formerly was the site of the butts where Minniebolers practised archery and shot at the popinjay. At the bottom, or east end, of the principal street there were the other two lanes, or vennals, one leading down to the church at the old cemetery and called the Kirk Vennal (now Kirkwynd) and the other named the Fore Vennal (now Castle Street) leading up to what is now Kirklandhill Path.

MAYBOLE - CARRICK'S CAPITAL

The town of Maybole in the seventeenth century was therefore mainly contained in the rectangle formed by the streets now called Abbot Street, John Knox Street, High Street and Kirkwynd. Abercrummie points out that the lower street was formerly the main, or principal, street of the town and this is understandable when one remembers that the main entry to the town from Ayr was by the Lovers Lane and the Bullock Loaning into Kirkland Street and thence along what was formerly Weaver Vennal to the Welltrees and out of the town to Girvan via Allan's Hill. This was the busy thoroughfare in those days (and indeed up to the nineteenth century) and later there was a tollhouse at Duncanland, when the Redbrae was formed, at the east end of the town and another toll at Welltrees at the west end. The two side vennals (Kirkwynd and John Knox Street) merely led up to a higher street which gradually became the site of new shops etc. as the older properties in the lower street became out of date, much as Princes Street in the new town of Edinburgh displaced the old High Street in the old town.

In the old principal street below the High Street and in Kirk Vennal there had been many pretty buildings belonging to the gentry of the district and in the winter the gentlemen with their ladies were "wont to resort and divert themselves in converse together at their owne houses". About the beginning of the 17th century there were twenty eight residences of the Carrick lairds in the town but by Abercrummie's time most had become ruinous and only the Castle at the foot of the High Street remained in good repair and was occupied by the Earl of Cassillis and his family. In those days this building was much larger than it is now and was built right across the bottom of the High Street with a great part of its outbuildings on the site now occupied by the Post Office and Public Library. Abercrummie writes of the streets being built up on each side with good freestone houses and remarks that many of them on the lower street (Ladywell Road) had pretty orchards which yielded a store of good fruit.

Naturally the reverend writer dealt fully with the local church at the foot of the Kirkwynd and describes it as "very capacious, well furnished and with seats below and lofts and galleries above, the principal gallery being that belonging to the Earl of Cassillis." At the east end of the aisle there was a Session Loft well adorned with two rows of seats for the accommodation of the people who were to be catechised. The school was formed in the east end of the church and only separated from it by a wooden partition. This is the same church which the Rev. James Wright wrote so disparagingly about a hundred years later and which finally became so ruinous it was abandoned and a new church built in 1808 in Cassillis Road.

Abercrummie points out that Carrick was a Bailliarie and belonged heritably to the Earl of Cassillis who exercised his power by depute and could appoint his own clerk. The Courts of Justice were held every Thursday in Maybole and the court dealt with all manner of crimes. The townspeople even in those days seem to have been inveterate poachers and it is recorded that the fines for taking fish in the close season gave a good revenue to the courts but "made a constant tax on the townspeople". In the whole of Carrick there was no other town than Maybole in the seventeenth century and although it was not a Royal Burgh, neither was it merely an ordinary Burgh of Barony, for it had a charter from the King erecting it into a burgh with a town council of seventeen persons with full powers to manage the common concerns of the town and with the right to elect from among the councillors, two Bailies, a Clerk and a Treasurer and the town council also had the privilege of creating Burgesses. The Earl of Cassillis, as Superior, and in accordance with the Charter, had the right to appoint the Bailies but the council in the seventeenth century disputed this right and tried to appoint their own Bailies. After much argument the Earl's right was confirmed and it was not until two centuries later that the rights of burgh privileges became outdated and the affairs of the town were dealt with by Police Commissioners who blythely dealt with matters to their own satisfaction and paid no attention to the Superior's claim.

Abercrummie was an observant and knowledgeable country parson and his description of the district in his day is interesting. He states "the land is more suitable for pasturage than crops" and this is true to this day and undoubtedly the good grazing land in Carrick produced the famous Ayrshire breed of cattle which is now world famous. In the seventeenth century the district was self supporting and indeed exported agricultural produce to surrounding areas and great droves of cattle were sent to English markets, as well as to markets throughout Scotland. The Carrick cattle were much sought after as "the special quality of the beefe that pasture in the moore countrey have flesh that is very sweet and pleasant and the fat of them keeps soft lyke that of pork." There were plenty of farmyard poultry such as "hens, capons, ducks, geese and turkeys and an abundance of partridge, black cocks, plover, etc." and all these were so cheap that "the very poorest of the people eat them in their season at easie rates, besyde other sea fowles, which are brought from Ailra (Ailsa Craig) of the bigness of ducks and the taste of solangees". From Maidens and Dunure the fishing boats provided "ling, cod, haddowes, whytings, herrings and makrell" while the Rivers Doon, Girvan, and Stinchar provided such an abundance of salmon that the local people could not dispose of them all and many were sold to other districts around Carrick. The lochs were full of trout, pike and eels and when one reads Abercrummie's description of these natural products which were available to the "very poorest of the people at easie rates" the "bad old days" do not seem to have applied very much in the district, at least with regard to food supplies. It must be remembered that the town was small in these days with comparatively few inhabitants and the people in the district were mainly farmers in a small way who grew much of their own food and it was not until the eighteenth century with the growth of the weaving trade, when the townspeople gave up their crofting to produce blankets, etc., and the great influx of Irish vagrants enlarged the population, that poverty and want became rife in the town as reported by the later writers in the Statistical Accounts of the eighteenth and nineteenth centuries.

This seventeenth century article is the first full description of Maybole and the district of Carrick and the Rev. Abercrummie spared no pains in detailing the interesting items which he had observed and learned from the local inhabitants of his day. He describes many prehistoric remains throughout the district, the many wells and springs in the town, the various great families of Carrick with their country mansions and "nyne churches all built of good freestone and covered with skleits", and the orchards with their terraces laden with peaches, apricots, cherries and other fruits. He even gives an interesting item of news regarding a jackdaw and magpie who paired together at Ardmillan near Girvan, built their nest, and raised their fledglings who resembled the jackdaw more than the magpie, and the whole article is well worth reading by those interested in the early history of the old Kingdom of Carrick.

Chapter 5

EIGHTEENTH CENTURY

At the end of the eighteenth century the Rev. James Wright, who was inducted Minister in Maybole in 1770, wrote an account of the town and district for inclusion in the Statistical Account of Scotland and his article gives an interesting insight into the life of the townspeople of that period.

He was of the opinion that the town derived its name from the "ancient game called maypole, because in the town there was a piece of ground, about an acre in extent, called the Green of Maybole, where people from the town and district gathered for the purpose of enjoying the diversion of the maypole". This is the only instance where this derivation is given and as it is unlikely that maypole dances were in great vogue in the twelfth century it is hardly reasonable that the old town was so noted for this pastime that its name was a corruption of it. The Town Green (or Ball Green) was certainly the gathering place of the townspeople for generations and many sporting activities took place there such as archery, playing of bowls, football, etc. but there is no reason that maypole dancing should have been singled out to give a name to the town. In the seventeenth century the Magistrates of the Town passed a byelaw prohibiting the playing or "Byasse bowls" on the Town Green on Sundays, and Sir Walter Scott mentions Maybole in one of his books as one of the last towns in Scotland where the archery game of shooting at the popinjay was practised.

The Rev. Wright describes Maybole as situated on a ridge of high ground with a fine south exposure and amply supplied with excellent water from many springs and wells. He ascribes the excellent health of the eighteenth century townsfolk to the situation and good water supplies and mentions that Mr. David Doig, schoolmaster in the town and a woman also within the burgh both died in the 1780s aged 104 and 105 years respectively. He also records that in 1790 there were ten persons living within the town whose combined ages exceeded 900 years, so Maybole must have been a very healthy place and noted for the longevity of its townsfolk in those days. The population of the Parish had increased to about 3,000 by 1792 from the total of 2,058 recorded by Dr. Webster in 1755, quite a large increase in forty years.

The trade was mainly weaving and at the end of the 18th century there were about eighty cloth looms and two dozen cotton looms in use in the town, employing over three hundred weavers. This was a very large proportion of the townspeople as there were only eight hundred of the population within the Burgh over eight years of age. The produce from the looms was mainly woollen blankets and about 10,000 stones of wool was woven yearly giving approximately 300,000 yards of cloth or blankets which were sold for an average of one shilling per yard at the public markets in Maybole and Ayr, four such markets being held yearly in each town. The wool was purchased by cloth merchants and supplied to the weavers who were paid an average of $1\frac{1}{2}$d per yard for their work and therefore a weaver's wage at that time would be in the region of seven shillings per week which compared quite favourably with wages for other tradesmen at that period. The schoolmaster who taught in the small thatched schoolhouse at the foot of the Town Green had an annual salary of 300 merks Scots (£16.13.4$\frac{1}{2}$d stg.) while the ministers stipend was 63 bolls 2 pecks of meal and £73 Scots with the free occupancy of a manse and glebe.

MAYBOLE - CARRICK'S CAPITAL

About the end of the 18th century farming in the district was improving greatly and in 1797 the Carrick Farmers Society was formed, the members consisting of nearly all the local lairds, a great proportion of the farming community and, curiously enough, all the clergymen in the district. The first President of the Society was the Rev. John Ramsay of Kirkmichael who was the founder of it and a leading agriculturist in his day. Two cattle shows were held yearly and four regular meetings were held annually in the Kings Arms Hotel in Maybole when articles on farm management were read and discussed. Prizes were given for the best kept farms and for the best fields of green crops, etc. and books were purchased on new methods of farming and passed round the members. In addition there was a fund raised to give grants to members who met hard times and altogether it was a thriving and prosperous Society with funds amounting to £575 in 1837. The Society was in existence until the middle of the 20th century when, due to lack of support, it was disbanded and its trophies handed over to the Ayrshire Agricultural Society for competition in special classes confined to Carrick Farmers at the annual Ayr Cattle Show.

The writer of the Statistical Account was not greatly enamoured of the local school or church and described the former as "an old mean thatched house, very unsuitable to the eminent characters, which, at different times have been educated in it" and the church as a "large but mean structure". The only other building referred to in the town is "a very old building, commonly called the College, the walls of which are still standing, and the area within them is used for the burying place of the family of Cassillis". It is odd the minister only recorded these three buildings, as at that period the Castle and Tolbooth at each end of the Main Street must have dominated the other buildings and there were many other town residences of local lairds which one would have thought worthy of mention.

In the Rev. Wright's article he lays great stress on the number of the poor in the parish, which he states "was very considerable", and in his opinion this was caused partly because of the great numbers of unemployed inhabitants and partly by the large influx of Irish vagrants about this period. He complains bitterly that nothing was given by the heritors towards the upkeep of the poor who were wholly maintained from church collections each Sunday. As most of the heritors did not attend the church it was left to the townspeople who did attend to give contributions to the Poors Fund, and as the townspeople were themselves poor there was very little to distribute among the needy and it was, as the writer said, "a case of the poor maintaining the poor."

Chapter 6

NINETEENTH CENTURY

ABOUT fifty years after the Rev. James Wright wrote about Maybole another Statistical Account of Scotland was published and once again the local minister, the Rev. George Gray, compiled the information on the town and district as it was in 1837. He was Parish Minister from 1828 to 1840 when he was appointed Professor of Hebrew in Glasgow University. He differed from his predecessor in the derivation of the name and gives its meaning as "the heath ground above the marsh or meadow" which is certainly more acceptable than the Rev. Wright's contention that it is a corruption of "maypole".

The 1837 article is much more detailed than the earlier Statistical Account and deals at great length with the geology, zoology and botany of the district and the writer must have given much study to his subject. He also deals with the fossil organic remains found from time to time throughout the parish, giving special mention to the head of an elk which had been found when a loch was drained in the South of the parish. This head was in the possession of Mr. Kennedy of Drummellan at that time and compared favourably in size with a similar specimen in the museum of the Royal Society of Dublin. To anyone interested in these matters a study of the Rev. Gray's article in the *New Statistical Account of Scotland* will give much information regarding the geology, etc. of the district.

Like the earlier writer the Rev. George Gray laid great stress on the good health and longevity of the townsfolk and pointed out that endemic diseases were very infrequent and never severe. He stated "when the last infliction of the plague in Scotland prevailed throughout the whole country and raged with great virulence in Ayr and other towns it never reached Maybole and none of the inhabitants were affected during the cholera epidemic in the early part of the nineteenth century". This freedom from disease, and the great age of many of the inhabitants, is still common (although in the 1930s there were many diptheria cases) and there are many octogenarians living in the town at the present time. The fact that the town is built on a hillside with good natural drainage and the fresh air of the southern uplands constantly blowing from the south west may have a bearing on the fact that Maybole is one of the healthiest towns in Scotland and its inhabitants have every chance of outliving their alloted three score years and ten.

By the early 19th century many of the old castles in the district had become ruinous but there were still in good preservation the castles of Newark, Greenan, Dunduff, Dunure and Kilhenzie. Newark and Kilhenzie are still in good order but the others have now become derelict and only have a few walls standing to show their former grandeur. In 1837 there were many old ruins of castles such as Bridgend of Doonside, Smithstowne, Brockloch, Sauchrie, Craigskean, Beoch, Garryhorne, Glenayes, and Dalduff, but most of these ruins have long since disappeared and only the names of the farms which were built on or near the sites of the old castles recall them to mind. Within the town boundaries the Rev. Gray mentions the Castle at the bottom of Main Street and the Tolbooth at the top of the street, also the former house of Sir Thomas Kennedy of Culzean, then occupied by a noted townsman Mr. Niven of Kirkbride and now of the Bank of Scotland. He also specially detailed the house in Kirkwynd belonging to Kennedy of Ballemore, the house of the Abbots of Crossraguel at the Garden of Eden (in Crosshill Road) and states that at one time there were twenty eight houses in the town where the principal families of the district resorted to in winter, no doubt taking his information from Abercrummie's article, as most of these houses were reported as ruinous in 1686 and must surely have practically disappeared by 1837. Of modern buildings only the Parish Church is referred to by the Rev. Gray and he states "it is a plain structure with a steeple in the worst possible taste." The steeple seems to have found little favour with anyone as shortly after the church was built in 1808 Bailie Sinclair was discussing it with one of the heritors (the Earl of Cassillis) and remarked that it should have a "knock" in it as a ring had been left on each side in the shape of a clock face, and the heritor replied "A knock in it? It would be better knocked down."

As Maybole was the place where the courts of Justice for Carrick were held many important criminal trials took place in the old tolbooth and punishment by public hanging was frequently inflicted. The public gallows stood in a field at the top of Culzean Road, (traditionally said to be on the site where the late Mr. Cameron, an ironmonger in the town, built his house) and the road is still often called Gallowhill by the locals. The last person to be publicly hanged there, in 1718, was a man, Thomas Nelson from Girvan, who, when quarreling with his neighbour, struck him with a mattock or spade and killed him. There is little doubt but the Minniebolers would turn out in full numbers to witness the spectacle and relish the fact that it was a Girvan man who was meeting his fate that day, as tradition has it that from time immemorial the communities of Maybole and Girvan could never thole each other and every opportunity was taken by a "Minnieboler" to crow over a "Syboe" and vice versa.

In the 1830s the main industry was still weaving, as the manufacture of boots and shoes, which was to make Maybole so well-known throughout the country, had not yet been introduced. Wages had not increased for years and a common pay was 7/- per week for six days of anything up to fourteen hours per day. While it was mainly male labour, quite a number of women and young boys also worked on the looms and the street known as Weavers Vennal resounded all day long to the clack of the machines which were usually housed in a room with a clay floor a little under the level of the ground. These weaving shops, as they were called, were dark and damp and most weavers were badly affected with rheumatism in their later years. By this time the cloth agents had a great hold over the weavers and some had started to keep shops to supply provisions, etc. to the weavers. Many would get goods on credit and be indebted to the agents who would then supply the wool at their own price and the truck system became rife in the town. Finally the conditions of the weavers became so depressed, while the agents prospered, that the truck system and the arduous work in hand weaving became intolerable and gradually weaving died out and the other manufactures of boot and shoe making and the making of agricultural implements was introduced into the town about the middle of the 19th century.

With the new prosperity from the new trades however, idleness and drinking, which had been checked for half a century, became rife again, and many alehouses did a roaring trade on Saturday nights and carousals often lasted until Sunday mornings. It was quite common for men who received their wages on a Saturday to go straight to a public house and not leave it until every penny was spent and there was nothing to take home to the wives and families who had to fall back on the charity of their more temperate neighbours. It is strange to record the squalor and poverty of the bad times of the weaving industry and to find that increase in trade and better days did not improve, but indeed even make worse, the lot of many wives trying to keep a house and family together.

MAYBOLE - CARRICK'S CAPITAL

Although the influx of prosperity to the town did not improve the conditions of many of the inhabitants it undoubtedly increased the trade of the shopkeepers and also benefited the farmers in the district. The price of farm land and farm rents rose considerably in the parish about this period and the average rent for farm land was around £1 per acre. The first part of the 19th century was the most flourishing period in the town's history and the gross average weekly payment to all the workers was in the region of £600, which was a considerable sum in those days to be divided among a community of around 4,000 persons, the population having more than doubled in a short period, mainly due to the large influx of Irish weavers who came to the town about that time.

With the increase in population and the new flood of prosperity many small shops and businesses were started and a list of the shopkeepers, etc. makes interesting reading. About the middle of the century the businesses carried on in the town were as follows:

3 Hotels (Kings Arms, Sun Inn, Dunnering Inn).
12 Public Houses (selling spirits as well as ales).
30 Ales Houses. (For sale of ale only).
13 Carpenters shops.
3 Chemists.
4 Blacksmiths.
2 Watchmakers.
4 Bakers.
11 Shoemakers.
2 Dyers.
5 Butchers.
9 Drapers.
16 Milliners.
1 Ladies Staymaker.
1 Wigmaker.
6 Doctors.
11 Tailors.

13 General Merchants. (Grocers, etc.)
4 Nailmakers.
3 Tinsmiths.
6 Lawyers.

(No mention is made of stonemasons, plasterers or builders but there must have been some such tradesmen in the town at this period). When this list is compared with a list of the shops and businesses in the town a little over a hundred years later, when there are numerous empty shops in the streets and much fewer tradespeople to supply the needs of a population of around 5,000, it shows how Maybole must have been a thriving and industrious town in days now past. Then difficulty of transport to Ayr made it necessary for the town to be self supporting and all merchandise was bought locally. Easy transport to Ayr and Glasgow has killed the need for local tradespeople and in the 1960's few, if any, suits, hats, etc. are purchased from local shopkeepers and grocers and butchers and chemists are the main local suppliers nowadays. It will be noticed from the list of merchants in the mid nineteenth century that the womenfolk, as usual, were well catered for and there were sixteen milliners and a staymaker to meet the fashions of the times. The local people must also have been rather litigious as it needed six lawyers to deal with their affairs. Much property was being bought and sold then and the old deeds of many houses have strange descriptions, many being recorded as bounded by "a middenheid" on the adjoining property or by somebody's byre or stable wall and this does not make it easy nowadays to trace such boundaries when old property is being transferred to new owners.

During the early part of the 19th century great strides were made in the forming of new roads into the town and William Niven, the "leader" of the council, and described by a local worthy as "Lord God o' Maybole and master o' a' the 'lime kilns roon aboot," was responsible for a great deal of improvements to the local streets. Many were just lanes with gutters down the centre, as in the Foul Vennal (now Castle Street) and William

Niven urged that such streets be paved and new streets formed. There were thirty tollhouses in Maybole District and four of these were within the town or on its boundaries. The rights to levy tolls were rouped publicly in May each year and the rents offered in 1840 were as follows:

Duncanland Toll (at foot of Redbrae)	£200
Ladyland Toll (end of Whitehall)	£88
Gardenrose Toll (at Station Bridge on Culzean Rd.)	£41
Welltrees Toll (foot of Welltrees Street)	£220

The rents show that the greatest volume of traffic was by the high road from Ayr entering the town by Duncanland Toll and by the road over Allan's Hill from Girvan which entered the town at Welltrees. The rouping of the toll charges was a lucrative business for the local authorities in these days as the total rental of all tolls in 1840 amounted to £2,625, the highest rent of £335 being offered for the toll rights at Bridgemill near Crosshill and the lowest of £10 for the toll at Ladycross at the junction of the road from the Howmuir and the Crossroads above the town. The income from these toll rents mostly went towards the upkeep of the roads in the district.

In the years between the 1790 and 1837 Statistical Accounts great improvements were made in the farming industry in the district. Before 1790 there was hardly a fence on a farm and the houses were mere huts with thatched roofs and with gables generally built of turf. By 1837 the farm houses were nearly all solid stone built houses with slated roofs and the fields had been fenced off with hedges. The improvements were carried out by farseeing landlords who improved the value of their holdings by building good houses, draining the land and planting hedges for shelter and as boundaries. This was a good investment as is shown by the agricultural rental of the parish. In 1736 the total agricultural rental was £172, in 1785 it was £346 and by 1819 this had increased to £2,157. In the late 18th century the crops were poor, being mainly oats and barley with a few peas and beans, but forty years later the ground, having been drained, produced good crops of wheat and other agricultural produce.

Mr. McJanet, the farmer in Drumshang, was one of the most progressive agriculturists in the parish and carried out many experiments in reclaiming moorland on his farm and in the 1830's the Highland Society awarded him a gold medal for bringing into cultivation the greatest extent of waste land in Scotland within the shortest time. Stock had also improved and where formerly the cattle were mainly Galloways the Ayrshire Dairy Cow became the predominant farm animal and has remained the favourite breed to this day in the district. It is interesting to note that the model Ayrshire cow painted by Mr. Shiels in the 1830's for the Edinburgh University Agricultural Museum was one of the herd owned by Mr. Finlay of Lyonstone Farm.

An agricultural market was held in Maybole every Thursday but, from being a thriving market where stock and grain was originally sold, it gradually dwindled until only butter, eggs, cheese and a few minor articles of country produce were finally offered for sale, as with the improvement of the road to Ayr, the farmers preferred to take their produce to the larger market there and the Maybole market became defunct. In 1837 it was estimated that the annual cash value of agricultural produce in Maybole Parish amounted to £47,202, a very considerable sum in those days. Fairs were held in the town for generations in the months of February, May, August and November where farm servants were "fee'd" and goods of every description were sold and it was at one of these fairs in 1756 that Robert Burns' father and mother met for the first time at a booth near the foot of the High Street. The traditional site of the meeting is commemorated by a bust of the poet on the top of the gable of a shop at the bottom of the street.

The town had a post office and was the half way posting station for the stage coaches which passed daily through the town from Glasgow to Portpatrick which was then the main port for traffic to Ireland. The passengers on these stage coaches stayed overnight in one of the local coaching inns and continued their journey the following day, and the yards of the Sun Inn, the Dunnering Inn and the Kings Arms must have been exciting places on the arrival and departure of the stage coaches which would be one of the daily highlights in the town, when no doubt the locals would gather to discuss and criticise the travellers from the far away city of Glasgow who were brave enough to face the trials and hardship of a visit to Ireland There were also two stage coaches stationed in the town which ran twice a week to and from Ayr leaving at 7 p.m. and returning twelve hours later, and one coach ran twice a week to Girvan.

The Rev. George Gray naturally dealt at length in his article with the ecclesiastical state of the town and parish and gave very accurate details of the various churches and their membership. Taking the total population of the town and parish at 6,362 persons he gave the membership of the various religious factions as:

Established Church	5,033
United Secession	548
Roman Catholics	355
English Church	214
Methodists	104
Relief Church	54
Reformed Presbyterians	44
Anti Burghers	10

The balancing of his figures would point to the conclusion that Maybole in the 1830s housed no atheists or agnostics and it may be thought the writer was a little optimistic about the beliefs of the townspeople of that time. Churchgoing on Sundays was not much better than it is today and the average attendance at communion in the Parish Church was 1,300. The Roman Catholics and Episcopalians only attended their services very occasionally, when a minister of these persuasions could come from Ayr, there being no local priest or Episcopal Minister in the town. The ten Anti-burghers however were solid and strong in their belief and met each Sunday in different houses of their members when, unless illness intervened, there was always a full attendance of the whole flock.

All denominations, (except the Catholics) combined to form a society called the Maybole Association, and collections were taken from time to time in the parish church, the Secession meeting house and other places of worship throughout the town towards the cost of purchasing Bibles and Testaments from the Ayr and Edinburgh Bible Societies for distribution among the poor. A Tract Society was also in operation for a few years and many religious articles were printed for distribution among the townsfolk. The "Carrick Class", composed of all ministers in Carrick, met regularly to discuss the affairs of the church and many proposals were made that this Carrick Class be erected into a presbytery but the proposals never came to fruition. The members gathered in the different manses throughout Carrick in strict rotation, on the second Tuesday of each alternate month at 1 p.m. and the host read an essay on any subject of his own choice which was criticised, or applauded, by the other ministers. The meeting was closed by prayer and all the ministers spent the rest of the afternoon and evening with the host minister and his family in social enjoyment and members from a distance invariably stayed the night. No wonder manses in the old days were built so large when it was often necessary to entertain and house visiting clergymen from throughout the district. These meetings of the "Carrick Class" brought together all the clergy and established kindly relationship, unbroken by difference of party, and Carrick has always been noted for its tolerant religious outlook.

Schooling was an important issue about the same period and in Maybole and district there were thirteen schools, of which one was the parish school, one supported by subscription, two free schools and the remaining nine private, or unendowed, schools. Reading, writing and arithmetic were taught in all schools while in the parish school and three of the others, Latin, French and Greek were also taught, as was geography. The parish schoolmaster in 1837 was John Inglis, who was also a preacher of the Gospel, and his annual salary amounted to approximately £130 which was much higher than the stipend of £100 paid to Rev. Mr. Thomson who was minister in the United Secession Church. The other schoolmasters and schoolmistresses depended largely on the school fees paid by the scholars, or on subscription from local people, and on a whole their average salary amounted to about £80 to £100 per annum. Maybole was always interested in the schooling of its young people and most townspeople could read and write at a time when the majority of the Scottish people were illiterate and could only make a mark on documents and this is proved by nearly all old deeds of property in the town being signed by the people concerned and few, if any deeds, are in existence from the eighteenth century onwards where a seller or purchaser has made his cross instead of signing his name in full.

It can be taken from a perusal of the old Statistical Account of 1837 and other writings that most of the nineteenth century was indeed a prosperous period for the old town (with some bad patches) and this prosperity continued until the decline of the boot and shoe trade in the town in the early part of the twentieth century.

Chapter 7

TWENTIETH CENTURY

In 1950 a third Statistical Account of Scotland was published and once again it was a minister in the town who prepared the article on the Burgh of Maybole. The Reverend Alexander Williamson, minister in Maybole West Parish Church, was the writer and as he was for very many years resident in the burgh and had a great interest in local affairs there was no one better fitted to deal with the subject. From time to time he had written many articles for publication in local papers on the street names, the old worthies, Crossraguel Abbey, etc. and he dealt very thoroughly with the facts about the old town in his article for the Third Statistical Account. It is a curious fact that all articles on Maybole's history have been written by local ministers but no doubt in their visitations throughout the town and district they gained an insight to the place overlooked by other townsfolk.

During the period between the Second Statistical Account and the publication of the Third Statistical Account (a little over one hundred years) Maybole had risen from an impoverished little country town to become a thriving place of industry which produced boots and shoes for all districts in Britain and agricultural implements, from the famous works of Jack & Son, for all countries in the world. The last half of the nineteenth century was the boom period for Maybole and its townsfolk prospered exceedingly well. There was work for all and while wages were small (considered by present day standards) they were sufficient to meet all daily needs and leave a little over for pleasure. This is evident by the great love of sport in the town about the last decade of the nineteenth century and the first decade of the twentieth century when Maybole had a sports ground which equalled any in Scotland at that time, and many of the local men were famous as runners and cyclists throughout Britain. At that period there was also a very fine silver band, and a choral society, and concerts were given often by Frame, Lauder, Hamilton and other well-known Scottish artistes in Wyllies Hall, Jacks Hall and the Town Hall, when invariably every seat was filled.

About 1908, however, one of the larger shoe factories (Grays) closed down and gradually the industry dwindled and Maybole again returned to hard times. It is said over 2,000 of the townsfolk emigrated around 1910 many of them going to Hamilton in Ontario, Canada, where there is still a district known as "Wee Maybole". By the time the Rev. A. Williamson wrote his article the population had fallen from 5,500 in 1891 to around 4,200 in 1931 and had gradually increased again to about 4,800 in 1947.

He describes the situation of the town in similar terms to that given by the previous writers which is natural as geographical features do not change much in three hundred years. Housing is dealt with very fully and he details the total number of houses in the town as numbering 1,250, of which 40 were villas, 115 cottages, 32 in terraces and the remainder of the tenement type, mainly of two storeys, a few with three and one with four storeys. Of the total of 1,250 the Town Council had built and let 318 by 1950 but this number has been greatly exceeded since then and in May 1971 the 1000th Council House was formally opened. Overcrowding was prevalent in the 1940s and over 20% of the council owned houses had more than one family living in them. Most houses in the town had gardens attached and the usual services of water, sanitation, cleansing, gas and electricity were amply provided and Maybole compared favourably with any other town of equal size in Scotland. Mention is made of the Castle and the Tolbooth as in previous accounts and the only new buildings erected in the twentieth century of any note were the Carnegie Library in 1906 and Post Office in 1913.

It is interesting to note in the Third Statistical Account the detail of the tradespeople in the town and to compare it with the list given a little over one hundred years previously. In 1950 the shops and businesses in the town consisted of:

3 Bakers.
5 Butchers.
5 Cafes.
2 Chemists.
4 Confectioners & Tobacconists.
1 Milliner.
3 Drapers.
2 Fishmongers.
6 Grocers (one with an "Off" licence).
2 Ironmongers.
4 Newsagents.
7 Public Houses.
2 Licensed Hotels (Kings Arms and Commercial Hotel).
8 Shoemakers.
1 Watchmaker.
4 Hairdressers.
4 Greengrocers.
1 Radio Dealer.
1 Tailor.
3 Motor engineers.
1 Blacksmith.
3 Taxi Hirers.
3 Banks.
4 Doctors.
1 Dentist.

1 Optician.
1 Chiropodist.
3 Lawyers.
2 Picture Houses.

It will be noted that easy access to the county town of Ayr and to Glasgow had changed the trend of shopkeeping in Maybole and the ladies would appear to have taken their custom to the larger towns as fifteen milliners and a staymaker had gone out of business since the previous census of shops etc. had been taken. The townspeople had become more temperate and made do with two Hotels and seven Public Houses in 1950 compared with three Hotels, twelve Public Houses and thirty Ale Houses in 1837. Health must have improved with modern sanitation, etc. as four doctors sufficed for 4,800 people against the six required a hundred years earlier for a much smaller population, while half the number of lawyers could deal with legal matters. Blacksmiths had practically disappeared but were replaced by motor engineers, and taxi hirers and a radio dealer had started business with the advent of cars and wireless while two picture houses had displaced the former concerts and "penny geggies" which were set up from time to time in the Town Green.

The boot and shoe industry still existed to a certain extent but the great days when there was full employment in this trade had passed. About the turn of the century the Ladywell and Lorne factories were in full production and the trade which had been started by the foresight of John Gray and Charles Crawford in the nineteenth century and expanded by James Ramsay, John Lees, Robert Crawford, John McCreath and others had passed its heyday and by 1950 only the factories owned by Lees & Co. at Townend and McCreath in Society Street were still in existence. Maybole specialised in heavy footwear and the decreasing demand for this and the tariffs imposed by Eire (where a great amount of the local footwear had been marketed) did much to kill the local trade and in 1950 only 3,500 pairs of boots and shoes were produced weekly against a total of 20,000 pairs weekly early in the century. The Millar Tanning Company, (which had taken over the former Ladywell Shoe Factory) was busy at this period however and tanned leather from it was sold all over Britain. Unfortunately this connection with the boot and shoe trade has also gone from the town as the tannery closed down in 1969 and there is now no connection in the town with the great boot and shoe industry which made it such a thriving community for nearly a hundred years, with the exception of the firm of Harrison & Goudie which employs a few workers and strives to keep some connection with the boot and shoe trade in Maybole.

At the same time as the footwear industry prospered in the town the making of agricultural implements was greatly increased by Alexander Jack and Sons and by the beginning of the present century their implements were famous throughout the world. The agricultural implement industry was started in the latter half of the nineteenth century by the two firms of Alex. Jack and Thomas Hunter and gave employment to many of the townspeople. The two firms united early this century and continued until the 1950s when, like the footwear factories, trade diminished and finally the agricultural works closed down. At one time in the agricultural world the name of "Jacks" carried a guarantee of excellence in materials and workmanship.

The government of the town had changed since the previous Statistical Account and in 1857 the old Burgh of Barony had become an ordinary Police Burgh with a Town Council of twelve members, including the Provost and two Bailies. In 1950 the officials consisted of a part-time Town Clerk and Treasurer (who was also Housing Factor) and a full-time Burgh Surveyor. The J.P. Court for the district was held in the local Court House which was formerly the Tolbooth and this was also the meeting place for the Carrick District Licensing Court. The District Council members met in the District Office (formed in part of the town's old "Poorhouse") and these courts still continue to make their decisions in the old burgh.

Once again the ministerial writer of the Statistical Account wrote fully on ecclesiastical matters. In 1950 there were four churches belonging to the Church of Scotland, those being the Old and West Churches (both Parish Churches) the Cargill (once the Free Church) and the Kincraig (the U.P. Church). At that time the Cargill and the Kincraig Church were used separately although united under one minister, but shortly afterwards the two congregations combined in what was formerly the Cargill Church (which became known as the Cargill-Kincraig Church) and the Kincraig Church was sold to a local builder who demolished it and built private houses on the site. The combined congregations of the four churches totalled around two thousand members. In addition to these there were places of worship for the Episcopalians, Plymouth Brethren, Baptists and the Salvation Army, while the Roman Catholics, with a membership of three hundred had their own church at the foot of Coral Glen. A few townspeople who were Christian Scientists and Spiritualists travelled to Ayr for their services and it would appear religious observances occupied a fair share of public attention. The Rev. Williamson, like his predecessors, remarked on the tremendous indifference of the townspeople in their attendance at church services and it would seem the Minniebolers have never pleased their ministers in this respect.

About 1571 the parish churches of Maybole and Kirkbride (near Dunure) were combined and the list of ministers since then who served the community makes interesting reading and shows that Maybole had many brilliant men who made their mark in church affairs, among them being two who were Moderators to the General Assembly. The following list gives the names of the parish ministers since 1571.

1571 Alexander Davidson. (Reader at Kirkbride).
1572 Matthew Hamilton. (Reader at Kirkbride and Maybole).
1591 Hew Hamilton. (Reader).
1595 John McQuorn, M.A.
1599 David Barclay.

1608 James Bonar, M.A. (Moderator of General Assembly, 1644).
1655 John Hutchison.
1667 John Jaffray. (Episcopal Curate)
1673 William Abercrombie, M.A. (Episcopal Curate).
1688 John Hutchison. (Re-admitted).
1696 Alexander Fairweather.
1720 Robert Fisher.
1753 James McKnight, D.D. (Moderator of General Assembly) 1769).
1770 James Wright, D.D.
1813 Charles Logan.
1823 John Paul, D.D.
1828 George Gray, D.D.
1840 Andrew Thomson.
1843 William Menzie, D.D.
1870 George Porter, D.D.
1902 David Swan, B.D. (Assistant and successor until 1919).
1943 George Anderson, M.A.

Education was still of prime importance to the townspeople in 1950, as it had been for over two hundred years, and within the burgh there were (and still are) three well equipped schools, the Carrick Academy, the Cairn School and the Roman Catholic School, with two primary schools in the parish at Minishant and Fisherton. The Carrick Academy is the main school where all children are transferred after they have completed their primary training at the other schools, and is a well built modern Academy with every facility for a complete secondary training. Carrick Academy was one of the first schools in Ayrshire to provide a mid-day meal for the pupils and its advanced outlook on scholastic matters gives it a high ranking among the County Schools. The Cairn School is entirely primary and although the buildings are much older they had been completely modernised by 1950, and since then many improvements have been carried out and the playground has been enlarged. St. Cuthbert's Roman Catholic School is an elementary school and most of the pupils from St. Cuthbert's normally go to St. Margaret's in Ayr to complete their schooling. Evening classes were held in all schools during the winter months and over 200 persons attended each session to be taught needlework, cookery, woodwork, country dancing, art, drama, etc. These classes still continue and are well attended.

The Statistical Account points out that townspeople are well provided for in opportunities of recreation and in the Memorial Park, formed after the 1914-18 war, there is the nine hole golf course, four tennis courts and a bowling green all for the use of the townspeople and visitors. In addition there is one of the oldest private bowling greens in Scotland situated in Cassillis Road, formerly solely a men's club but in recent year ladies have been admitted as members. In the 1940s a junior football club was started and the old football ground, which had been the pitch for the local team who played Glasgow Rangers in a Scottish Cup tie just before the first World War, was reformed and became known as Ladywell Stadium. Many of the townspeople were keen anglers and there was always a great demand for membership in the local angling club which had the right to fish part of the River Girvan. There was also a strong Curling Club whose members usually played in Ayr Ice Rink but who took every opportunity to enjoy the game outdoors when there was keen frost, and the local curling pond at the "Beggar's Rest" was a busy place at such times with curlers and skaters of all ages enjoying their sport. With the exception of the Curling Club, which is now defunct, these recreational facilities are still enjoyed by the townsfolk and the golf club and bowling club are well patronised although the tennis courts are not so popular with the young people as they were in the 1940s.

Around 1950 there was a great upsurge of social life which was enjoyed by all after the dreary years of the second World War and nearly every week whist drives or dances were held in the Town Hall or one of the smaller halls in the town. There were also many guilds, clubs and societies with good memberships and in the winter months a full social life was enjoyed by most of the townsfolk. About this time wireless enjoyed a great vogue and in 1949 one thousand one hundred wireless licences were issued from the local Post Office while the two picture houses in the town were usually well filled every week night and had queues waiting to get in every Saturday night. With the advent of television the picture houses became more or less redundant and now one has been taken over as a warehouse and the other converted into a Bingo Hall and there are no picture houses in the town nowadays. In summer nearly every organisation had outings for their members and trips were often made to Aberdeen, Blackpool, etc. and indeed a favourite venue for a day trip was the Isle of Man.

The Rev. A. Williamson again stressed in his article for the Statistical Account the fact that Maybole was an exceedingly healthy place to live in and it is curious each writer made much of this point. It would seem there was a stereotype way to write a Statistical Account but probably this was because the instructions regarding it were given under certain headings which have been more or less similar in each case. Finally the writer ends his article by emphasising that Maybole is a friendly and couthy little town with a distinct feeling of unity among the townsfolk and what better description could be given for any town?

Chapter 8

COUNCIL RECORDS

THE old Council Records do not go back beyond 23rd December, 1721, (the older records having been lost in the Sheriff Clerk's Office, Ayr in 1745) but there is much of interest in the minutes from then on. They are sometimes very lengthy and sometimes very terse, depending no doubt on the mood of the clerk and his approval or disapproval of the decisions of his magistrates, which is not uncommon even at the present time.

Before the minutes start to be recorded there is given a detail of the Acts and Statutes pertaining to the Burgh which today seem strange but no doubt were of great importance in early times when full power was vested in the Magistrates and Councillors. It was ordained no inhabitant would wash clothes, etc. in the town wells, give lodgings to "idle or infamous persons" or sell meat or drink to them; no person was to buy more provisions than they required for their own use until the other inhabitants were supplied with their needs; no baker could refuse to bake in his ovens the loaves prepared by the householders themselves; that all goods displayd by traders for sale on market days should firstly be inspected by persons appointed by the Magistrates to examine same and if they were found wanting in any way the trader would be fined, and many other interesting facts which give an insight as to how the town was run by a small community in the early eighteenth century. Many of the bye-laws could be brought back today with benefit to the townspeople and the old fathers of the community showed great practical commonsense in dealing with many things which are now a cause for concern to many ratepayers. The "idle and infamous persons" were then given short shrift as there was no psychologist to plead they were maladjusted citizens and sellers of inferior ware were immediately brought to book before they could foist their goods on the public.

The first minute of 23rd December, 1721 records that Bailies John McFadzean and Hugh Malcolm and fifteen councillors were present when it was reported that, from the list of councillors submitted to him, the Earl of Cassillis had appointed Hugh Malcolm and Alexander Binning of Machriemore to be Bailies until Michaelmas 1722.

In September 1772 the councillors met and decided to stent (rate) the inhabitants of the town in the sum of Sixty Pounds Scots (£5 stg.) in respect of payment of the Schoolmaster's salary, the upkeep of the town clock and payment to the bell-ringer for ringing the curfew each night throughout the year at 8 p.m. and also the rising bell at 6 a.m.

In October 1772 the councillors rouped the customs in the Burgh and accepted the offer for same of Forty Two Pounds Scots (£3.10/- stg.) by John McGully, Innkeeper in Maybole, and at the same meeting they leased the annual grazing on the Balgreen (Town Green) to Alexander Girvan for Three Pounds Scots (5/- stg.). Councillors Thomas Ronald and Robert Alexander were appointed to visit the markets in the town and to apply fines for any misdemeanours by the traders, and the town officer was instructed to attend them on their visits to protect them against disgruntled traders should the occasion arise, whilst another councillor was instructed to examine the town wells and ensure they were kept clean.

In April 1723 the minutes report the anxiety of the councillors with regard to vandalism in the churchyard and it was decided that a voluntary collection be made in the town for the purpose of raising money to fence the cemetery and churchyard. It would seem that vandalism is not a new problem and was as common two hundred years ago as it is today.

On 6th July 1731 the Magistrates and Councillors met to deliberate on the necessary repairs to the High Street, also the avenues and "inlets" to the town and ordained that "the haill inhabitants come out provided with horses, carts, sleds, spades, shovels, picks, mattocks and other implements as shall be required and work on repairing the streets on six days yearly from six in the morning till six in the evening". Such was the way of dealing with road maintenance two hundred years ago, a practical and simple method where all shared in the upkeep and over-heads were negligible.

In November 1744 the councillors decided that all public proclamations should be made from the steps of the Town Cross in High Street by "tuck of Drum". A new drum was purchased for the town crier and this was in use until May 1774 when it was broken in "an unseemly brawl" and the town crier was given a handbell to ring before making his proclamations throughout the town. The price of the handbell is recorded at 15/- Sterling and this same handbell was known to be in the Town Chambers at the beginning of this century but unfortunately it has now been lost. Another interesting handbell was in use for many years and was known as the "Deid Bell of Maybole". It was late 17th century and measured $5\frac{3}{8}$ inches in diameter, was very roughly cast and had no inscription or marks of any kind on it. It was rung in the streets by a bellman or town crier who intimated a townsman had died and gave the time of the burial should anyone wish to attend the funeral. This bell was an exhibit in the Glasgow Exhibition of 1911 and is now preserved in the Glasgow Art Gallery and Museum at Kelvingrove.

In June 1745 the question of maintaining the streets again was the subject of discussion and the councillors confirmed that the townsfolk were to gather stones and sand for the roads on three days in June and three days after harvest and those who owned horses and carts and did not turn out were to be fined Eighteen Shillings Scots (1/6 Stg.) for each day's absence.

In 1747 heritable jurisdiction was abolished throughout the country and the full control of the town's affairs were vested in the Magistrates and councillors. The Earl of Cassillis received £1,800 as compensation for the loss of his superior rights but continued to claim the right to select the Magistrates for many years afterwards.

The first financial statement shown in the town records is for the two years, Michaelmas 1747 to Michaelmas 1749. The total receipts amounted to £635.11.10d. Scots (about £53 stg.) made up of stents, custom duty, malt duty and burgesses fees and the highest charges were £40 for two years' salary to David Doig, Schoolmaster, £60 for three years' accounts to William McClymont for keeping the town clock and ringing the curfew, while £3.12.0d. was paid to Mr. Hamilton, Saddler, for a saddle as a prize at the horse race at the Lammas Fair. It is interesting to note the council was paid £1.13.0d "for revising the accounts". In the two years detailed the town funds were in credit to the sum of £141.16.10d. Scots (about £12 stg.) which makes one think when the present day town's accounts are published. It is also an interesting sidelight to note that the clock-keeper and bellringer was on a par with the schoolmaster as regards salary.

The townspeople seem to have been worried about mad dogs roaming the streets in 1753 as in July of that year the councillors made an edict that all dogs be "wormed and muzzled" before 5th July and any person owning a dog and not doing so would be fined Three Pounds Scots (5/- stg.) and any dog found unmuzzled after that date would be killed and the person killing it would be paid the sum of One Shilling Sterling. Three years later in December 1756 the dog problem again cropped up following complaints to sheep being worried by "dougs and biches" and the council decided that no one within the burgh should keep a dog without a special licence from the Magistrates and should any dog worry sheep the owner of it would pay Twelve Pounds Scots (£1 stg.) in damages to the owner of the sheep. In 1763 the question of dogs roaming loose was again raised in council and once again fines were imposed on the owners of such dogs.

On 26th October, 1758 the council met to consider the proposal that a new church be built on the North West side of the Balgreen, on the site of an old meeting house. The councillors agreed to the proposal on condition that the Heritors of the Parish allowed a council loft to be formed at one end of the church and that the Town be freed of any of the expense of building the church. Much discussion must have taken place between the Heritors and the Councillors as on 4th May, 1759 it is reported that the Heritors had decided to rebuild the church on its present site at the foot of the Kirkwynd and that the Council would not be entitled to a loft, or even part of the seating on the floor of the church, unless they contributed towards the cost of the building. The council nominated three members to meet the Heritors and to stress the absolute importance of the Magistrates and Councillors having a loft of their own in the new kirk and also that part of the area below it be reserved for townspeople. The council agreed to pay part of the cost of the building of the new church, commensurate with the area of the council loft and the townspeople's seating area, on condition that the rents from the townspeople's pews be repaid to the council. If the Heritors did not repay the seat rents the council were to have the right to charge the value of them against the town's revenue. By October, 1761 the church had been rebuilt and the council decided to sell the seats in the ground area to provide the money for their share of the rebuilding costs. These were rouped in January, 1762 and brought in a total of £97.17.6d.

Some councillors of the eighteenth century appear to have been remiss in their attendance to their duties as on 9th June, 1760 a meeting was called for 4 p.m. but it was not until 6 p.m. that sufficient members turned up to form a quorum. The magistrates were extremely indignant and immediately passed a resolution that all members must in future attend all meetings punctually, unless they had a reasonable excuse, and any members turning up late or failing to attend would forfeit one shilling sterling for their lateness or absence, the Magistrates being the sole judges as to whether the excuses were valid or not.

In October 1773 traffic on the High Street had increased to such an extent that it was found the Town Cross was causing an obstruction to coaches and carriages and it was decreed that the Cross be removed and the site marked by a "paved freestone cross formed within a stone circle level with the street and neatly paved with small thin pebbles which the Magistrates and Councillors ordain will be the Cross of the Burgh of Maybole in all time thereafter". The shaft and steps of the cross were broken up but the stone forming the head of it was built into the inner gates of the Castle and is still there. This stone has a moondial on one side, a sundial on another side, the date 1707 and a rampant lion on the third side and the coat of arms of the Earl of Cassillis on the fourth side. The site of the old cross is now marked by an iron cross set in the asphalted roadway midway up the High Street.

The Foul Vennal (now Castle Street) had been a constant worry for years because it was unpaved and had an open drain down the centre of it and in January 1775 the owners of the properties in the Vennal paid £7 sterling to the Council for the purpose of causewaying the street. The work was carried out and shortly afterwards the name was changed from Foul Vennal to Post Vennal because the post vans were stabled in it.

On 16th February 1779 the Council appointed John Duncan as Schoolmaster in succession to David Doig and fixed his salary at Twenty Pounds Scots (£1.13.4d.) being the same as the salary paid formerly to Mr. Doig. This salary of £20 Scots per annum was the same in 1779 as was recorded in the financial statement of 1747 and there seemed to be no consideration of a rise in pay for the poor Schoolmaster. It must be taken into account however that the teacher had the right to collect fees from his pupils and had many perquisites which increased his income considerably.

Sanitation would appear to have been a constant subject of discussion in council as complaints were often raised regarding the townspeople dumping their refuse in the "bystreets and town inlets" and on 26th October 1782 the councillors instructed the towncrier to go round and proclaim that all such refuse be removed within eight days and if this was not done all inhabitants owning horses and carts were to be called on to remove all such refuse. Such dictatorial methods by the council seem strange today but they appear to have been effective as no further complaints on this subject are again recorded.

In November, 1790 the records show that the council built a slaughterhouse in the burgh with cattle yards attached and it was ordained that no cattle should be slaughtered unless in the place provided for such a purpose.

The town's finances must have been in a perilous state in 1791 as on 12th February of that year the Treasurer reported there were no funds available to pay the tradesmen employed in building the market house and they were "very clamorous" for their wages. A loan of £30 stg. to meet such expenditure was raised and the Bailies were taken bound to ensure repayment of same.

The riotous behaviour of some of the townspeople was the subject of a meeting held on 13th August 1792 when complaints were heard by the councillors from some of the steadier Minniebolers that "several inhabitants in the town and suburbs (Kirkland Street, Coral Glen and Dailly Road) gave lodging and entertainment to vagrants and randy beggars who go through the streets blaspheming and cursing and swearing to the disturbance of the inhabitants". The Councillors promptly dealt with this matter by clapping a fine of Two Pounds Scots (3/4d. stg.) on any person giving lodging to such "randy beggars", the person informing on the landlord or landlady guilty of such misdemeanour being paid half the fine collected by the Magistrates. Such a practical solution to a problem might well be enforced today with profit to all.

The European crisis at the end of the eighteenth century when Napoleon was at the zenith of his power seems to have reached out to all corners of the country and on 12th February 1797 the "Magistrates and Councillors of the Burgh of Maybole" held a special meeting to "consider the present crisis of public affairs and to express their loyalty to the Sovereign" (George III). It was resolved to offer His Majesty a Corps of Volunteers from "respectable" inhabitants of the burgh and neighbourhood, consisting of one hundred and fourteen men, to be called "The Loyal Carrick Volunteers", and the Earl of Cassillis was to be asked to take command of the troop "as a mark of attachment to his Lordship for his zeal at all times in promoting the public good". The "Carrick Loyal Volunteers" were duly enlisted from the "respectable" inhabitants of the district of whom seventy seven were townsmen, and the regimental roll contained many names common in Maybole to this day. The men were issued with weapons as varied as the Home Guard weapons of the Second World War (swords, pistols, axes, spades, shovels and a few firelocks) and the Earl of Cassillis mustered them for drilling on the Balgreen. Unfortunately there must have been some not so "respectable" members of the corps as it was regretably recorded that on the third occasion of their drilling on the Town Green their "drunken and riotous behaviour" forced the Earl and the Magistrates to reconsider their scheme to raise a force in defence of their country and the Carrick Loyal Volunteers were disbanded and did not turn out again for drilling. The Councillors no doubt decided to risk a probable invasion by Napoleon to a more than possible disturbance to the lieges by one hundred and fourteen armed men out on a spree. In February 1798 however, the Magistrates again came to the help of the Government "at this critical period when the nation is threatened by the invasion of an Enemy whose aim is the destruction of our Religion, our Laws and our Liberty", and a voluntary subscription was raised by them to send to help the funds for the war against Napoleon. By January 1798 rumours of war had taken a back seat to more important local business and the councillors were engrossed in raising money to repair the roof, build up the chimney and repair the windows in the "Dancing Room" in the Courthouse and the Earl of Cassillis came to their assistance with a gift of £21 sterling.

In April 1800 it is recorded £100 was paid to the Road Trustees to enable them to form a road from Lyonstone in a direct line to the Town of Maybole. This is what is now Park Terrace and Cassillis Road from the foot of Lovers Lane to Duncanland Toll.

In May 1804 the question of the removal of the Castle kitchens, etc., which then spread across to where the Post Office now stands, was discussed with the Earl of Cassillis and it was finally agreed in April 1805 that these would be taken down and a road formed through the Castle yards to join up with the road formed from Lyonstone to Duncanland Toll in 1800. This was done and the New Yards (or Cassillis Road as it is now called) came into existence at that time.

In April 1805 a petition was submitted by the Wool Merchants of Glasgow that the Maybole Cloth Market be held on a Tuesday instead of a Monday as had been the custom. The Wool Merchants pointed out they had to leave Glasgow on a Sunday to be in time to attend the Monday markets and their leaving their houses and travelling to Maybole on the Sabbath was frowned upon by their ministers. The Magistrates, being godly men, (as Maybole councillors have always been) quite saw the point and decreed that all Cloth Markets in the town be held on Tuesdays, commencing at 6 a.m. on the Beltane and Lammas Fairs and at 8 a.m. on Hallows Fair but the Candlemas Fair was to be held on a Thursday. Bills were posted fixing the dates of the Cloth Fairs as follows:

> Beltane Fair—Last Tuesday of April.
> Lammas Fair—Las Tuesday of July.
> Hallow Fair—Last Tuesday of October.
> Candlemas Fair—First Thursday of February.

The Wool Merchants of Glasgow expressed their satisfaction with these arrangements and for nearly half a century thereafter they travelled to the Fairs in Maybole four times a year without fear of lectures from their ministers for breaking the Sabbath. At this period a woollen mill was worked at Welltrees Square by a Gilbert Goudie and a "skinnery" had been started next to it by a Hugh Girvan. Both were councillors and no doubt they lobbied that the request of the Glasgow Wool Merchants be granted as they formed the main customers of Gilbert Goudie and Hugh Girvan who would be anxious to attract the Glasgow traders.

In 1806 the vexed question of a new church again arose and on 20th August a petition was submitted to the council asking the Magistrates to "add their utmost exertions to promote the building of a new church". A committee was formed to join the Heritors in pressing for a new church and the council pledged support for the project with the proviso that their commitment towards the cost would not exceed £300 sterling. On 17th January, 1807, however, after discussion with the Heritors this sum was increased to £450 (a loan of £400 being taken by the council from Hunters Bank in Ayr to meet this expense) and in 1808 the new church was finally built in New Yards, the pews being rouped on 22nd December 1808 for a total sum of £276.10.0d. A stipulation was made at the public roup of the seats that only a burgess, or a widow or a child of a burgess would be allowed to bid for the seats. The names of the successful bidders are listed in the records and many of their descendants still live in Maybole.

In the early part of the nineteenth century the councillors would seem to have been a convivial body of people as in 1806 the principal sums expended from the town's coffers went to pay "Miss Piper, innkeeper in Maybole" (Red Lion Inn) for supplies to the council, and some councillors pointed out the expenditure on refreshments amounted to more than four times the Schoolmaster's annual salary. This was not unusual, however, as on the evening of 6th June, 1797 the sum of £2.9.8d. stg. had been expended by the councillors at a party they held in the Kings Arms Hotel to celebrate the King's Birthday. The "Common Good Fund" of those days must have often been deleted to meet the needs of the good men and true who watched over the affairs of their fellow townsmen.

In March 1807 the council paid £4.1.8d. to acquire the ground at Welltrees where "the water issues from the rock at the spout below the tree" and this ground was later tidied up and a wall built round the well which supplied the townspeople in that "suburb" for nearly another hundred years.

The town authorities decided in October 1808 to instal street lighting throughout the town and fourteen oil lamps were purchased and fitted in High Street and Weaver Vennal, the other streets being left for the inhabitants to find their way about in as best they could on dark winter nights. In the accounts for 1810 the sum of £7.19.3d. is shown as having been expended "on oil for the lamps of Maybole". At the same meeting it was decided to engage a town "scaffengere" to sweep and clean the streets and it would seem the councillors were indeed becoming very civic minded in the early 1800s.

In July 1814 Hugh Davidson, Parochial Schoolmaster, petitioned for an increase of salary as he had employed an assistant since Martinmas 1810 and paid him out of his own salary. Mr. Davidson pleaded that his salary and other emoluments afforded but a small amount to defray "the unavoidable expense of keeping a wife and family" and to pay for an assistant. The councillors (all married men) were sympathetic to the plea and increased the salary by £1.13.4d. per annum.

On Saturday 1st September, 1817 a great part of the ceiling of the grand new church in New Yards fell down and William Niven of Kirkbride was appointed to meet the Heritors and discuss the question of having the repairs carried out. As it had only been built nine years previously it would seem all old tradesmen's work was not so good as it is often said to have been.

The Financial Account for 1817 records that the "Dancing Room" in the Town Hall had been let for various functions throughout the year. A Dick Harper paid 2/- for one night's let for a wedding, a "Company of Strolling Players" £1.4.0d. for a week's let to produce plays and Mr. Ferguson, Dancing Master, paid £1.12.0d. for two months' let of the Hall to hold his dancing classes.

Around 1817 there arose among the townsfolk a popular clamour for Burgh Reform (although there is no reference to it in the minutes of that year) and on August 4th 1820 it was reported that a Process of Declarator had been served in December 1817 by Thomas Bell and others against the Magistrates and Councillors, pointing out that by the existing method of election of councillors the burgesses had no voice in the nomination of Bailies or Councillors and demanding that this position be altered to give the Burgesses a say in such matters. The councillors did not look kindly on such a radical suggestion as election by popular vote and strongly opposed the proposal. As usual the Earl of Cassillis was drawn into the argument but he, by a letter from his Factor, Charles D. Gardner, on 13th April,

1818 ably threw the ball back to the Magistrates and more or less told them to settle their own difficulties but indicated he supported the plea of the townspeople. At the same time the Earl claimed that he, as Superior, had the sole right to nominate the Bailies although he had not exercised this right since 1792. This put another cat in the dovecote at the old Tolbooth and the poor councillors had to battle on two fronts. The matter finally went to the Court of Session where a decision was given in favour of the councillors continuing in the even tenor of their way. In these days the councillors were elected more or less for life and on the death or retiral of a member the remainder chose his successor and also chose the Bailies from their members, and the council was really a closed shop. The Magistrates and Bailies contended that the Charter of 1516 only laid down that the original councillors should be elected by the burgesses and thereafter the councillors would "choose the new" according to a statute made in 1469 in the reign of James IV. Most of the papers relating to the dispute are extant and make interesting reading with arguments ably supported by both the councillors and the reformers but the Maybole burgesses were to wait many years before getting representatives elected by popular vote, a right which is taken as a matter of course nowadays with no thought given to the lengthy battle to obtain this right.

The councillors appear to have been generous victors of the battle as on 21st October, 1820, it is recorded that William Niven the "leader" of the Council proposed that a short leet of five members be drawn up and submitted to the Earl of Cassillis for him to nominate two Bailies, this being a "courtesy gesture only because of the long friendship which had subsisted between his Lordship and the Council". The Earl was equally generous however, and, although still claiming his right to nominate the Bailies, left it to the councillors to elect the Bailies. So ended a three year period in the town's history when reform was first mooted and arguments were fierce but the townsfolk seemed to accept the continuance of the old rule with equanimity and settled down again to their "byasse" bowls and "gowf" and the enjoyment of the dances and dramas by the "Strolling Players" in the "Dancing Room" in the old Tolbooth.

It is noted in the Town Records that from this time on William Niven is always referred to as the "Leader" of the council and there is no doubt but that he was a forceful "Leader" and made a "one man council". As he was intensely interested in the town however, his dictatorship does not seem to have been a bad thing and proves that very often the most successful committee consists of one, so long as he is the right one.

By 1834 gas was replacing the old paraffin lamps throughout the country and on 19th March of that year the Maybole Gas Company opened their new Gasworks in Dangartland. This was a great occasion and the townspeople took the opportunity to make it a holiday and flocked to the opening ceremony which must indeed have been a colourful scene. The Magistrates and Councillors, the Freemasons, Shoemakers, Wrights, Tailors and other guilds all marched in procession, in full regalia, with their banners flying and with the local band to keep them in step, from the Town Green to the Gas Works, where, after the usual driech speeches, the gas taps were finally turned on and Maybole became lit up. Many of the citizens must have followed suit as the Secretary of the Local Masonic Lodge complained bitterly about the number of whisky glasses that had been broken by the brethren during the evening's harmony after they had "processed" to the opening ceremony at the Gas Works. These private gas works continued for over a hundred years until they were Nationalized about 30 years ago and in 1969 piped gas was introduced under the gas grid scheme and gas is no longer made in the old works. Few, if any houses are now lit by gas, electricity having been introduced to Maybole in the 1920s and nearly all lighting is now by electricity, but many of the housewives still swear by gas for cooking and will not part with their gas stoves.

In 1843 the Magistrates discovered the local sexton was digging up graves after interments in the old cemetery at the foot of Kirkwynd and selling the coffins to local undertakers and he was heavily fined for this grave misdemeanour. It did not deter him however as sometime later he was again fined and discharged from his duties for other misdeeds. Perhaps he needed the money to pay his first fine.

By the middle of the nineteenth century the weaving trade in the town was in a very bad state of depression and on 1st April, 1849 the Council met to consider the question of relief for the unemployed hand loom weavers. It was decided the Council should meet the Heritors and try to take measures with them to provide work for the poor and needy in so far as possible. Later it was decided they should be given work breaking stones for the new roads being made at that time and the unemployed of that period had to work for their "dole" as the councillors "were of the opinion it was not good for a man to be paid for doing nothing."

In June 1848 new dates were fixed for the Town Fairs which had been altered to suit the Glasgow Wool Merchants in 1805.

Tuesday had become the fixed days for markets in Ayr and many trades people attended the county town on these days in preference to trading at the smaller Maybole Fair and the civic fathers altered the Maybole Fair days to Thursdays instead of Tuesdays in the hope of "bringing mair profit" to the townsfolk.

On 29th January, 1849 a petition was submitted to the Magistrates from a large number of the inhabitants of the Burgh objecting to the proposal by the members of the Free Church to use the vacant piece of ground adjacent to the Church as a burial ground as it was "considered unsuitable because of the proximity to St. Cuthberts Well which was one of the chief sources of water for the townspeople". The "Free Kirkers" on 24th June had buried one of their members in this area without making application to the civic heads for right to use the ground for such a purpose and the Magistrates decided to "strenuously object and go further into the matter". After lengthy discussions with the church members it was finally agreed that no further burials would take place in the Kirkyard and the members of the church would have the right of burial in the new private cemetery at Tunnoch when it was opened. (The new cemetery was formally opened in 1851). Many of the Free Church members were party to the pressure for Burgh Reform in 1817 and would seem to have been "ag'in the Government" in many ways and were indignant that they were not allowed to run their own affairs and bury whom they liked in their own God's Acre. Finally however they succumbed to public opinion and agreed that no further interments would take place "for fear of pollution to the town well". The person buried was a well known local doctor and the inscription on the tombstone reads:

"Sacred to the Memory of William MacFarlane, Surgeon, Maybole, who died on 21st January, 1849, a victim to faithful discharge of professional duty from a poisoned puncture received at a post-mortem examination for the public interest". Underneath the inscription is added (evidently at a later date): "The body of the lamented deceased is the lonely occupant of this ground, the Free Church congregation to whom it belongs having relinquished their right of sepulchre therein in consideration of having obtained in perpetuity the fourth part of the Private Cemetery at Tunnoch". So ended another episode when the all powerful council brought to heel those townsfolk who thought they could deal with their own affairs in their own way.

In April, 1853 the question of extending the Ayr-Dalmellington Railway line to Maybole and Girvan was the subject of discussion between the councillors and promoters of the railway. Lengthy meetings were held and finally in October 1953 it was decided the railway line should stop at Maybole and not be continued on to Girvan as originally proposed. The Secretary to the Railway Company reported that from traffic tables he had prepared he estimated shareholders in the company could expect at least 10% return on money invested. The Council agreed to recommend the project to the inhabitants of the town and urge them to give support by taking shares. Many townspeople did this and, as foretold by the Company Secretary, the railway prospered and the shareholders did exceedingly well from their investments. The railway station was first formed at Redbrae and later the line was formed to where the old Coal Lye was sited and where the Carrick Co-operative garages are now built. A little later the railway was taken on to Girvan and the present railway station was built, thus completing the Ayr-Maybole-Girvan railway line first mooted in 1853.

The townspeople were strongly "anti-papist" and the local Orangemen made things rather difficult for the Roman Catholic minority every twelfth of July. On 10th July, 1854 a letter was received by the Magistrates from Sheriff Robinson, Ayr, stating that, as the Orange Lodge members would not give an undertaking not to parade on the twelfth, he proposed to send to Maybole a detachment of the Ayrshire Yeomanry on that date to keep the peace.

Th Orangemen however cared not a jot for the "Sour Milk Jocks" and gaily met on the morning of the Twelfth, with banners flying and the Orange Band to lead them and "processed" along Weaver Vennal and out the Crosshill Road to join their Crosshill brethren. The Magistrates tried to stop the procession but wisely retreated when they realised nobody could turn aside the Maybole Orangemen and the Crosshill and Maybole contingents duly joined forces at Ballochbroe. A band of Roman Catholic townsmen bravely challenged them there and the annual Donnybrook started, when the two factions gleefully assaulted each other, and men who were bosom friends for three hundred and sixty four days of the year tried their utmost to crack each other's heads in the full knowledge they would sympathise over each other's wounds the following day. The Magistrates and Sheriff did not appreciate the high spirits of the Minniebolers and the Ayrshire Yeomanry detachment was speedily dispatched to Ballochbroe to quell the disturbers of the peace with a show of force. The Orangemen and Catholics however, although bitter enemies for the time being, were still all true Minniebolers and would brook no interference in their private affairs and they promptly banded together in common cause against the "interlowpers" and made it so hot for the troopers they had to retreat. The two factions then again blythely attacked each other but the Yeomanry, after a brief spell of rest, again interfered and finally broke up the party. The *Ayr Advertiser* of 13th July, 1854 gave a brief account of the affair and reported "The Orangemen of Maybole and Crosshill processed, despite the Sheriff's proclamation, but were stopped by Sheriff Robinson and local Magistrates at Maybole and by Mr. Dykes and Bailie Muir, Justices of the Peace, at Crosshill, assisted by the Yeomanry Cavalry. The musical instruments and staves were taken from the parties and near Crosshill where the procession stoned the force employed in preserving the peace, one of the ringleaders was apprehended and sent to Ayr prison". Such was the very much watered down report on the "Battle of Ballochbroe", no doubt carefully worded not to demean the powers of the Sheriff and Magistrates, but any Maybole man will stoutly aver that on the 12th July, 1854 the townsmen put to flight the "Sour Milk Jocks" and defied the powers of the Sheriff who had ordered them not to "process". Tradition has it that the young officer in charge of the troop rashly ordered his men to fire over the rioters and some persons were slightly wounded which brought everybody to their senses very quickly indeed. No mention is made of this in any report of the affray but old townspeople who had heard the story from people who were present at it stoutly maintain this was a fact and the "Battle of Ballochbroe" could well have developed into a civil riot if anyone had been seriously wounded.

In 1857 the Town Council, very similar to its present form, came into being and became known as Police-Commissioners under an Act introduced "to make more effectual provision for the Policing of Towns and populous places in Scotland and for paving, draining, cleansing, lighting and improving same and permitting twenty one or more householders in any such burgh to petition the Sheriff of the County to define and specify the boundaries of such Burgh". The reformers of 1817 had waited forty years for such a body to govern their town but finally the old ways had passed and the first election of Commissioners was held on 29th May, 1857 when the following twelve Councillors were appointed:

> Thomas Dykes, Estate Factor.
> William Rennie, Banker.
> Peter Sinclair, Grain Merchant.
> James Weir, Merchant.
> David McClure, Ironmonger.
> William Brown, Banker.
> James Rennie, Innkeeper.
> William Galbraith, Merchant.
> John Fergusson, Clothier.
> Alexander Jack, Wood Merchant.
> Charles Crawford, Shoemaker.
> John Rankine, Farmer at Broch.

These were all men of substance with interests in the welfare of the town and the townsfolk were well content to leave the town's affairs in their capable hands. At the first meeting of the Commissioners on 1st June, 1857, Thomas Dykes was appointed Senior Magistrate and William Rennie and William Brown, Junior Magistrates, while William Hainay was engaged as Town Clerk and Thomas Rennie as Treasurer and Collector. Their first duty was to fix the rates for the ensuing year and a rate of 1/- per pound was passed for the year 1857-58. In April 1860 the council met and agreed that the Burgh Police and the County Police Force should merge and Councillor James Murdoch was appointed to represent Maybole on the Police Committee for the County.

MAYBOLE - CARRICK'S CAPITAL

In May 1867 the members of the Carrick Instrumental Band were in trouble because they would not turn out to practise, "the younger members being otherwise employed", and it was decided their instruments would be taken from them and given to the Rifle Corp. Probably it was thought the Rifle Corp would make better use of the instruments as, being composed of older and mostly married men, the members would not be "otherwise employed" as their courting days would be mainly past.

In May 1868 the Councillors agreed to accept the estimate of Mr. Lambie, Builder, Maybole to form a new street from My Lords Well at the junction of New Yards and Castle Road to the foot of Kirklands Street at Pat's Corner and when this was done the new street was named St. Cuthberts Road. The following year an ornamental iron pump was erected by public subscription at My Lords Well (so called because it had formerly been the well in the Castle Yard to supply the occupants of the Castle), and this pump was a land mark in the town until it was removed in the 1930s.

The question of a new Town Hall had been mooted for some years and finally on 15th January, 1877 the councillors agreed to obtain plans for a new Hall to be built next to the Court House on ground purchased from Mr. Donald, Kilmarnock for the sum of £120. It was proposed that funds for the project be raised by the townspeople taking £5 shares and later in the year (15th October) this was altered to a resolution to form a Stock Company with shares at £10 each. Five years later (April 1882) Bailie Lambie reported he had approached various parties throughout the town to take shares in the proposed Town Hall Company, but the canny Minniebolers had not looked kindly on the proposal that they should pay for the grand new building they had pressed the Council to erect, and as the shares could not be sold, it was resolved to let the matter rest awhile. In November 1885 it was agreed to make over free of charge, but subject to certain conditions, the ground for the new Town

Hall to the Commissioners of Police, and let them get on with the building of it.

In October 1877 it is recorded that the Railway Company intended to improve the station and to remove the bridge which crossed the railway "a little to the south of the present station and not to erect another in its place". This meant that all the traffic (foot and horse) would require to use the road at Gardenrose House (where the present Station Bridge is sited) and the Magistrates would not agree to the Railway Company's proposal unless a new foot bridge was erected by them where the old bridge had been placed near the north end of the Free Church. This was agreed and "Buchty Brig", as it is now known, was erected the following year.

On 19th July, 1878, the Magistrates, Councillors and friends held their annual outing to Croy Shore, being transported by Mr. McCubbin's brakes, and no doubt being ably served in other needs by the said respected owner of the Kings Arms Hotel. No trace of expenses for the day can be found in the accounts and each councillor would probably share in the cost and the lesson of 1806, when the cost of refreshments had been raised, seems to have had effect seventy years later. This practice of the councillors having a day's outing has continued to the present time and formerly the Provost was host for the lunch and the two Bailies for the tea but latterly the outing has been combined with the "Water Trip" and charged against council expenditure.

In 1879 unemployment again was rife in the town, the weaving trade having declined and the boot trade not yet into its stride, and meetings were held to discuss the problems of the poor and needy. The sum of £26.16.8d. was raised by public subscription and the Right Honourable Thomas Kennedy of Dunure gifted one hundred tons of coal for the benefit of the unemployed. It was agreed to use the money raised to meet any loss incurred by the council from engaging the unemployed to break stones for road making and to distribute the coal amongst the most needy.

On 13th October, 1881, the Magistrates agreed to permit Mrs. Law to raise a memorial over the Green Well in the Town Green in memory of her late father Thomas Dykes, who died on 12th June, 1879, and who was for many years Factor to the Marquess of Ailsa and first Senior Magistrate in the town under the Police Commissioners Act and this Peterhead granite monument still stands in the Town Green and is known as the "Dykes Memorial".

On 19th May, 1882, at a joint meeting of the Town Council and the Police Commissioners it was reported there had been a disastrous fire that morning in weavers' houses in Ballony resulting in the death of three women, Mrs. Campbell and Marion and Helen Byron, and the loss of all the possessions of the other cottagers. It was agreed the Council would give a donation of £16.10.0d. towards aiding the people who had lost all their possessions and it was later reported that a total of £39.19.6d. had been collected for the fund from the townspeople.

The Town Green (formerly the Balgreen) had been a source of annoyance for many years, being unkept and overgrown with weeds when it was not a quagmire after rain, and in February, 1892, it was finally decided to have it put into order, sown out in grass, with walks through it and a railing erected round it, at the cost of £300, of which £150 had been collected by public subscription. Two years later the work was completed and on 23rd March, 1894, the Councillors met and marched up the School Vennal to the Green which was formally declared open by Bailie Guthrie and afterwards the councillors had dinner in "Wyllies" Inn (now the Carrick Hotel) to celebrate the occasion. The Town Green had the original railings round it until the Second World War when they were removed to aid the war effort in the collection of scrap iron for ammunition. The trees were planted in 1894 and many are still standing although some have died and been removed.

In September, 1895, the Rev. Roderick Lawson and a few other townsmen offered to supply, free of charge, a new bell for the bell tower in the old Tolbooth and the offer was gratefully accepted. The old bell, (19" in diameter) which had been the curfew bell for two hundred years, was removed and placed on an ornamental oak stand, and now graces the present Council Chambers. An inscription on it states: "This Bell is founded at Maiboll by Albert Danel Geli, a Frenchman, the 6th November, 1696 by appointment of the Heritors of the Parish, and William Montgomerie and Thomas Kenedy, Magistrates of the Burgh." The new bell,, which still warns the townsfolk it is time for church on Sundays and tolls for past Provosts, etc., weighs 20 cwts., is 49" in diameter, has the note "F", and was cast by Murphy, Bell Founder, Dublin in 1896. The inscription on it reads: "J. Murphy, Founder, Dublin. Presented by a few friends to the Burgh of Maybole. James Ramsay, Provost, Christmas 1895". The curfew bell was rung in the town at 10 o'clock each night until the Second World War when the custom was discontinued much to the regret of many older townsfolk who would be glad to have the old custom revived.

By the end of the nineteenth century the Commissioners gave way to the Provost, Bailies and Councillors as continue to this day and the members of the twentieth century council deal with more modern matters which are mainly common knowledge to all townsfolk. Since the turn of the present century the Council Minutes deal mostly with rating, housing and the usual everyday problems of a small burgh. In the earlier part of the century they record the mourning of the townspeople on the death of Queen Victoria in 1901 and the subsequent rejoicing at the coronation of King Edward VII in 1902. Much the same pattern of sorrowing and rejoicing occurred on his death in 1910 and the crowning of King George V in 1911 and there seems to have been a ritual proceedings for such events, as the council made more or less similar arrangements on each occasion. Deaths of crowned heads warranted church services and tolling bells and coronations gala days with medals for all the children.

The second decade of the twentieth century records the townspeople's efforts in the First World War and the usual town's affairs were put in the background until the old Town bell rang its victory peal on 11th November, 1918. During the war reference is made in various minutes to concerts, fetes and collections being made to collect funds to send parcels to the men on service and to entertain them on their return and from the sums collected the townspeople did not fail in their efforts to raise money for these purposes.

After the war the council again resumed their usual business of running the town and started building Council houses at Cassillis Terrace, etc. and many road and street improvements were carried out. Again in 1936 the townspeople mourned on the death of King George V and cheered on the proclamation of the Prince of Wales as King Edward VII but no coronation celebrations were held as he abdicated on 17th December of that year. In May 1937, however, King George VI was crowned and the Council royally entertained the townspeople. A large beflagged arch of green foliage was erected across the High Street at the site of the old Town Cross, the elder generation were entertained with a meal and a concert in the Town Hall and the children once again had their sports gala in the Sheep Park and 989 of them received Coronation Medals. It was in this year that the Council sold the old German gun which had stood in the Town Green as a memento of the First World War and the money received for it (£2) was gifted to the funds of the British Legion.

In 1938 the Council discussed the urgent need for a new Police Station and agreed it be built on a site in Ladyland Road. Although the members of the Council had changed throughout the years the methods had not altered much since the days when the civic heads had decided a new Town Hall was required as it was not until 1965 that the new Police Station was built. In the same year (1938) a Council Minute records that complaints had been made that tenants of council houses were drying their washing on their back greens on Sundays and in this instance the councillors of the 1930s emulated their predecessors of the 18th century by issuing a notice forbidding such desecration of the Sabbath under penalty of a fine. It is good to see that the old despotic spirit of the councillors had not been completely submerged by twentieth century democratic rules and regulations. In 1938 it was reported that the population of the town was 4,545 and that the council had built 222 houses since the first housing scheme was commenced in 1919, this being 20% of all houses in the Burgh. It was in this same year that two old Minniebolers, D. & J. Sloan of Glasgow, gifted a Sports Pavilion for the Public Memorial Park and the new Carrick Cinema in Welltrees Street was formally opened on 11th July when the Provost, Bailies and all Councillors attended the opening ceremony and, according to the Minutes, "enjoyed a display of first class films afterwards".

The years 1939 to 1945 again record the horrors of war and the council records deal mainly with air raid precautions, the housing of children from the large cities, the billeting of soldiers, the formation of a prisoner of war camp at Ballony, the ploughing up of part of the Memorial Park and the collection of iron railings from the Town Green and private houses to provide scrap metal. Concerts and dances were again held to raise funds as had been done in the first war and parcels were sent to the troops and money collected to entertain those who returned. One amusing minute in the dreary record of war time was a complaint in July, 1942, that at the Saturday night dances held to raise funds many of the dancers "jitterbugged" and the councillors solemnly passed a rule that only one "jitterbug" dance could be held at any Saturday night dance. Presumably the "jitterbugs" could dance merrily away to their hearts delight on any other night of the week but were solemnly curtailed to one such dance on a Saturday night.

Since the Second World War the minutes of the Council have again reverted to the usual humdrum records of providing sanitation, water supply, street repairs and all the things so necessary to any community. The minutes are now more mundane in so far as they record little of the flashes of genius and practical application to problems dealt with by the old civic heads who held power over all and were the demigods of their day. The power of the Councillors has been greatly curtailed and the constant changing of the composition of its members (unlike the old days when a councillor was more or less elected for his lifetime) seldom allow any outstanding personality to shine (although there were a few, such as Provost McCubbin and some others) and the couthy and homely feeling of the small town, where its own problems were solved by its own folk, has passed away. The days when "Leader" Niven and Bailie Guthrie could definitely solve a problem on the spot and tell the townsfolk what to do have been forgotten and now nearly every matter arising in the council has to be referred to some Government or County Department. At the present time the "Wheatley" proposal that local councils be cast aside and the country "regionalised" hangs like the sword of Damocles over the councillors' heads but it is to be hoped that the Minniebolers will never lose their age long right to govern their old town's affairs by their ain folk.

It is indeed unfortunate the older records from the sixteenth century until 1721 were lost at the time Bonnie Prince Charlie put the fear of death in the lowland Minniebolers and they sent their minutes for safe keeping to the Sheriff in Ayr who promptly lost them. It would make interesting reading to see what the Councillors of that time thought of John Knox when he visited the town in 1562, the mustering of the Maybole Covenanters to march to Bothwell Brig in 1679, the celebration of Mass in the "Auld College" in May, 1563, the fight at Ladycross when young

Bargany was killed in 1601 and the many stirring events which took place in the "auld toon" from the granting of the Charter in 1516 to the time the records are extant. The notes by the Rev. Abercrummie in 1686 are the only written records (apart from some other Charters, etc.) which give an insight on the town in its early days and naturally they are not so complete and pithy as recordings of the council meetings would have been, from the first meeting in 1516 to 1721, and it is indeed unfortunate these minutes were lost by the Sheriff of Ayr.

Chapter 9

BURGESSES

In the Charter dated 1516 power was granted to the townspeople to make "free burgesses" and this was an honour much sought after by old Minniebolers. They were originally to be "admitted, created, and received for good deeds done, and to be done by them, to the said town" and had to be "good and loyal subjects of His Majesty". The Charter stated they would have the right to elect annually Bailies and all other Officers in the Burgh and it may be presumed they elected the first council of civic fathers. As time went on, however, the councillors gradually started to elect their own nominees to replace vacancies caused by the death or retiral of council members and based their claim to do so on a Statute of 1469, in the reign of James IV, which ordained that "Touching on the election of officeraries in Burghs as Aldermen, Bailies and other Officeraries, because of great contention yearly for the chusing of same, through multitude and clamour of cummunes simple persons — the auld Council suld chuse the new." There are no records of any annual elections by the burgesses of the council and certainly this was not done in the eighteenth century, although the councillors faithfully submitted a list of council members to the Earl of Cassillis for him to name the two Bailies for the ensuing year, until nearly the end of the century when this procedure was dropped until it cropped up again in the reforming dispute of the 1820s. The burgesses at that time tried to regain their right and maintained the Town Charter granted powers to them to "elect annually" all councillors and the matter was taken to the Court of Session who ruled the charter did not supersede the earlier Statute. It was not until 1857 that the burgesses regained the right to elect their councillors annually when the Police Commissioners superseded the old councillors.

Originally burgesses were created free of charge but later a fee was made for admittance to the Burgher Roll, One Guinea being charged strangers and ten shillings for sons of burgesses. Most well doing townsmen applied to be admitted as burgesses as they obtained quite a few privileges over their fellowmen and many minutes of the old Council refer to the admittance of Burgesses and state the fees collected. A burgess ticket was necessary before one could trade in the burgh, it entitled one to buy seats in the church and, of course, only burgesses had any chance of being elected to the council.

No records of admittance of burgesses can be traced before the eighteenth century but certainly all councillors and traders would be on the roll. The custom of selling burgess tickets was dropped about the middle of the nineteenth century but in recognition of their services to their town and country many of the townsmen who served in the Boer War were admitted. There have been no new burgesses for many years, although the Freedom of the Burgh has been conferred from time to time on some ex-Provosts and also on President Eisenhower of America in October, 1946. An old list of Burgesses in Maybole between 1834 and 1837 is still in existence and the following excerpt from it gives many names which are familiar in the town to this day.

List of Maybole Burgesses

1834	Nov.	6	Allan Hunter Jr.	Grocer.
,,	,,	20	John Spellman.	Residenter.
1835	Jan.	8	Richard Cowan.	Plumber.

1835	Oct.	1	Charles Crawford.	Shoemaker.
1838	Aug.	2	Thomas Holligan.	Weaver.
,,	Oct.	4	William Forsyth.	Grocer.
1839	Nov.	7	John Hannay.	Grocer.
1840	Dec.	7	John Campbell.	Baker.
1843	Jan.	5	William Baird.	Shoemaker.
,,	,,	21	John Hindmarsh.	Weaver's Agent.
,,	Jly.	20	Hugh McCrindle.	Tailor.
1846	Oct.	7	Thomas Dunlop.	Weaver.
,,	Nov.	9	Thomas Dykes.	Factor.
1847	Oct.	9	John Austin.	Wright.
1853	,,	3	Peter Sinclair.	Gamedealer.
,,	,,		Arthur Muir.	Draper.
,,	,,		William Galbraith.	Merchant.
,,	,,	4	Alexander McWhirter.	Draper.
1860	Sept.	28	John Kennedy, Jnr.	Grocer.
1863	Oct.	5	Adam Gray.	Shoemaker.
1864	—		Joseph Pealing.	Cattledealer.
1868	Oct.	7	Adam Goudie.	Merchant.
1872	,,	19	Robert Allan.	Auctioneer.
,,	,,		James Lambie.	Clothier.
,,	,,		John Gray, Jnr.	Shoemaker.
,,	,,		Malcolm Gillespie.	Innkeeper.
,,	,,		John Cameron.	Ironmonger.
,,	,,		David Templeton.	Watchmaker.
1874	Jne.	5	Robert Muir.	Grocer.
,,	,,		John McGeachie.	Flesher.
,,	,,		Mathew Guthrie.	Baker.
,,	,,		John Watson.	Private
,,	,,	5	John McMath.	Flesher.
,,	,,		James McKissock.	Draper.
,,	,,		James McCubbin.	Draper.
,,	,,		Thomas France.	Ironmonger.
1876	Oct.	13	Robert Allan, Jnr.	Accountant.
,,	,,		John Gilmour.	Clerk.

MAYBOLE - CARRICK'S CAPITAL

1876	Oct.	13	Richard Hunter.	Joiner.
,,	,,		John Riddoch.	Plasterer.
,,	,,		Hugh Hunter.	Innkeeper.
,,	,,		John Marshall.	Millowner.
,,	,,		James Gray.	Shoemaker.
,,	,,		James Gibson.	Solicitor.
,,	,,		John Chapel.	Teacher.
,,	,,		David Brown.	Solicitor.
,,	,,		Thomas Rennie.	Banker.
,,	,,		John Dunn.	Carrier.
,,	,,		James Goudie.	Weaver.
,,	,,		John Gray.	Shoemaker.
,,	,,		George Wilson.	Weaver.

It will be seen that all included in the list were men of substance with a stake in the town's trade and an interest in its welfare. The Grays and Crawfords started the great shoe industry. Hindmarsh was a notable wool merchant, Marshall brought fame to the old firm of Jack & Sons and the others were all sound tradespeople, etc. who depended on the custom of the people in the town and surrounding district. Many old Burgess tickets must still be laid away in old drawers, etc. in houses in the town although most would probably be lost or destroyed when older people's possessions were disposed of on their deaths, as few of the younger generations would appreciate how prized they were by the holders who were proud to be Burgesses in the old Capital of Carrick.

74

Chapter 10

INDUSTRY

THROUGHOUT the centuries there have been many varied trades in the town but to Minniebolers weaving and shoemaking have been the main ones and they both brought prosperity to the town. Unfortunately the townsfolk concentrated so much on these trades that, when tastes changed and the Maybole products fell from favour, there was nothing else to turn to and after the sunny times there were long periods of dull times with unemployment and hardship.

Originally agriculture in one form or another was the principal employment in the town and district and all townsfolk were connected with it in some way. Everyone was entitled to share the common grazings at what are now Whitefaulds and Lyonston Farms and gradually a system evolved where common barns were erected to hold grain, and yards and buchts were formed to pen cattle and sheep when they were brought in from the grazings at night, as there were no hedges or fences to keep stock from straying and they had to be constantly herded. It is believed that in the fifteenth and sixteenth centuries the Minniebolers reared huge flocks of geese, grazing them on the marsh below the town, which is to this day known as "The Bog" although it has been drained and is now fertile farm land. These geese were driven in the evenings up a narrow lane, still known as the "Croft" or "Croft-e-geish", (the croft of the geese), to the goose pens sited in the Ladylands near the railway station, and this part of the town seems to have been chosen for the penning of all the agricultural animals, as the goose pens, cattle yards, town pound for stray horses, barns for grain and sheep pens were all in the area between what is now the railway station and the Cargill-Kincraig Church. The present names still refer to these, as Buchty Bridge is where the sheep buchts were sited and Barns Road was the site of the public barns. Once a year the geese, when fattened and ready for market, were driven through a layer of tar and then through sand which stuck to the tar and made "bootees" which saved wear and tear on their feet when they were driven in great flocks to markets, sometimes as far away as Carlisle. This method of tarring and sanding seems to be peculiar to Maybole district although it is said the same practice was carried out by gooseherders in parts of Yorkshire.

The first recognised manufactory trade was weaving and by the eighteenth century most of the townsfolk had given up crofting and set up hand looms in their houses. It was then a family trade and the looms were set up in the lower rooms of the houses, which had earthen floors, the weaver and his family living in the apartments above. While the menfolk worked the looms the women and children were kept busy washing, cairding and spinning the wool for the looms and this was the common lot of nearly all Minniebolers for some generations. To begin with it was mainly blankets and rough cloth which was produced but gradually weavers from North Ireland infiltrated and cotton looms were set up and Maybole clacked its way to prosperity and sold its produce to Glasgow merchants who distributed it throughout the country. Because the weavers were mainly individualists and would not combine to set up mills but preferred to work at home and sell their cloth to merchants it was understandable why the weaving trade declined when the powerloom was developed and large mills began to produce cheaper cloth and this was the death knell of weaving in Maybole.

With the failure of the weaving trade there was a great deal of unemployment and labour was cheap and easily procured and about the middle of the nineteenth century some small shoemakers who had been producing boots and shoes mainly in their own homes or having it done by other shoemakers on piecework rates, decided to start boot and shoe making in a large way and they built factories and trained and employed the old weavers. These firms prospered exceedingly well and by 1883 there were eight large shoe factories, (three with tanneries and currying departments), employing 1,184 workers and producing 12,360 pairs of boots weekly. The main factories in that year were:

John Gray & Co. (Ladywell)	498 workers	4,500 pairs per week		
T. A. Gray (Lorne)	283	do	3,000	do
Charles Crawford	156	do	2,000	do
Robert Crawford	118	do	1,500	do
James Ramsay	51	do	550	do
Other factories (3)	78	do	810	do
	1,184		12,360	

By 1891 there were ten shoe factories in full production employing 1,500 workers and producing about one million pairs of boots and shoes annually. Shops were opened throughout the whole of Britain, named "The Maybole Shoe Shop", (one being opened as far away as Manitoba) and these sold the products of the factories direct to the customers. The list of factories in the town at that date were:

John Gray & Co.	Ladywell
T. A. Gray	Lorne
James Ramsay	St. Cuthberts
Charles Crawford	Kirkwynd

John Lees & Co.	Townend
William Boyd	St. Helens
Maybole Shoe Factory	Drummellan Street
J. M. Rennie	Greenside
G. Dick	Ladyland
McGarvie & Co.	Society Street.

The boot and shoe industry continued to provide work for nearly all the townspeople until 1907 when the Ladywell Factory, which was the largest in the town, had to close down (an event which was reported in the local press as "a major tragedy") and once again many Maybole men were out of work and there were hard times, as there had been when the weaving trade failed. Many shoemakers emigrated with their families to Canada (some estimates give 2,000 persons as the number that left Maybole at that time) and some went to work in the shoe factory at Shieldhall. The cause of the failure was once again the insularity of the Maybole men, who would not change from the craft of making shoes by hand to making them by the machines which had been invented about that period. The owners of some of the smaller factories, however, were more far sighted and gradually Crawford, Ramsay and Lees installed modern machinery and absorbed the remainder of the shoemakers who had stayed in Maybole. The First World War was a boon to the shoe trade as large army orders were obtained and full employment again came to the townspeople. The workers started at 6 a.m. and worked to 6 p.m. and there was a short period of well being among them, but after the war trade again fell away. The rubber wellington boot had displaced the farm worker's heavy boot which was one of the main products of the Factories and the loss of the Irish market, through heavy tariffs imposed, was a great blow, and gradually trade dwindled, factories closed and finally only Lees & Co. and McCreath & Co., who had started a small factory in Society Street, were left. The Second World War again brought a short term of full employment but as before, after the war ended, shoemaking as the main manufactury in the town fell into the doldrums. Lees & Co. continued to produce boots and shoes and modernised their factory. They started trading in other commodities and were the only large employers of labour up until June, 1962, when unfortunately their factory was completely destroyed by fire and this was really the end of the hundred years of shoemaking when Maybole craftsmen were famous for their products throughout the whole of Britain and the old jinkle had it that:

> "Go where you will through Scotia's land,
> You'll see our boots on every hand,
> It's Maybole on which Scotsmen stand,
> This auld toon o' Maybole".

McCreath's carried on for a few years after the disastrous fire at Lees' but in 1968 competition from larger factories, cut rate prices in the trade and their unwillingness to lower the high standard of their products finally forced them to close, and apart from a small factory run by Messrs Harrison and Goudie, which employs a few men and deals mostly with special orders, the boot and shoe trade in Maybole is now a memory like the weaving trade.

The tanning of leather, which was ancillary to the shoe trade, also flourished during the period from the 1850s to the 1960s and originally some of the factories had their own tanneries. These were, however, finally replaced by one large tannery at Ladywell which was owned by the Millar Tanning Co. Ltd. This company took over the buildings (which had been erected by John Gray) when the Ladywell Tannery & Shoe Co. failed in the first decade of this century and started the Ladywell Tannery with 45 employees. The company prospered and continued in business until May 1969 when once again the march of time and the change to the method of making shoes with materials other than leather forced it to close down and the last link with the old leather trade was swept away.

MAYBOLE - CARRICK'S CAPITAL

At the same time as the shoe manufacturers started their industry in the town another farseeing and forceful personality laid the foundations of what was to become one of the best known agricultural implement businesses throughout not only Britain but many countries in the world. This was Alexander Jack who began business with a capital of £10 and made masons' mallets in a small mill at Auchendrane near Minishant. In 1852 he also saw that labour could be got cheaply in Maybole from out-of-work weavers and he started in a small way to make carts, etc. for the surrounding farmers. The business grew rapidly and he built at "Townhead", at a cost of £6,000, the works which became widely known as "Jacks" and employed over one hundred men. With the expansion of trade, and the efforts of his successor, Mr. Marshall, after Mr. Jack died in 1877, another smaller implement firm which had been carried on by Mr. Thomas Hunter (who started in a small blacksmith's shop sited at the foot of the "Castle Brae" where H. & T. McQuiston's ironmongery shop now stands and later built a factory near "Brandy Row" in Alloway Road), was absorbed into the business and early in the twentieth century the famous firm of Alexander Jack & Sons was producing every type of implement for farmwork. Their products were exhibited at Agricultural Shows throughout the whole land, many being bought by farmers in Canada, Australia, etc. The firm started their own moulding shop for the metal work required, employed their own fellers for the timber, and their own painters, sawyers, cartwrights, etc., and produced the finished implements from raw materials. They experimented on improvements to ploughs, grubbers, turnip, sowers, etc., were the first to make the rubber-tyred wheels for carts in 1932 and produced the famous Oliver ploughs demonstrated so ably at ploughing matches by Mr. Houston who was a famous ploughman in the district early this century.

In those days ploughing matches were regularly held at Tunnoch and other farms round about where all the local ploughmen gathered to show their skill. It was a brave sight to see pair upon pair of gaily bedecked Clydesdales steadily drawing the ploughs so earnestly guided by shirt sleeved experts who were entirely oblivious of the comments of the numerous critics who always gathered at a "peughing match". There were prizes for nearly every competitor, from the most skilful to the poorest exponent of the art, the oldest and the youngest, the married ploughman with the largest family, the competitor with the most colourful braces, etc., and everyone, competitors and spectators alike, had a wonderful time. Such days are now past and the handsome Clydesdales have given way to the tractor, which is perhaps more practical, but can never have the magnetism to the spectator of a "furr and land" pair with satiny coats and steaming nostrils on a crisp frosty morning drawing a straight rich brown furr soon to be covered with a seething line of noisy seagulls.

Up until the First World War the firm had a great influence in the agricultural implement world but from then on the business waned, and fewer and fewer men were employed until after the Second World War it finally was taken over by the firm of John Wallace who carried on the business until the 1960s when, like the shoe industry, it finally had to close down. It is strange that both industries started in the town about the same time, gained country wide fame and finally died out about the same time. Unfortunately Maybole's geographical position made it impossible for employers to compete with the products of new factories which had been built nearer larger centres of population where transport was cheaper to such centres and where raw materials were more easily procurable. Goods could be sent much cheaper from places like Kilmarnock by rail direct to English markets and Kilmarnock has now large shoe factories and agricultural implement works while Maybole has neither.

In the eighteenth century the women of Maybole were famous for their needlework and their speciality was "flowering", in which some were expert, and their work was much sought after throughout the whole country. Two women were the acknowledged mistresses of this craft and these were Ann Jenkinson and Janet Inglis, both of whom lived in the Kirkwynd. This was the start of the famous Ayrshire embroidery and this unique style of white embroidery on muslin and cotton gave work to a large number of the local womenfolk whose husbands worked the looms which made the cloth to be embroidered.

Two lemonade factories started up business in the town about the end of the nineteenth century, one (McPherson's) in the factory in Society Street which was later taken over as a shoe factory by McCreath and Sons, and one (Gellatly's) at the corner of Crosshill Road and Drummellan Street. Artesian wells were sunk on each site and the water proved most suitable for the manufacture of lemonade and the factories were both successful for many years. The lemonade was put into bottles which had a twisted neck and were sealed with a small glass ball which had to be "plunked" down into the bottle to allow the contents to be poured, and some of these bottles with the glass marbles in them are still to be found in many of the out premises of houses in the town. The factories enjoyed a good business while the shoemaking trade was in full swing and the products were mainly sold to the local people but when trade became bad and many of the inhabitants emigrated there was little demand for the lemonade and both works closed down.

During the Second World War part of Ramsay's old shoe factory was taken over by Hutchison & McCreath, Grain Merchants, as a store, and for some time experiments were carried out in trying to process a quick cooking oatmeal for porridge but the experiments were not successful and the proposal to start a factory to process meal fell through. When Crawford's factory was demolished Hutchison & McCreath built a large store on the site. The business was later taken over by West Cumberland Farmers Society but it has also gone and the buildings are now occupied by McQuater Bros., local grain merchants, who have a thriving trade with the local farmers.

MAYBOLE - CARRICK'S CAPITAL

Although weaving, shoemaking and agricultural implements are the industries mainly associated with the town throughout the centuries there have been other trades which started up, flourished for a time and died out and are now forgotten by most of the townspeople. At the end of the seventeenth century a Frenchman, Albert Danel Geli, set up a bellfoundry (said to be near the site occupied by the gasworks) and carried on his business for a few years. He cast the bells for some churches in Scotland after he cast the old town bell for the steeple of the Tolbooth, which is the only remaining bell in Ayrshire that he cast. It is not known how long he remained in Maybole but in 1696, one year after he cast the town bell, he removed to Irvine and there cast a bell for the laigh Kirk in Kilmarnock but this bell has not survived. In 1702 Geli moved to Aberdeen and took over a bell foundry there which had formerly belonged to a Patrick Kilgour. In this foundry he cast many bells, the last known one being cast in 1713, and his work greatly improved and his later bells are said to be much finer than the first known one which he cast in Maybole.

In coaching days there was a great deal of money brought into the town through Maybole being the "half-way house" between Glasgow and Port Patrick, at that time the port where people sailed to Ireland. There were three famous coaching houses, the Dunnering Inn, the Sun Inn and the Kings Arms and all travellers stayed the night in one or other of these inns when journeying to and from Ireland. Relays of coach horses had to be kept and a great many people worked at the inns and while this may not be classed as a "trade", it was certainly a busy industry which gave a lot of employment to the townspeople.

The 1960's brought much unemployment to the town, as in the early years of that decade the boot and shoe factories of John Lees & Company Ltd., and John McCreath & Sons Ltd., both closed down, as did the famous agricultural implement works of Alexander Jack & Sons Ltd., and, as these firms had given employment to most of the townspeople, it seemed that once again Maybole was facing a period of hardship. The Town Council, however, faced up to the problem with all the force and energy of the councillors of last century and due to the efforts of the councillors in 1967 Maybole was granted "Development Area" status by the Government. This was a tremendous step towards attracting new industries to the Burgh as it made financial and tax incentives available to any new industry starting up in the area while the great number of unemployed provided a ready pool of labour.

The Town Council, with great foresight (and in the face of much criticism) committed itself to a policy of acquiring all vacant industrial buildings and sites suitable for industrial development, at the same time taking the difficult decision, in a period of great shortage of housing, to provide houses for key-workers of incoming industry. The Council also committed itself to assist incoming firms to finance the purchase of existing factories or to build new ones, using the new powers given to Local Authorities under the Industrial Development Acts.

This was a courageous attitude by the Council as it meant stepping out of the past century of leather working and agriculture implements into a new and unknown era of unknown trades, and Minniebolers, like people in all small communities, are loth to depart from old customs. Time has proved the Councillors to be right and although their early efforts met with some setbacks, they persisted in striving to attract new industries and now the town has seven completely new industrial firms, and two new factory buildings which provide about 450 new jobs of which over 100 are for male workers.

One of the first new industries to start was the making of slippers by Monteith's Ltd., a Glasgow firm who took over Townend Factory but unfortunately after a short period this firm went into liquidation. Then the John Wallace Group of Companies which had taken over the old Jack & Sons implement works closed down their works in Maybole and these two closures were not a happy start to the promise of better times for the townsfolk. Since then, however, progress has been steady and new firms have brought their industries to Maybole and it would seem that good times will come again and the old Burgh will flourish as in years long past.

In 1967 the old implement works of Alexander Jack & Sons were purchased by the Town Council and part of it was resold the same year to the American firm of International Packaging Corporation who are one of the world's leading manufacturers of presentation cases and whose parent company is based in Rhode Island, U.S.A. This firm completely modernised the buildings to provide 60,000 square feet of factory and office space and at present employ 39 men and 137 women.

Another part of the old works were taken over by the firm of William McCulloch & Son who were formerly blacksmiths in Maidens and this firm, who employ 7 men, are now carrying on the tradition of agricultural implement makers, etc., in the old buildings made famous by Alexander Jack & Sons.

The Council purchased the former warehouses of John Lees & Co. Ltd., in Alloway Road which had escaped damage when the disastrous fire in 1962 destroyed the factory buildings and in 1968 sold them to a printing firm from Yorkshire who specialise in colour printing. This firm was formerly known as Northern Gravure Ltd., but is now called Clyde Gravure Ltd., and it is associated with the old established London based printing firm of Ripley & Co. Ltd. The premises have been completely modernised and reroofed and extend to 18,000 square feet and the company presently employ 18 men and 9 women.

In 1968 the Town Council, with great foresight, granted the use of the Town Hall to the firm of Jersey-Kapwood Ltd., of Nottingham, to allow them to set up sewing machines to train local women to make ladies lingerie, blouses, etc. Although the townspeople lost the use of the Hall for social functions and dances for over a year, all were only too glad to know that new industry was being introduced into the town and that prospects of local employment were steadily improving. At the same time the Council acquired the disused Railway Goods Station at Redbrae and cleared the site and then sold it to Jersey-Kapwood Ltd., who built a modern factory with 15,500 square feet of floor space. The machinery was then cleared from the Town Hall and installed in the new factory and it was formally opened in July, 1969, by Dr. J. Dickson Mabon, Minister of State. The factory is one of the most modern of its kind in the country and the firm at present employs 12 men and 149 women. Early in 1971 the Jersey-Kapwood factories in Scotland were amalgamated with Saracen Ltd., of Northern Ireland, who are within Carrington Viyella Ltd. Since then a large building at Maybole Station has been taken over by the firm and converted into a modern warehouse where an extra 6 men and 5 women are employed. On 1st January, 1972, the company became known as Saracen Ltd.

In 1969 the Council pursued their effective policy of acquiring old industrial buildings by purchasing the old implement works of Hunters Ltd., in Alloway Road and in 1970 they resold them to the packaging firm of Wm. Clark Stephen Ltd., a family business which started in Glasgow in 1919. This firm, which specialised in the manufacture of cardboard boxes, had steadily expanded and in 1964 started a Screen Process Printing Department. Eventually this department grew to such an extent that new premises were required and the firm decided to transfer the whole printing department to the 13,000 square feet factory in Maybole. The firm now employ 20 local people and is still very much a family business and the present Managing Director, Mr. Robert McGhie Stephen is a grandson of the founder of the firm, the late Wm. Clark Stephen.

Another new industry was started in 1971 when the old gas works site in Drummellan Street was cleared of its gasometer and sheds and a modern factory of 3,000 square feet with separate works canteen and offices were erected by a group of Ayr businessmen headed by Mr. Thomas Gray of Messrs Hunter & Gray, Fish Salesmen, Ayr. This company is called Sea G. - G. Ltd., and the firm installed in the new factory the most modern plant for processing and freezing fish. It specialises in producing "Scampi" (now a favourite sea food made from prawns which is in great demand) and most of the fish and prawns are purchased from the fishermen who land their catches at Ayr harbour. This company already employs 7 men and 40 women and the venture is proving so successful that it is planning further expansion in the near future.

In 1971 the Town Council, which had purchased the old boot and shoe factory formerly occupied by Messrs McCreath and Sons in Society Street in 1969, resold the buildings to Hunter Wilson & Partners Ltd., and these companies moved to Maybole from Ayr in July 1971. Hunter Wilson and Partners design a comprehensive range of equipment for High Tensile Fencing based on the most modern metallurgical conception which is erected by special techniques particularly suitable for moorland areas where access is difficult. Stainless Steel Silencers Ltd., design exhaust conversions in stainless steel for a wide range of cars. These companies at present employ 9 men in the works in Society Street with others employed outside on erection contracts. The buildings cover about 7,000 square feet, most of which has already been modernised and new buildings will be developed as required.

In the 1960's the old established Maybole firm of McQuater Bros., Grain Merchants, took over the old factory originally built by Messrs. Ramsay, Boot & Shoe Manufacturers, and occupied after the boot and shoe industry closed down by Messrs Hutchison & McCreath, Seed Merchants, for some years McQuater Bros. have now excellent works and storage premises, employ 25 men and 3 women and carry on a thriving business with the farmers throughout the district.

In the short space of five years all these new industries have started up in Maybole, giving employment to over 100 men and

350 women and much credit must be given to the local Council for their continued efforts to bring work to the area after the old trades of boot and shoemaking and agricultural implement making died out. It shows the spirit of the Minniebolers is as prominent today as it was a hundred years ago when the weaving trade collapsed and the civic fathers had to look for other means of employment for the townspeople and introduced the boot and shoe trade which prospered for over a century. It may be unfortunate that most of the new industry predominantly employs female labour and the majority of the townsmen have to commute to Ayr, etc., to find employment but no one can tell what the future may bring and expansion in the new trades in the town may, at a not too distant date, give full employment to the townsmen as well as their womenfolk.

Many confirmed pessimists (who, like the poor, are always with us) are voluble in their arguments that there is much unemployment in the town and that the future holds no promise of better times, but facts disprove this when thought is given to the number of jobs open to the people of Maybole. In addition to the 450 jobs in the new industries over 430 men are employed by the local builders, joiners, plumbers, etc. This does not take into account the employment for shop assistants, Post Office workers, Burgh workmen, and many other positions which accounts for at least another 200 jobs. Altogether there are at least over 1,000 jobs available within the town which compares favourably with the number employed at the end of last century which was considered one of the most thriving periods of the town's history. In 1883 approximately 1,180 people were employed in the boot and shoe industry out of a total population of approximately 6,500, while today there is employment for over 1,000 persons from a greatly reduced population of around 4,500 townspeople. When these facts are considered in a true perspective it must be admitted that times are not really so bad as the pessimists declare.

Chapter 11

STREET NAMES

HISTORY is often bound up in street names and although many streets in our old town have been renamed over the years a study of them can be most interesting and show how different communities, trades, etc., grew, flourished for a while, and dwindled away only to leave in the name a record of their existence. Unfortunately about the end of the nineteenth century (and even in recent years) there were many alterations to street names and descriptive old names such as Smithy Brae, Weaver Vennal, New Yards, etc., have been changed to what are considered more "genteel" names. The old names will always be remembered by the older residents, however, and even by the younger generation who hear their elders speak of Ladywell Road for instance as Weaver Vennal, and it is to be hoped that the old names will not be entirely forgotten by coming generations.

To many it will be surprising there are over seventy streets in Maybole and every street name has a meaning attached either to local events or people or to national events such as the coronation of Queen Elizabeth which is commemorated in Queens Terrace.

Abbot Street. At one time the Abbots of Crossraguel had a town house in this area. Near it stood the Black House which was one of the oldest houses in Maybole before it was demolished in 1967. It belonged to the Dominican Friars who dressed in black robes, and, being itinerant preachers, had resting places throughout the country. At one time the Black House was occupied by a Prebend of the Collegiate Church, which was built just behind the house. Near to it, where the new houses on Crosshill Road are built, was the garden for the Abbots House, and the area is still known to the older folk as "The Garden of Eden".

Academy Quadrant. So named because it is adjacent to the Carrick Academy. It is part of the Council Housing Scheme between Kirkoswald Road and Culzean Road.

Allans Hill. This was one of the oldest exits from the town to Dailly and Girvan and is believed to be a corruption of the Gaelic "Alt-nan-hill" or "hill beside the burn", in this instance the Cairders Burn where the weavers of Maybole used to "caird" or wash and comb the wool for weaving. Another derivation of the name is from the Anglo-Saxon "aelron" (or alder tree) but the Gaelic derivation is the most fitting.

Alloway Road. Descriptive in itself and is the road to Alloway.

Ayr Road. Again just the road to Ayr and is only the short part of the highway from the foot of the Lovers Loaning to Lyonston Farm.

Ballony. A very old name in the town and formerly a small farm. Believed to mean the house or dwelling place of John. It was formerly outside the town boundary but about the end of the nineteenth century the farm lands were purchased for the town's sewage works and refuse coup and were used as such for many years until the new sewage works were formed near Littleton Farm in the 1960s and the public coup was moved to an old quarry at Kirklandhill Farm in 1969. On the farm lands was formed the town's first football pitch where before the first World War the Maybole Football Team played Glasgow Rangers in the first round of the Scottish Football Cup. The game is remembered by the older townspeople but the score conveniently forgotten. The present football pitch at Ladywell Stadium is on the same site as the original ground.

Barns Road and Barns Terrace. The public barns for the town stood on this area and the townspeople had the right to store their grain etc. in these barns. Where Barns House now stands was the town "pound" where stray horses were impounded until their owners could bail them out. This was the forerunner of the present method of dealing with cars wrongly parked, or left unattended for too long, and towed away to a "pound" by the police.

Cairnfield Avenue. Named because it is near the Cairn School which was built on a field which at one time had a cairn in it to mark some forgotten incident in local history. Before the local council built Cairnfield Avenue it was a large field owned by the Carrick Farmers Association and for very many years was the site for the local Agricultural Show which was one of the highlights of the year's activities for the local people.

Cargill Avenue and Cargill Road. Commemorates the time when Donald Cargil the great Covenanter preached at the conventicle held in May, 1681, on the lands of Cargilstone Farm, just outside the town. A large stone marked the site of the conventicle and part of this stone is built into the wall of the Cargill-Kincraig Church in Barns Road. The conventicle was held in the field on the Cross Roads behind the Covenanters Memorial which was erected to commemorate the death of the Maybole Covenanters who were taken prisoners at the Battle of Bothwell Brig.

Carrick Street. Refers to the region of Carrick of which Maybole is the ancient capital. Carrick means "hilly or craggy place" and is mentioned in Roman history about 80 A.D.

Cassillis Road and Cassillis Terrace. Formerly called New Yards as the ground was occupied in olden times by the stack yards of the Earl of Cassillis. It was a custom to pay farm rents at one time partly in kind and the grain and straw paid in kind was carted to the lands adjoining Maybole Castle, which was then the town residence of the Earl of Cassillis, and stored in the "yards". This was used for feeding cattle given by other farmers as rent for their farms and the cattle were held and fed in the yards until they could be sold at market. The Rev. Roderick Lawson (who was responsible for changing many of the couthy and descriptive street names) persuaded the civic fathers to change the name from "New Yards" to Cassillis Road, thus still connecting the road with the Earl of Cassillis, but to most townspeople it is still the "New Yards".

Castle Street. Named because of its proximity to the Castle. It was first known as the "Fore Vennal" but later became the "Foul Vennal" because a drain ran down the centre of the street and in wet weather it was rather unpleasant and the Councillors arranged for it to be causewayed in 1775 to remedy its foul condition. The name was changed for a short time to "Post Vennal" because the Mail or Post vans were stabled there, but about the end of the nineteenth century it was finally changed to Castle Street. It is a pity the commonplace "Street" was used and not the ancient Scottish "Vennal" so often come across in Edinburgh, and surely every bit as suitable for the ancient Capital of Carrick.

Chesney Grove. Named after a well-known benefactor to the town, Mr. Harold Chesney. Although an Englishman he came to Maybole, married the daughter of a well-known Provost, James Miller, and became a staunch "Minnieboler" by choice if not by birth. He was ever ready to help in all matters relating to the town's welfare and the Councillors, when the new street was formed, perpetuated his name in "Chesney Grove" in recognition of his many services to the town.

Coral Glen and Coral Hill. It is strange to find such a name in an old Scottish town but it has no connection with blue seas and coral strands. Originally the old quarries from which the stone was quarried to build the old houses in the town stood in this glen and through time the "Quarry Glen" was corrupted to "Quarrle Glen" and finally to "Coral Glen". There are also deposits of "quarl" or fireclay in the glen and probably this also was corrupted in time to "Coral". In "The Glen" is the well-known "Cockydrighty" or "Wee Spout in the Glen" with the inscription above it, "Ye may gang further and fare waur". A small lane running parallel to the Coral Glen was known locally as the "Sma' Glen". It was in the "Sma' Glen" that the "Lodging Houses" housed most of the "randy beggars" which the douce townsfolk complained about to the Council in 1792 and the last of these "Lodging Houses" still stood, and was in use, until after the first World War.

Crosshill Road. Merely the road to Crosshill. In former days the "Garden of Eden" was here and last century a lemonade works and the slaughter house stood in this street. The ground behind these buildings was for many years used as a fairground and, until the Council built a housing scheme on the site, the once pleasant "Garden of Eden" was a derelict wasteland. It must have at some time been used for burial purposes as when the area was cleared for building some very old tombstones were found buried in the ground.

The Croft. The steep lane leading from Whitehall to Welltrees Street is commonly called "The Croft" but the full and correct name is "Croft-e-geish" meaning the "Lane of the Geese". Centuries ago many townspeople kept flocks of geese which were driven daily to graze on the marshlands round the "Bog" and each night again driven up "The Croft" to pens sited near Ladyland Road.

Culzean Road. Until the end of the nineteenth century this was known as "The Shore Road" being the way the townspeople flocked on summer days to Croy Shore. Now the name signifies it is the way to Culzean Castle, for so many years the home of the Kennedies, the Kings of Carrick, and now one of the best known properties belonging to the National Trust for Scotland. It was in this area on a field known as the "Muster Lea" that the Maybole Covenanters gathered, or "mustered", to march off to defend their cause at Bothwell Brig in 1679. The town gallows, where public hangings used to take place, were sited at the top end of Culzean Road on a spot now occupied by a house known as "The Knowe". Prior to being named "Shore Road" the name given to it was "Gallow Hill" a name still used by many of the older residents. It was near Whitefaulds Farm on Culzean Road that McAdam first experimented with his new style of roadmaking which gave the world "macadamised" roadways and made transport so much easier.

Dailly Road. Again now merely descriptive as the road to Dailly but formerly known as Masons Row. The old name was a corruption of "Maison Dieu" (House of God) and a Hospice or "spittal" connected with the Old College stood here at one time. Where the "Sma' Glen" joined Mason's Row the site used to be known as "Bryce's Corner". A well-known local character, Rab Bryce lived here, who enjoyed nothing better than a "guid gaing fecht". In one such differences of opinion after a ploughing match when he was wielding a stick to good effect he was asked whose side he was on and answered, "on nae side ava; I'm just for ma ain han'."

Drummellan Street. About the end of the nineteenth century this was one of the old streets renamed at the instigation of the Rev. Roderick Lawson, and was so called because the lands around it belonged to Mr. Kennedy of Drummellan House (formerly known as "Machrie Mhor" as far back as 1721). The old name of the street was "Dangartland", a name still commonly in use, because at one time it formed part of the estates of Dangart in Colmonell Parish. Mr.

Kennedy of Drummellan proposed to form a new street to the south east of, and parallel with, Drummellan Street and plans were drawn up for it but the street was never formed. The name of the new street was to be Primrose Lane in honour of Mr. Primrose Kennedy of Drummellan who was a Provost of Ayr and whose memorial in the form of a granite obelisk stands at the south end of Sandgate in Ayr. Local people nicknamed the proposed new street "Blue Pansy Street" and among the older folks this name is sometimes used for Drummellan Street.

Dunlop Terrace. This is one of the streets formed in the new housing scheme built on the steep slope between Whitehall and Ladywell Road and was named after Provost John Dunlop who was for many years Housing Convener in the Town Council.

Enoch Road. A street in Gardenrose housing scheme, formed in 1970 and named because it overlooks East Enoch Farm.

Gardenrose Path. This road led to Gardenrose Farm and at one time was one of the exits from the town. The street really takes its name from a house (commonly called the Bumbee because the householder kept bees) which used to stand where the railway bridge is in Culzean Road and not from the farm of Gardenrose which was built much later. Locals know the road better as "The Near Path" to distinguish it from "The Far Path" or Kirklandhill Path.

Glebe Terrace and Glebe Crescent. These roads were formed on the lands of the glebe belonging to the manse of the Old Parish Church and are self explanatory.

Glenalla Road. A street in the Gardenrose housing scheme so named because it faces Glenalla Fell, a well-known hill above Crosshill.

Greenside. This roadway circles the open space known as the Town Green and is most suitably named. Formerly, it was here the townspeople practised archery, played bias bowls, "gowf" and held fairs. At one time the authorities forbade the playing of "bias bowls" as the townspeople were neglecting their archery practice. Sir Walter Scott in one of his novels mentions Maybole as being one of the last towns in Scotland where the archers' sport of shooting at the popinjay was practised. In the 18th and early 19th centuries the grazing on the Ballgreen was rouped annually by the Magistrates of the town and the usual rent was about 5/-.

High Street. Now the main street of the town although formerly only a roadway between the Tolbooth at the top and the Castle at the bottom of the roadway. These buildings sat across the street at one time and the only approaches to it were up the Kirkwynd and what is now John Knox Street. The street was much broader in former days but the newer buildings on the south side were built in front of the older buildings, many of which still stand behind the present shops and this narrowed the roadway considerably. The Town Cross originally stood halfway up the street but was removed in October, 1773, because it was obstructing traffic and the site is now marked by an iron cross set in the middle of the roadway. It was in this street that Robert Burns' father first met his future wife, Agnes Brown, at a booth erected for one of the Town Fairs and the spot where they first met is marked by a bust of the poet set on top of a gable over a shop near the bottom of the street. Although Rev. Roderick Lawson states this street was at one time called Main Street, there is no reference in any Town records at any time to such a name, although it is marked "Main Street" on an old ordnance survey map of last century. Abercrombie refers to it as High Street and the council minutes of 4th June, 1745, ordained that the "High Street" should be causewayed. The name originally merely meant is was the High Street up the hill above Abbot Street which was then the main street of the town. On 5th November, 1744, it was ordained that all public proclamations would be made from the Cross in High Street and such proclamations should be preceded by "tuck of drum".

Hicks Avenue. Named by the Town Council to commemorate the services given to the burgh by Provost Thomas Hicks, who for many years was a member of the Council and took a great interest in the town's welfare.

Hutchison Street. The houses here were built by a man called Hutchison and the street was named after him. Locally the street is commonly called "The Hill" which is a most suitable name as it stands high with a wonderful view over the Southern uplands.

Inches Close. Derived from the Gaelic "innis" meaning a narrow place and a most suitable name as formerly it was just a narrow close or lane. For some years it was named Buchanan Street, but fortunately the old name has been resumed and it is hoped will remain. It has been said the street was called after an old worthy nicknamed "Inch-aboot" but this is most unlikely.

John Knox Street. The old name, still in common use, was Red Lion Brae so called from a public house "The Red Lion" which was in the street. It was earlier known as the Back Vennal leading up to High Street. It was in a house in this Street in 1592 that the famous debate between Quintin, Abbot of Crossraguel, and John Knox took place and again the Rev. Roderick Lawson persuaded the civic fathers to change the name to commemorate this event. Fortunately this change was quite logical and not too harmful to the history of the street names, as many others were which were changed for no good reason. The house in which the debate took place became an inn known as the "Red Lion" and after it was closed another inn at the foot of the hill took the same name.

Kildoon Drive. A new street formed in 1969 by the Town Council in the private housing development at Gardenrose Farm, and so named because it looks to Kildoon Hill. The old spelling was "Culdoon" and not "Kildoon" and the name means "the brown hill".

Kincraig Avenue, Kincraig Court and Kincraig Crescent. From the Gaelic "Cean-no-creige" meaning the end of the rock or hill. In this instance the names refer to the site being at the end of the hill above the town where a small croft known as Kincraig once stood.

Kirkland Street. The name is self explanatory as the lands here belonged to the old Church built at the foot of the Kirkwynd and it is an excellent example of how names arose from simple and logical beginnings.

Kirkwynd and Kirkport. The road down to the old church of St. Cuthbert. "Wynd" is the old Scots word for road or street and "port" means gate. This was a most important street at one time and many baronial mansions for the surrounding nobility were built here. It was in the Kirkwynd, about halfway down the hill, that the "Little Chamber" stood, where disputes among the inhabitants were settled at a form of court and where "swords and daggers" were to be left in the "outer chamber" before the disputants entered the "Little Chamber". In the 19th century the Kirkwynd was renamed "Grey Street" by the Town Council but fortunately it soon reverted to its fine old original name.

Kirklandhill Path. The road to Kirklandhill Farm and known locally as the "Far Path". Before the railway was formed this road was a continuation of the Castle Brae and at that time ran down the side of the Cargil-Kincraig Church.

Kirkmichael Road. Formerly known as the "Cottage Road" because it led to the Cottage of St. Johns just outside the town but now it merely indicates it is the road to Kirkmichael Village.

Kirkoswald Road. Again indicative of it leading to the village of Kirkoswald. At the junction of this road with Coral Glen stood a wall locally known as Parliament Dyke where the local worthies met to settle the affairs of state. Before then a smithy stood on this spot, known as Crossmillhead, and this old name is often referred to in old titles of properties in this area. The smith at Crossmillhead was a well-known worthy and the smithy was a gathering place for many of the local people who sat and argued on the wall outside the smithy on good days and round the forge on bad ones. When the smithy became derelict and was taken down the dyke remained and became the gathering place of the locals, giving rise to the name Parliament Dyke.

Ladyland Road. This street was formed on lands belonging to the Church of St. Mary and means the lands of Our Lady, again a simple and descriptive name.

Ladywell Road. Until the early 1950s this street was known as Weaver Vennal (or simply "The Vennal") and was one of the most suitably named streets in the town. This was the main street of the Burgh for centuries and in it lived most of the weavers who made Maybole famous in the 18th and 19th centuries as one of the best known weaving towns in Scotland. The old descriptive name was changed in 1952 by the Town Council to Ladywell Road, meaning the road to Our Lady's Well, which is at the foot of the Bog Brae at the former Miller Tanning Company's factory.

Ladywell Terrace. Similar to Ladywell Road and adjacent to Our Lady's Well.

McDowall Terrace. Formerly a group of old houses known as Duncanland which was the oldest name in the town and commemorated Duncan, Earl of Carrick, who granted the first Charter of the district in the 12th century. About 1966 the old houses were demolished and new houses built by the local council and the name altered to McDowall Terrace in honour of the then Provost of the town.

Manse Street. Named after the old manse of the Parish Church at Kirkport which at one time stood on this site.

Miller Terrace. Commemorates Provost James Miller a well-known Provost and benefactor to the town in the first half of the 20th century.

Miller Street. Simply named after the builder of the houses in the street.

Minnoch Crescent. A street in the Gardenrose Housing Scheme which looks towards the well-known hill of Shalloch-on-Minnoch.

Mochrum Avenue. A street in the new council housing scheme at Whitefaulds built in the 1940s and named because Mochrum Hill overlooks the area.

Murray Gardens. When the Council built a new housing scheme on the lands of old Ballony Farm, the street was named after Provost Thomas Murray, who was then Provost of the town.

Old College Lane. The lane leading along the side of the old Collegium and is one of the oldest lanes in the town.

Park Terrace and Park View. These two rows of red sandstone houses were built about the end of the 19th century with an uninterrupted view over the Lyonston or Sheep Park, which, until the 1950s was a beautiful natural park used by the townspeople for playing football, cricket, etc. and the name is self explanatory.

Queens Terrace. Named in commemoration of the coronation of Queen Elizabeth in 1953 as the street was formed at this time.

Red Brae. At one time, before the railway was formed, it was a continuation of the High Street to Ayr past Lumsden Home and joined Kirkland Street at Duncanland Toll. The street was partly formed through a cutting in the hillside and, as the earth was reddish coloured, the street was commonly called the Red Brae and finally this became its official name.

Roderick Lawson Terrace. When the council built this street in the 1950s they decided to name it after the Rev. Roderick Lawson, who was Minister in the West Church in Coral Glen for many years last century and who took a great interest in the town.

St. Cuthberts Road and St. Cuthberts Street. St. Cuthberts Road formed in 1868 was named after the Patron Saint of the town and has been so called since it was formed from a path down the side of a burn which led from My Lord's Well (or the Pump as it is commonly called) to Abbots Place (or Pat's Corner) at the Old Cemetery. The old name of St. Cuthberts Street was Smithy Brae or locally "Smiddy Brae" because a smithy once stood in this street where Gladstone Place now stands. Unfortunately this was another of the old descriptive names wiped away when the mania for renaming streets was so rife at the end of the 19th century. St. Cuthbert was once a shepherd lad near Melrose and became one of the most revered saints in Britain. His bones, or rather his well preserved body, was carried from place to place by the Monks of Lindisfarne, when they were fleeing before the Danes and it is said it rested in Maybole district for a time and therefore St. Cuthbert became the Patron Saint of the town.

School Vennal. One of the few descriptive names fortunately remaining in the town. This vennal or street led from the top of High Street to the Ballgreen where the school was sited in the 17th and 18th century, and the name is so clear and meaningful it is hoped it will never be altered by well meaning but often so misguided, street name reformers.

Seaton Street. The first house built in it was occupied by a man named Seaton and the name of the householder remained when other properties were built. The old quoiting ground was in this street which led down to "Bryces" grain stores, now converted to a haulage contractor's garage.

St. John's Lane. A path connecting Cassillis Terrace and The Loaning named because it is formed on lands formerly belonging to the proprietor of St. John's Cottage. For years it was officially unnamed, but locally nicknamed "Calcutta Lane" because it was unlit and a member of the Council once likened it to the Black Hole of Calcutta. The lands on which St. John's Cottage now stands was formerly known as "Bogend".

Society Street. In this street in 1824 the Maybole Benevolent Society built a house for letting to "workpeople and their families belonging to Maybole" and because of this the street was named Society Street. Maybole was one of the first towns in Scotland to form a Benevolent Society which built workmen's houses.

Swan Court. The old manse for the Parish Church in Cassillis Road stood here for about one hundred and fifty years. In 1967 it was demolished and a new council housing scheme built on the site. The name commemorates the Rev. David Swan who for many years was minister of the old Church and resided in the Manse. In this instance the Council deserve credit for choosing such a suitable and attractive name.

The Loaning. Formerly the Bullock Loaning and at one time the north entrance to the town. It was down this lane or "Loaning" that the townspeople drove their cattle to graze on the common grazing lands around St. John's Cottage in the days when all townspeople had the right to graze on free lands.

Vicarland. A simple and concise name plainly descriptive of the fact that the land belonged to the Church at one time. Part of this area was formerly known as "Garleffan" meaning "the place of the Druid's Stones".

Wellington Street. Originally named in memory of the great Duke of Wellington. Commonly known to the older townspeople as "The Peameal Row" because it is said the person who built the properties was so miserly he fed his family mainly on peasemeal.

Whitehall. At one time the Carmelite Friars owned a house sited approximately where the Royal Bank now stands. As the members of this order wore white robes, the house was known as the Hall of the Whitefriars, and when the street was formed the name Whitehall was given to it. After the Carmelite's house was demolished an Inn was built on the site and named the Sun Inn which became a famous coaching inn.

Whitefaulds Avenue, Whitefaulds Crescent and Whitefaulds Quadrant. These streets in the Council Housing Scheme take their names from Whitefaulds Farm, as the scheme was built on part of the farm lands. At one time stock was grazed or "folded" on these lands which were rather poor, with a whitish weak grass and the local name of the "white folds" or "faulds" has happily remained to this day. It is a pity, however, that the name was trebled as this is the area near where McAdam experimented in roadmaking and when the roads were formed it would have been a wonderful opportunity to have commemorated the fact by naming one of them "Macadams Way".

Welltrees Street. The spring at the foot of the hill locally known as the "Welltrees Spout" gives its name to this street. Formerly there was a large tree beside the well, but this was thought to be dangerous and was cut down in May, 1939, although when it was felled it was found to be perfectly sound and would have stood for many years. The street is locally known as the "Kildoup" and it has been said there was a malt kiln in the street which gave rise to the local name. This can hardly be correct, however, as a street running from Whitehall (at the site of the House of the Carmelites) went straight down to the Black House at Abbot Street and this was then known as the "Kildoup" being a corruption of "kil-dubh" the Gaelic for "Black Church". It was only in the 19th century that the street was formed to turn sharply to the right near the junction with Whitehall, to join up with Weaver Vennal near the foot of the Croft. This new street continued to be called "Kildoup" until it was changed at the end of the 19th century.

While every street in every town must be given an official name for rating and postal purposes, it is common practice for local people to give nicknames to streets or to certain areas or houses in them. These local names are often more descriptive and humorous than the official names and Maybole does not lack in such unofficial names. These have been handed down from generation to generation and it is hoped will never be forgotten as much of the history of the old town is wrapped up in them. The following are some of the local names with which the true "Minnieboler" replaces the names shown in the Valuation Roll.

New Yards. Now Cassillis Road and the explanation for the old name has already been given.

Peameal Row. Wellington Street and again previously explained under this street name.

Pat's Corner. At the corner of Kirkland Street and Crosshill Road. A man called Pat O'Hara had a well-known public house here and his name is still given to this area.

Bumbee. At the road bridge over the railway on Culzean Road. Formerly Gardenrose Toll stood there and the owner kept an apiary of "bum-bees" in the garden. In former times it was the accepted place to settle schoolboys' quarrels and all schoolboys were aware of what was meant when he was challenged to "meet at the Bumbee" after school hours.

Sebastapool. The open space at the bottom of the Kirkwynd behind what used to be a barber's shop (Scobie De Morrow or De Blitt) in front of the entrance to the old cemetery. It was here that the weavers and shoemakers settled their disputes as did the schoolboys at the "Bumbee". Curiously enough a narrow passage led from here to St. Cuthberts Road and this passage was locally known as "Bumbee Lane".

Mushroom Row. The row of small cottages in Kirkland Street in front of the entrance to the Cairn School. These houses were built so quickly it was said they rose like mushrooms.

Brandy Row. Now offices of the building firm of M. J. Callaghan Ltd. in Alloway Road but at one time a block of tenement houses. At a card game in a local public house the players became rather tipsy and one, who had been losing a great deal of money, put up the tenement property to cover his stakes. He unfortunately lost on the evening's play and the winner claimed the property which ever afterwards was known as Brandy Row, as a concrete example of the evils of drink and the devil's cards.

Townend. A row of cottages near Brandy Row on the High Road to Ayr which were the last houses in the town in this road.

Townhead. The area at Duncanland Toll. This was the top end of the town at the old Duncanland houses.

Johnstone's Close. Formerly Jardines Close and was entered originally from High Street before the shop (The Chit Chat) at the junction of Kirkwynd and High Street was built. In the second part of the 19th century the properties in the yard were purchased by William Johnstone, a master slater, and although the Council officially named it Waverley Place it is commonly known as Johnstone's Close.

Smithy Brae. Commonly known as "Smiddy Brae" and is now St. Cuthbert's Street and described under that street name.

Black House. Now demolished but it formerly stood in Abbot's Street next to the "Auld College" and was the oldest house in Maybole. It was built originally for a Prebend of the old Collegium.

Runcie Row. The nickname given to part of Ladyland Road because the houses in it were built by a man Runcie who owned a shoe factory at one time in the hall at the bottom of the Greenside.

Primrose Lane. A local name for a proposed new street at Dangartland, or Drummellan Street as it is now called, and the origin of the nickname is given under the description of that street.

The Breek. A house with this name formerly stood near the Cairn School and the old name was often used by the older townspeople. It is now demolished and forms part of the school playground. The origin of the name is unknown.

The Royal Billy. A house in Welltrees Street was once used as the headquarters of the Orange Lodge in Maybole and it was locally known as "The Royal Billy" or more commonly just "The Billy". Tradition has it that when the Orange Flute Band was first formed its members decided to practise in the house, but at the first rehearsal the noise of the big drum brought down the ceiling and afterwards the band practised in the garden behind the house.

Gallow Hill. Now Culzean Road but to townspeople still the "Gallows" Hill or "Gala Hill" in memory of the fact the town gallows stood here. Maybole people still gleefully remember that the last man hanged here was a Girvan man for killing his neighbour in 1718. Eye witnesses to the crime could not be produced but the fact he was a Girvan man was sufficient to convict him in the eyes of his Maybole judges. The rivalry between the "Tacketies" and the "Syboes" still exists but in a less lethal form.

The Bench. The local nickname given to the house which stood at the bottom of Kirkland Street near Pat's Corner. A small raised front garden at the house was shaped rather like a cobbler's bench and gave rise to the name. The house was demolished in 1969.

Parliament Dyke. At the head of Coral Glen where iron railings now separate the Glen from Kirkoswald Road there was formerly a low dyke or wall which was at a height that made a comfortable seat for old worthies and the origin of the nickname is explained under the item referring to Kirkoswald Road.

Cockyrighty. The spring in the Coral Glen which discharges from the hill on which the West Parish Church is built and often simply known as the "Wee spout in the Glen".

The Pump. The site of the well which supplied Maybole Castle and which, as it originally stood in the Castle Garden, was known as My Lord's Well. When the Castle kitchens, etc., which originally blocked the bottom end of the High Street were removed and Cassillis Road was formed a pump was erected over this open, or draw well, by public subscription in 1806. In 1869 when the new road (St. Cuthbert's Road) was formed from the junction of the Castle Brae with New Yards to join up with Kirkland Street at Pat's Corner this old pump was removed and an ornate iron pump erected which stood until the 1930s. It was then removed and a circular plot formed with a low stone wall to form a roundabout at the junction of the roads. Although the pump has gone forever, the old name still remains for the site. Unfortunately in some recent instances the site has been described as "The Cross" in various publications and it is to be hoped the Council will correct this when it appears in documents, as of course "The Cross" is sited in the centre of High Street.

Buchty Brig. The metal bridge over the railway at the northern end of the ground surrounding the Cargil-Kincraig Church. Before the railway was formed "buchts" or pens stood on this site adjoining the public "pound" in Barns Road and the name derives from these buchts.

Bowsie Brig. The local name given to the road bridge on the Kirkmichael Road at the end of the former park at Lyonston known as the Sheep Park because it was an original condition of the lease to the Council that only sheep would be grazed on it while it was used as a park by the townspeople. The name is often thought to be connected with "bowsies" or ghosts. The original spelling, however, is "Bowser" (easily corrupted to "Bowsie") and as the old word for a spring is "Bowser" it merely means the bridge by the spring which rises just above the bridge and is thought to be seepage from the "Hart" or "Heart" Loch.

Hen's Castle. The local name given to the house on the corner between Castle Street and High Street which was rebuilt by a local man who always called his wife "Wee Chooky Hen" and who installed her with pride in her "castle".

The Doll's Eye. This is a nickname for the house built in the south-east corner of Greenside and which has an outside balcony along the back wall giving access to the upstair houses. The origin of the nickname is unknown.

Bryce's Corner. Part of Dailly Road and origin of the nickname is given under the description of this street as is "Mason's Row" which is the part of Dailly Road near Bryce's Corner.

The Paths. These are the "Near Path" and the "Far Path" as explained under the present names of Gardenrose and Kirklandhill Paths. Forsyth's Path was the lane leading up to the fields behind Viewfield at Townend and was named after the man who originally owned the fields.

Kildoup. The old name for Welltrees Street and is one of the old local names explained under Welltrees Street.

Bog Brae. The path leading down to Ladywell Tannery and originally the path where the townspeople drove their geese to graze on the bog or mire below the town which gives rise to the name Maybole or Minniebole, being the town above the mire. This path was originally the bottom part of the Croft until Welltrees Street cut it in half.

Lovers Lane. Every rural town has its Lovers Lane and Maybole is no exception. This was originally the road into the town from the north and joined up with the Bullock Loaning. At the top of the Lovers Lane many years ago there stood a large oak tree known locally as "The Lily Oak" which was a great gathering place for the local shoemakers on a summer evening.

Tippersweill. The site of a locally famous well which was sited beside the old road to Kirkoswald, which runs from Whitefaulds Toll to meet the present road to Kirkoswald near the road end to Cultizeoun Farm. A little cottage stood beside it until it became ruinous after the first World War, and not far from this cottage stood Peden's Thorn, a thorn tree commemorating the famous covenanter who preached in the district. It was in the old cottage near the well at Tippersweill that the famous local character "The Eastern Princess", who hoodwinked the elite of London was born. It is said the name is a corruption of "Tippler's Well" and it may be it was thought its water blended well with whisky.

The Fleeing Yett. The name given to the original entrance to "Machrie Mhor" or Drummellan House as it is now called. This gateway had two square stone pillars set sideways to what is now the main or low road to Ayr at the end of the row of trees known as "The Twelve Apostles" (the Twelve Disciples was a row of trees at Kirkmichael House) on the straight level piece of roadway beyond Lyonston Farm. "Fleeing" means sideways or aslant and "yett" gate, and a favourite walk at one time for the local lads and lasses after church on a Sunday evening was down the "Low Road to The Fleeing Yett". Since the advent of the motor car few walkers are now seen on this road and other favourite roads such as the Cross Roads, the Whinny Knowes, and the Capenoch, are also deserted.

The Measured Mile. This was the local name for the part of the roadway on the Cross Roads from the milestone at West Enoch Farm to the milestone near the Covenanters' Memorial. This distance was meticulously measured and was the training ground for the famous Maybole sportsmen such as the Allans, the famous cyclists, and the runners, Milroy, Rodger, etc.

Market Place. The area at the foot of Kirkland Street which was the site of the old market where agricultural stock and produce was sold.

The Hill. A local name for Hutchison Street.

Fulton's Folly. The old name given to the house now known as Carrick House at the corner of Carrick Street and Ladyland Road. It was originally built by a man Fulton, who could not afford to complete it and it lay unfinished for some years. It was then completed and formed to house two families, then converted for one family. For many years it was a doctor's residence and after the first World War it was entirely converted to the desirable house it now is.

Tolbooth. The old name for the clock tower at the Town Hall which was originally part of the town house of the Blairquhan family. The building finally was used as the town gaol, court hall and "dancing room" (and was so described in a Council Minute, dated 12th January, 1798), before it was demolished to allow the present Town Hall to be built in 1887, at a cost of around £3,000. The main tower and part of the "dancing room" (now the "Lesser Town Hall") was left standing and this tower, which is still called the Tolbooth, was the recognised gathering place for the townspeople every Hogmanay.

Spooncreel. The name given to a building consisting of three shops with a dwelling house above erected adjoining the old Tolbooth steeple when the buildings of the Blairquhan House, which stood across the roadway to where Cameron's Garage is now sited, were removed. The gable of the building facing down High Street was rather rounded in shape and resembled a "Spumecreel" (a basket used for gathering seaweed and potatoes, etc.) which through time was corrupted to "Spooncreel". This building was demolished in 1967 and the old Tolbooth now stands out in its original dignity.

The Burgher Corner. An old name sometimes given to the corner at the bottom of John Knox Street where it joins Ladywell Road and where in 1797 the United Presbyterian Church or "Burgher Kirk" was built. This church had 555 sittings, but in 1880 the church fell into disuse and was formed into a tenement building when the new Kincraig Church with 400 sittings was built in Culzean Road. The old tenement building was demolished in 1960 when the Council Housing Scheme was built in John Knox Street.

The Clachan Brae. The hill at the cemetery on the Crosshill Road and was the local name for the hill one had to climb on the road to the small clachan, or village, of Crosshill.

The Slap. The old road, now disused, from Allan's Hill to Abbey Mill and Kirkoswald. For generations weavers and shoemakers gathered there to play "pitch and toss" which along with marbles was a favourite sport of the townspeople.

Sunnyside. An old row of houses in front of Park Terrace on the road to Ayr. Now demolished.

The Runnel. A roundel of trees at Lochlands Farm and formerly the gathering place of local Orangemen.

Near Wood. A strip of woodland at top of Gardenrose Path. A house called "Fineview" formerly stood at the top of the wood and the agricultural houses built there took the name from it. The house was occupied by a man called Fulton who at one time had a pet white roe deer which was shot by a gamekeeper and caused quite a furore in the town.

Stey Leas. The road to Howmuir and an old road to Ayr. The Preaching Brae is half way up this road and commemorates the time Donald Cargil preached to the local townsfolk on the adjoining lands of Cargilston. It merely means the steep road by the fields or meadows.

The Bog. The local name for Ladywell shoe factory which finally became a tannery until it closed down in 1969. It was built on the low ground at the top end of the mire or bog which gave Maybole its name and occupied the site of an old mill which once stood at the bottom of Ladywell Lane. In 1869 there was a row of houses next to the mill and one of the housewives, Sarah Carey by name, decided to kill the bed bugs in her wooden built in bed by singeing them with a candle, but she was too thorough and her house caught fire. The fire spread to the adjoining weavers' cottages and the whole row was destroyed. Mr. John Gray purchased the site and built a shoe factory on it, naming it The Ladywell Boot and Shoe Factory but the locals still referred to it by the old name of the former mill, which was "Bogmill" and all succeeding generations of Minniebolers have known it simply as "The Bog".

The Iron Rails. Part of Weaver Vennal from the top of the Bog Brae to the foot of the Kildoup. Old weavers' houses once stood here and when they became derelict and were removed the council erected iron railings to keep people from falling over the steep embankment.

The Barracks. A local name given to a large two storey tenement which used to stand next to Connolly's Garage at the foot of Kirkland Street.

Reform Place. The street leading from the foot of Kirkwynd to the Old College Lane was originally named this because the houses were built about the time of the Reform Bill.

Chapter 12

BUILDINGS PAST AND PRESENT

MANY of the old buildings in the town have been swept away in the course of time to make room for more modern buildings as sites within the burgh have always been scarce for new developments and it is difficult to get suitable building ground on the sloping hillside on which Maybole is built. Many interesting old buildings are therefore gone and mostly forgotten, such as the old manse in Manse Street, the "Maison Dieu" at Welltrees, the Old College Provost's house in John Knox Street, and all the noblemen's houses in Weaver Vennal and Kirkwynd. If these still remained there would have been a wealth of interest in such old buildings and although many would argue it is right such old houses should be cleared away, Maybole has undoubtedly lost a great deal of its ancient character although it has gained much in the way of modern houses, which, though perhaps not so picturesque, certainly have the modern conveniences so necessary nowadays, although it is a pity that modern planners can not afford to build in the old traditional stone of the district and give character to the houses instead of erecting rows of brick and roughcast boxes. The first housing schemes erected in the town in the 1920s were built for cheapness and did not show much imagination, but fortunately this period passed and the houses erected during the last few years were better designed and blend better into their surroundings. Unfortunately the last Council Housing Scheme started at Gardenrose in 1969 is once again a monument of poor foresight on the part of the Council as the houses are without doubt the greatest of all blots on the Maybole landscape. Sited on one of the most prominent positions above the old town, the whole scheme is dull and drab and well deserves the nickname it has already earned as "The Barlinnie of Maybole".

The oldest building is the Collegiate Church at the foot of John Knox Street, affectionately known to Minniebolers as the "Auld College", and, although now ruinous, its main walls have withstood the ravages of six hundred years, having been built in 1371. The older church built at the foot of Kirkwynd when the charter by Duncan was granted to the Cistercian nunnery of North Berwick in 1216 was small and over one hundred and fifty years old when Sir John Kennedy of Dunure, ancestor of the present Marquess of Ailsa, decided that the growing village of "Maibol" deserved a larger and finer place of worship and he built and endowed a Chantry Chapel, part of which still stands, while no trace remains of the earlier church. Sir John built it "For the purpose of celebrating daily Divine Service for the happy state of himself, his wife Mary and their children" and ordained that the Provost and Prebendaries of the Church "shall celebrate Mass daily, and if anyone fails without reasonable cause, he shall be amerced in four pence for each default", a large and substantial fine in those days. He also ordained the fines should be paid monthly and the money collected shared out among the priests who had attended the services, thus ensuring prompt retribution for misdemeanours.

The Church was dedicated to the Virgin Mary and endowed with the rents from many of the surrounding lands and practically the whole land on which the town is built was in possession of the Collegium and this is shown by the local names of Ladyland, Ladywell, Ladycross, etc. On 18th May, 1441, this Chapel was elevated to a Collegium and had the distinction of being one of the finest in Scotland in its time and was served by a Provost (or Principal) and three Prebends. It remained the important place of worship in the district until the Reformation in 1560 when Roman Catholicism was abolished in Scotland and the Mass declared illegal. Although the Minniebolers were for the most part supporters of the Reformation some, as usual, paid little attention to edicts passed outwith their own Kingdom of Carrick and continued to worship as before in the Auld College, and in April, 1563, over two hundred men of Carrick met to celebrate Mass in defiance of the laws of Scotland. They came prepared for trouble as they were armed with "jakkis, speris, gunnis, and other wapins" and no one dared to intervene as they worshipped their God in the ancient manner. They tried the patience of the Reformers too much, however, with their blatant disregard of the laws of the land and the leaders were arrested, a not unusual occurrence for Carrick men. One was put in ward in the Castle of Dumbarton and two others (Hew and David Kennedy) were imprisoned in Edinburgh Castle to remain there "during the will and pleasure of the Queen".

The Provost lived in a house in Back Vennal (now John Knox Street) just above the Collegium (this was later formed into an inn known as The Red Lion and gave the name to the street for many years) and it was in this house in September, 1562, that the debate between John Knox and the Abbot of Crossraguel took place, the Provost at that time being Andrew Gray. The Prebends lived in the "Black House" (occupied by the Fitzimmons family until it was demolished in 1967), a house at the Welltrees and in a house known as James Gray's house behind the College which was occupied by Miss Thom up until the first World War when it was finally so ruinous it became uninhabitable.

After the Reformation the roof of the "Auld College" was removed and the building fell into a ruinous state and it was used only as a burial place for the Cassillis family and some others in the district who helped to reroof the old building many years later. The old vestry became the family burial ground of the Earls of Cassillis and there is a large stone detailing the members of the family interred in this old Collegiate Church and the ground around it. The first name on it is David, the first Earl, killed at Flodden; then Gilbert, second Earl who was murdered at Prestwick; Gilbert, third Earl who died at Dieppe in France (he helped to arrange the marriage of Mary, Queen of Scots to the Dauphin of France but refused to allow the crown of Scotland to pass to France and was believed to have been poisoned because of his stubbornness); Gilbert, the fourth Earl (who roasted the Commendater of Crossraguel); John, the fifth Earl (who slew young Bargany at Ladycross) and John, the sixth Earl, known as "the grave and solemn Earl", a great churchman and a Commissioner to the Westminster Assembly and the husband of Lady Jean who was wrongly accused of eloping with a gypsy. In addition there are the graves of John Kennedy and his wife, Margaret Hamilton, daughter of the first Lord Bargany and their son, Sir Archibald Kennedy (who shot Gilbert McAdam, the Covenanter, at Kirkmichael) and over their tombs is a large square stone set in the wall and carved with the arms of the Kennedys' and Hamiltons'. Some of the lairds of Baltersan are also buried in the old Collegiate, one being James Kennedy who died in 1609 and who stated in his last Testament, "I ordaine no vain in my buriall, but to burie me without serimonie and by honest friends". Members of the Kennedies of Kirkmichael also had the right of burial there and Provost Kennedy of Ayr, who lived at Drummellan (or Machrie Mor), is interred among them, his tombstone having the hopeful epitaph: "He cannot return to us, but with God's help we hope to go to him."

While the old ruins show signs of alterations and additions from time to time the original building is easily traced. It measures 54 feet by 6' 6" with the adjacent vestry measuring 16 feet by 8 feet. Some window tracery still exists and the doorway is beautifully carved with a dogtooth design, while the Sedilia, Piscina and Holy Water Font can still be partly seen on the right wall. After the Reformation the "Auld College" and its temporality reverted to the Cassillis family (whose predecessors had originally donated them) and it was kept in fair preservation for some time but finally became so ruinous that a public subscription was raised by the townspeople in the 1880s to clear up its surroundings and build the walls round it which stand to this day. After this the Marquess of Ailsa and his successors maintained the buildings and grounds in pretty fair preservation until the 1940s when the Fourth Marquess of Ailsa handed it over to the Ancient Monuments Department of the Ministry of Works which has carried out many repairs and is now responsible for the preservation of this, the oldest building in the town and one of Scotland's most interesting ecclesiastical relics.

Whilst the townspeople may be commended for their strong religious principles through the centuries it is regrettable they cannot be complimented in their taste in the buildings they erected as their places of worship. There is no record of the style of the first church building in the days of Duncan but it can be assumed it was only a small and mean building, whilst the Collegiate is more interesting for its antiquity and prominence in its day than its design. The kirk built by the Reformers at the foot of Kirkwynd was a source of adverse criticism by all its ministers and was merely a box with a roof over it and so badly built it was in need of constant repair. Indeed for the last two years it was in existence, before the New Kirk was built in the Cassillis Road, the minister (Dr. Wright) preached to his congregation in the churchyard, refusing to allow them to enter the church in case it should fall on them. There were other churches in the district in early days, the most important being at Kirkbride, near Dunure, another at Auchendrane near Minishant, with smaller chapels dotted here and there but these have all disappeared and not even a few stones are left to mark their sites. From records available none of the old Maybole churches were very well built and there are constant references to pleas for repairs to be carried out on them.

The oldest church still in use in the town is the Parish Church in Cassillis Road which was built in 1808 to replace the ruinous kirk in the old churchyard at Kirkport. There was no change evident in the attitude of the Minniebolers with regard to their religious buildings and they again erected a square box with a roof over it and a steeple which defies description. This steeple was originally fitted with a weather vane but it proved to be too heavy and was removed some time later. The original design does not seem to have included the horse shoe gallery, which was in existence up until the latest alterations to the church in 1928, as the access stairs to it would surely have been better designed if it had been intended to form part of the building in the first instance. This gallery was a constant source of worry, as it had a bad sway when the people all moved out together at the end of the services, and many old worshippers breathed sighs of relief when it was finally taken down. Originally the vestry, or robing room, was at the base of the steeple and there was a door to the body of the kirk in the back wall. No allowance was made for heating the building and the congregation shivered throughout the winters until finally, in 1841, two stoves were fitted against the back wall and their position can still be traced where the outside corbelling was cut to allow the smoke pipes to be carried up above the eaves. About the same time as the stoves were fitted gas lighting was introduced and the Auld Kirkers considered themselves to be really an up-to-date and progessive body of people. In 1872 central heating was installed and the door in the back wall was built up to allow a heating chamber to be built. This necessitated a change in the layout of the church and the whole seating accommodation was altered. In 1883 the Parish Hall was built on the rising ground behind the Church and has been little altered since then with the exception that a porch has been added to the front door. The hall stands on the ground where the communion preachings used to be held and members of the congregation listened to sermons from various preachers whilst waiting their turn to "go to table" and take Communion within the church. The preachers sheltered in a form of sentry box while the congregation sat on the hillside and many took "bannocks and cheese" with them to sustain them through the long hours they often had to wait before it was their turn to take Communion. In 1890 the "kist o' whistles" was installed by the congregation and the vestry, being required to house the organ mechanism, was moved to its present position. In 1900 the congregation again subscribed to the entire redecoration of the church and the two large stained glass windows were fitted in the front wall at this time. Later other stained glass windows were fitted in memory of John Marshall (of Jack & Sons); as a memorial to the fallen in the first World War, and in memory of the Rev. David Swan who was minister for so many years in the Auld Kirk. In 1928, three years after the Act of 1925 which relieved the heritors of their responsibilities, the whole church was entirely remodelled, the seating being altered, the pulpit moved to the east wall, the horse shoe gallery removed and a small gallery fitted to the west wall but nothing could be done to relieve the starkness of the exterior and it can only be said the building is more functional than beautiful.

In 1844 the "Free Kirkers" built their church in Barns Road, near the site of the old public barns and granaries, and once again the opportunity to build a worthy building was lost. It was built in the form of a headless cross and is a stern forbidding building which an old residenter once likened to the old public barns which had once stood near the site. Fortunately it was not burdened with a steeple like the Auld Kirk and there was much truth in the old jingle:

"I'm the Free Kirk, the wee Kirk,
The Kirk without the steeple,
And you're the Auld Kirk, the cauld Kirk
The Kirk without the people".

when one thinks on the Auld Kirkers shivering at services before the stoves were installed. A small belfry was incorporated originally in the Free Kirk but in early days it did not have a bell in it and the bell to call the congregation to worship was, for a time, fitted on brackets on the front wall. Later a bell was fitted in the belfry which is topped with an attractive little louvred turret. The outstanding features of the church are three lancet windows to each gable which relieves the monotony of the tall gables, each of which are surmounted with a cross. The church was originally named Cargil Church but when the congregations of this church and the Kincraig Church united in the 1950s the two names were combined and it is now known as the Cargil-Kincraig Church. Its original name commemorated the fact that Donald Cargil, the great Covenanter, had preached in the district. On the outer east wall of the church a square whin stone is inset (so high above the ground it is practically impossible to read it) with the inscription: "This is part of the stone beside which Donald Cargil is believed to have conducted a Conventicle on the farm of Cargilstone during the Covenanting period 1638-1688". The stone in question was a large whin boulder which marked the spot where Donald Cargil preached to a large gathering of townspeople near Ladycross in May, 1681, just before he was hanged in Edinburgh two months later. When he preached at Ladycross there was a price of 5,000 marks on his head but no Maybole man thought of betraying him. The stone was broken up in the nineteenth century and mainly used in the building of the Covenanters' Memorial on the Cross Roads but part of it was dressed and inscribed as above and set in the wall of the "Free Kirk" as the building will always be known to the local people.

The "Free Kirkers" however, seem to have had more architectural taste when the question of building a manse for their minister was mooted as they erected at "Townhead" an attractive villa which for many years was the Free Church Manse. This house was built at the top of Kirkland Street opposite Duncanland Toll and is now occupied by the Burgh Surveyor and the manse park is now the site of the Roman Catholic School.

On a Sunday in 1906 the Cargil Church was practically destroyed by fire and, when it was rebuilt, a small porch was added to the main front door and some other alterations were made, including the formation of an attractive window in the back wall and a new top to the belfry. When the organ was installed in the church about forty years ago, unfortunately it was sited on the back wall and spoiled the beauty of the large window but as Minniebolers are fond of saying "things maun aye be someway", and once again artistic ideas were submerged in the flood of practical thoughts about cost of installation, etc. In 1882 the congregation built a hall, attached to the rear of the church, with a vestry, etc. and while it is useful, it did nothing to make the church building more attractive.

Both the Auld Kirk and the Free Kirk are built on, or near, springs and since they have been built there has been constant trouble with both buildings requiring repairs for dampness, dry rot, etc., and the cost of maintenance has been high in each building. The workmanship of "the good old days" was certainly not so wonderful as one is led to believe, at least where these buildings were concerned, as in both many instances of bad and slipshod workmanship has come to light when repairs have been carried out. The Parish Church especially was built with poor materials and in 1830, 1836, 1868 and 1879 the heritors had to pay large sums to renew ceilings, joists, floors, etc., the cost in 1830 being £450, a considerable sum in those days to spend on repairs to a building which had been erected only twenty years previously at a cost of around £4,000.

In 1842 the West Church (locally known as the Glen Kirk) was built in Coral Glen, the cost being mainly met by Sir Charles Fergusson of Kilkerran. Once again it was built in what could be described as "The Maybole Kirk" style and there is little to commend it from an architectural point of view. It is a pleasant enough building, however, with an ornamental open bellcote on the gabe facing Coral Glen and its gables and walls are relieved with finely proportioned long arched windows. It was of better workmanship than the two earlier churches and, being sited on top of a hill, rather than on the side of one, there has been little trouble in keeping dampness from damaging it. It serves the west part of the town admirably and has the most attractive surroundings of all the churches in the burgh. It was the church where the Rev. Roderick Lawson preached for so many years and his successor, Rev. Alexander Williamson, was also minister for a long period and both these men were keenly interested in their adopted town and wrote many articles about it.

The three churches, the Auld Kirk, the Free Kirk and the Glen Kirk were all built in the early part of the nineteenth century and it can only be surmised the Minniebolers of that period were hard headed true sons of their Covenanting forefathers who counted the cost and thought the sermons more important than the churches, as it cannot be honestly said any great thought was given to their design from an architectural point of view. Perhaps there was still a lingering feeling that there should be no beauty or fripperies which could possibly remind the congregation of the Popish splendours their forefathers had helped John Knox to overthrow.

The Episcopal Church at the foot of Gardenrose Path was built about the end of last century and is a small neat building with a simple dignity unfortunately marred by being crammed into a small site. It had a metal framework bell tower with a little high pitched bell, the sound of which was so familiar to the townspeople, until the tower was removed during the second

World War to help the war effort in the collection of scrap metal. The interior is more attractive than any of the larger churches, with a fine arch to the altar on the east wall.

The Roman Catholic Church at Allan's Hill was built in 1878 and has the most commanding site of any of the church buildings in the town, being well situated on the crown of a small hill and, although small, its site makes it look quite imposing. It has an attractive steeple at the side of the front gable which has a rather fine window in it. Its interior is enhanced with an arch round the altar which is placed in a vaulted recess and the roof is supported by arches which have heads carved on the springers. Local tradition has it that these heads were carved by an old tramp mason who turned up one day during the building of the church and asked for employment in hewing the stones. He proved to be so expert he was given the job of carving the heads to the arches and it is believed he modelled his carvings on the heads of some of his fellow workmen and carved one in his own image. These heads were originally painted in life like colours as to hair, lips, eyes, etc., but early this century they were all painted a uniform fawn colour much to their detriment and it is to be hoped that someday they will be repainted in their original colouring.

In 1914 at a cost of £1,720 the Baptist Church was built in Carrick Street and it is a small rectangular, brick built structure, with a red sandstone front gable and porch with an arched doorway. Like the Episcopal Church it is crammed into a very small site which does nothing to improve its appearance and it would seem building sites were either scarce (or expensive) when these churches were built. It was built, mainly through the efforts of Pastor Ramsay, to replace the former meeting place of the Baptist congregation which was a hall in Abbot Street near the Old Cemetery and which is now used by the Roman Catholics as a recreation hall.

The most attractive church ever built in Maybole was undoubtedly the Kincraig Church in Culzean Road. This was built as a United Presbyterian Church in 1880 to replace the old "Burgher Kirk" at the foot of John Knox Street which had served the congregation from 1797. The old church was converted into a tenement building which stood until the houses in John Knox Street were demolished and new houses built in the 1960s. The new church in Culzean Road was a fine red sandstone building with a neat stone steeple and a beautiful window with stone tracery and four stained glass panels in the front gable to the main road. It was well proportioned inside and was an attractive little church with a most convenient hall attached. It was evident that by the end of the nineteenth century more thought was being given to church design by the townsfolk and this, the last church to be built, was a great improvement on the older kirks. Unfortunately (from a buildings point of view) when the Cargill and Kingcraig congregations decided to amalgamate it was decided the Cargill Church should be used as a congregational meeting place and the Kincraig Church was sold to a local builder who demolished it and built houses on the site. The Church hall was converted into a dwelling house and now only the name of Kincraig Court remains to remind the townfolk of the fine church which once stood there. The Kincraig Manse which adjoined the church was retained as a manse for the minister of the Cargill Kincraig Church and Cargill Manse (which was next to Kincraig Manse in Culzean Road) was sold and is now a private house.

An Evangelistic Hall, built in 1879, stood in the Kirkwynd on the site of the old "Little Chamber" (where men of Maybole met to settle their disputes in olden days and had to leave their swords in an anteroom lest they came to blows) and this was finally used as the meeting place of the members of the Salvation Army for many years. It was a plain, brick pointed building of no merit whatsoever and it was no great loss to the town when it became derelict and was demolished in 1969 to make room for a car park.

The Castle is now the oldest inhabited house in the town having been built about the middle of the sixteenth century (no exact date can be given but it is believed to be around 1560). It was the town house of the Earls of Cassillis who spent most of the winter months in Maybole in those days and was the largest and finest of the twenty-eight lairds' houses which were written about by Abercrummie in 1686. It was built in the style of a typical Scottish castle, with square tower and round turrets, and strong enough to protect its occupants from unfriendly neighbours, of whom there were many at that time. Originally it stood across the bottom of the High Street with the gates to the courtyard facing up the street and with a great part of it on the site now occupied by the Post Office. The main door was originally at the side of the square tower which faced up the High Street. The main hall was above vaulted cellars which still remain and above the hall were the sleeping apartments. The retainers' quarters were on the other side of the gateway which gave entrance into the castle yard which was built round the well now locally known as "The Pump"'. The buildings were L shaped with the base forming the part still in existence and the longer side built where the Post Office and Public Library now stand and the part now demolished housed the servants, grooms, smiths, and other persons necessary for the service of a nobleman in the sixteenth century. The tower is capped by a lovely little oriel window looking up the High Street (described by McGibbon and Ross in their books on Scottish Castles as "a rare specimen"), with heads carved round it which local people wrongly believe represent the heads of Johnnie Faa and his gypsies. The corbels to the roof of the little room at the top of the tower (known as the Countess's Room) are carved with male and female heads and symbols of fertility. A square recess about fifteen feet from the base of the tower originally held a stone carved with arms of the Cassillis family. The walls are extremely thick (in some places about seven feet) and it must have originally been a safe retreat in troublesome times when the Earls could live in it, with their own men around them in the small township clustered on the hillside below it. It was from Maybole Castle that the Earl of Cassillis and his men sallied forth to the fight at Ladycross in December, 1601, when young Bargany was killed in the bitter feud between the Cassillis and Bargany families. Locally there is an old tale of the Countess of Cassillis being imprisoned in the "Countess's Room" at the top of the tower, after she had allegedly eloped with Johnnie Faa, King of the Gypsies, but while the story is a delightful one, facts disprove it.

As years passed the Earls spent less and less of their time in Maybole, and gradually the old Castle fell into a state of disrepair and it became practically abandoned except for a few old retainers who lived in some of the outbuildings. In 1805 the Earl of Cassillis agreed with the town council that the part sited where the Post Office stands could be demolished to allow a road to be formed from the foot of the High Street to Duncanland Toll at the bottom of Redbrae. When the old buildings were removed the Earl decided to repair the old Castle and in 1812 reroofed it and built the additions which are now the Marquess of Ailsa's Estate Offices and the living rooms above, also the Dining Room and new kitchen premises. The gardens and park had walls erected round them and from 1812 the Castle has remained as it is now and it has been the home of Lord Ailsa's Estate Factors from then until the present day. In 1919 fire broke out in it and part of the roof was destroyed and had to be repaired. It has a commanding position at the bottom of the High Street and makes an attractive entry to the town from the Ayr Road and when the Library (1905), Post Office (1913) and the building at the head of the Kirkwynd (1894) were erected the builders harmonised the new buildings with the old Castle by making crow stepped gables, etc., and this little corner of Maybole has a dignity which can compare with any part of any town in Scotland.

MAYBOLE - CARRICK'S CAPITAL

In olden days another Castle stood at the top of the High Street, facing down the street to Maybole Castle, and the street was closed at both top and bottom of the hill by these two buildings which stood, like watch-dogs, over the Minniebolers as they thronged the booths set up in the High Street at the quarterly fairs or gathered to listen to proclamations from the drummer on the steps of the Town Cross. This building was originally the town house of the Lairds of Blairquhan and again was built in the usual style of Scottish castles with strong walls, a tower, and turrets. It is not known when it was originally built but it is believed to be older than the Castle. The building was quite large and occupied part of the site now occupied by Cameron's Garage and the Royal Bank. About the end of the seventeenth century it was formed into the Court House and Tolbooth for the town, when a great part of the building was removed, and only the tower, part of the Lesser Town Hall, and a square building with a raked crow stepped gable were left. There are many old prints showing this building in the early nineteenth century and they give a good picture of the Town's jail and Council House and the Seal of the Burgh is a representation of the old Tolbooth. The prison cells were under the Court Room and they must have housed many prisoners in their time, as the Courts of Carrick met there and dealt out justice to all accused of every type of crime from poaching to murder. When the Court Room was not in use for the meetings of the Councillors it was let out as a "Dancing Room" and to actors to present their plays and many of the prisoners in the cells below must have had a few sleepless nights when the fiddlers played reels for the dancers above them. The old "jouggs" for the necks of prisoners used to hang above the door at the bottom of the tower and the "stocks" for their feet lay in a room at the top of the tower, but the "jouggs" went amissing about the end of the last century, and the "stocks", although still in existence in the 1930s, have also been lost.

In the 1880s it was decided Maybole must have a proper Town Hall commensurate with the needs of the thriving burgh and the old buildings with the exception of the tower, were swept away and the new Town Hall built in 1887, and it stands so to this day, with a few minor alterations to the interior. It has accommodation for 750 people and is the gathering place for all the townsfolk at dances, whist drives, public meetings, etc. The "Lesser Town Hall" incorporates part of the old Council Chamber and "Dancing Room" and the tower was fitted last century with a new roof with a clock in it, the original clock having been set in the stonework of the tower. Since it was built the Town Hall has seen much life and gaiety within its walls and all Maybole folk recall with nostalgia the nights of the great balls held by the "Yeomanry", the "Masons" the "Boolers" and the "Curlers". These were the great events of the winter's season in the town up to the 1920s and few Minnie-bolers have not attended some of these balls, the men with their patent dancing pumps and a fresh collar in their pockets and the ladies in their finery and redolent with a "pennysworth of scent from Dr. Girvan's pharmacy". All beaus called for their lady friends with a cab from the "Kings Arms" and danced until three or four in the morning, it being a point of honour never to miss a dance, and to have as many partners as possible. When one sees a modern dance hall with its bored looking patrons ambling round all night with the same partner "the bad old days" seem, somehow, to have been not so bad after all.

When the old house of Blairquhan was formed into the Tolbooth, and a great part of it demolished in 1800, a small, oddly shaped building, was permitted to be built on the site of the demolished buildings next the tower and this later became three shops with a dwellinghouse above and was known as the Spooncreel. The Council in later days tried to have it removed and when the new Town Hall was being built acquired it and started to demolish it. Some trouble arose about the titles, however, and finally the civic fathers had to replace the roof, which they had removed, and the building remained with its shops until 1967 when it was finally acquired by the town and demolished. Its removal opened up the old tower and, as the surrounding area has been neatly paved, it now again stands up in its glory as it did over four hundred years ago. Few towns in Scotland can boast of a castle at each end of its High Street and McGibbon's "Scottish Architecture" remarks on the air of antiquity in the description of Maybole which states: "This little town, which stands on a hillside sloping to the south, may be cited as a good example of the local centres or provincial country towns of early days. Such centres were then, when roads were bad and travelling dangerous, much more numerous than now, when travelling is easy and rapid, but few have preserved their pristine features so little altered as Maybole. Here we still find the Castle of the Lord of the Bailery standing guard at the east end and that of the Laird of Blairquhan at the west end of the main street whilst the remains of the Collegiate Kirk nestles quietly in the centre". These remarks still apply to the old town today and every Minnieboler has great affection of these three old buildings.

The next outstanding building erected in the town after the Town Hall was built was the Carnegie Public Library at the foot of the High Street. The foundation stone (engraved with the Town Coat of Arms) was laid in 1905, when the whole population turned out to see it well and truly laid by the local Free Masons, with the town band leading the Magistrates and Councillors in procession to the site. It was built mainly from funds donated by the Trust formed by Andrew Carnegie, the great Scottish philanthropist, to provide such buildings in Scottish towns and is a handsome stone building which blends admirably with the old Castle across the street from it. The doorway is extremely fine and has a handsomely carved coat of arms over it. A native of Maybole, Robert McQuater who died in Dublin in 1902, bequeathed £1,000 to the Magistrates and Council and this sum was expended in forming the recreation rooms in the building. It contains a billiard room, games room, reading room and lending library, and is a great asset to the town. Most Maybole youths have learned to play billiards there (often unknown to their mothers who somehow or other never looked too kindly on the game as suitable for their sons), the older men of the town enjoy their dominoes and draughts in the games room and the lending library supplies all types of books for the more studious and sober citizens.

In 1912 an old house next to the library (belonging to a local contractor, "Tup" Dobbie, a well-known Minnieboler) was demolished and the Post Office built on the site, again in a style to harmonise with the old Castle and is a handsome building of sandstone and granite. It was the main Post Office for the district until after the first World War when it was demoted to a sub post office under the control of the Ayr Postmaster. In its early days the postmen delivered the mail three times daily during the week and once on Sundays throughout the town, and the red bicycles of the postmen with the heavy mailbags on the front carriers were a common everyday sight throughout the country districts and in the villages of Kirkoswald, Crosshill and Kirkmichael. The Straiton mail was taken by a pony and dogcart and anyone wishing to go to the village could always be assured of a lift by the driver of the mail gig. Nowadays the gig and the colourful bicycles are a thing of the past and small red motor vans hurtle like hornets with the *Daily Express* to Glenalla, etc.

In 1876 the "Ladyland School" was built in Carrick Street at a cost of £6,000 and it was a square sandstone two storey building to which the youths of the town crawled slothfully for over forty years until it was destroyed in a Sunday night in January, 1920, when they joyfully watched it burn to the ground. Some years later, after much wrangling regarding a site, the Carrick Academy was built in Kirkoswald Road in 1927 and while it is not a thing of beauty it serves its purpose well and is one of the finest schools in Ayrshire.

The Cairn School was built in 1890 on the site of an old building known as "Cairn House" and there has been little external alteration to it although in the 1930s extra class rooms were added and the old rooms modernised. Many older people remember with affection Miss Duncan, Miss Brannan and "Skin" Nisbet the headmaster who all taught for many years in it, and afterwards the headmaster was A. B. Coburn who took a prominent part in the town's affairs.

In 1878 the Roman Catholics built their own school next to their Church, and it stands to this day, although it is no longer used as a school, a new one having been built at the head of Kirkland Street (in "McGeachies" field) in the 1940s. Unfortunately the new school is a box like building which, although practical, like the Carrick Academy it cannot be said to be ornamental. Prior to the Roman Catholics building their own school the youthful R.Cs. attended the other schools in the town and could turn up ten minutes late in the mornings as they stayed outside until the other pupils said morning prayers. In the 1860s there were five schools in the town, the Parish School at Greenside, the Industrial School at Greenhead, the West Church School (which had the largest number of pupils) the Free Church School and the Episcopal School, but these were all closed in 1876 when the new school was opened.

About the latter part of the 19th century a "Poorshouse" was built in Ladyland Road with accommodation for forty-eight inmates and it was built to house the "destitute persons" from the parishes of Maybole, Kirkoswald, Kirkmichael, Girvan, Dailly and Barr. It was used for this purpose until after the first World War when, due to centralization of the social services, there was no further need for it and it was converted partly into the District Offices and Labour Exchange and partly into offices for a local firm. The local firm gave up their part some years ago and it is now used as a Youth Centre and Welfare Centre. The building still stands as originally built and retains its stern forbidding look so characteristic of all Victorian "Poorhouses".

Around the end of the nineteenth century many fine villas were built in the town, especially up the "Shore Road" and behind the station, and the old town started to spread up the hill. The local council about twenty years ago arranged to get water from Ayr County Council to supply this area and it was possible to build council houses up the Culzean Road and at Whitefaulds where the lack of a good water supply had previously prevented the building of too many houses. In 1968 the council acquired the lands of Gardenrose Farm and it was planned to erect a large housing scheme with an area laid aside for private development, on the site of the farm. This means that the old town, which nestled for over eight hundred years on the lower slopes of the hillside is now spreading upwards and soon an old townsman who has been away for many years will find it difficult to visualize his old hometown, where new buildings are springing up above the "Shore Road" and old buildings so well-known to him in "Weavers Vennal" and the "Dangartland" have been cleared away and replaced with modern ones.

The buildings on the High Street are a mixture of old and new with some very old (such as the Kings Arms Hotel) and some (such as Templetons Stores) brand new and determined to outshine, in a modern way, their douce elders. The street has just grown, like Topsy, and some buildings have gables to the roadway, some are solid stone fronted, others chromium and glass (and as hygenic as operating theatres) but on a whole the old street still has the couthy atmosphere of the main shopping centre of a provincial country town and McGibbon would not alter much his article on Maybole if he was again to write on Scottish Architecture.

These are the main buildings in the town but two other fine buildings are Ashgrove Home and Lumsden Home, both built originally as private houses and both taken over this century by

Glasgow Corporation as holiday homes for children from Glasgow, who were in need of holidays in rural surroundings. Ashgrove Home was originally "Craigengillan" and was built about the end of last century by James A. Gray, owner of one of the shoe factories and it is said he built it at the top of Kirklandhill Path so that he could look down on the "Bog Lum" which was the chimney stack of Ladywell Factory and a well-known landmark to older residents in the town. Lumsden Home was built by a local doctor and was originally known as Redbrae House and there are many lurid tales of the gruesome happenings in an outhouse built next the retaining wall where it is said the doctor used to dissect human bodies in his experiments. Local lore has it that he was not too particular as to the source of his subjects and, if there be any truth in the tales, there must have been some local "Burke and Hares" in the district about a hundred years ago. It is interesting to note in the Town Records that in 1843 the local sexton was prosecuted for digging up corpses in the old cemetery and selling their coffins and it may be the sexton found an easy and profitable way of disposing of some of the contents of his second hand wares but this can only be conjecture as certainly neither the vendor nor the purchaser would speak about their business transactions.

Many old buildings have been swept away with the march of progress and the town has lost the "Sun Inn", the "Dunnering Inn", the "Whitehall of the Carmelite Friars", the "Black House", the "Little Temple" in Kirkwynd, the old Parish Manse, John Knox's House and the houses of twenty-six lairds but there are still enough old buildings left, and attractive new ones will no doubt be built, to keep Maybole as a "good example of a local centre or provincial town".

In 1963 the Scottish Development Department made a survey of the town and issued a list of "Buildings of Architectural and Historic Interest in Maybole". The buildings were graded in importance under categories A, B and C and noted as being of architectural interest of importance from a historical point of view and the following is an abbreviated extract from the notes issued by the Department:

Note: A=Buildings of National Importance.

B=Buildings of Local Importance or good examples of some period or style.

C=Good Buildings which are fair examples of a period or in some cases happen to group well with some categories A and B.

Name of Building	Description	Category
1. Old Parish Church	1829; refurnished 1882, 1742 bell—a large square rectangular shaped hall with tower centrally placed on south side.	B
2. Saw Mill and Factory, Cassillis Rd., now premises of Messrs. Jack.	Early 19th century — Bull-nosed masonry; 2 storeys on raised embankment; 7 sash windows, those on ground floor being round headed; simple eaves with gutter; slate roof has 3 hipped gables.	C
3. No. 14 Cassillis Road.	Forms part of same range as Nos. 16 and 18; stucco, 2 storeys, 4 sash windows; plinth, 2 bands, moulded eaves, rolled skews; ridge roof, single splayed dormer; round headed doorway to right has fanlight.	B

4. Nos. 16 & 18 Cassillis Road.

Early 19th century — Pink ashlar; plinth, 2 bands, moulded eaves; 2 storeys; 11 sash windows, centre palladian window on 1st floor above elliptical arched carriage way; 2 panelled doors with fanlight to right and left; ridge roof, 4 square dormers, rolled gable skews.

5. Nos. 22, 24, 26 and 28 Cassillis Rd.

Pleasant vernacular range circa 1840; stucco, 2 storeys; No. 24-26 has modillioned cornice; No. 28 has centre recessed doorway flanked by columns.

C

6. Maybole Castle.

Town mansion of the Lords Cassillis, hereditary bailiffs of Carrick. The plan is of the simple quadrilateral form with a square projection at the south-west angle containing the principal stair which ascends to near the top where the turret is corbelled out and formed into a handsome prospect room with a bow window to the west. The large angle turrets, the ornamental and remarkable

A

form of the dormers, and the enriched chimney heads, point to a late date or the first quarter of the 17th Century and was probably built by John, sixth Earl, who was appointed Extraordinary Lord of Session at the Restoration — The castle has been enlarged in more recent times and is now occupied by Lord Ailsa's factor.

7. Tolbooth.

Little now remains of the old mansion of the Lairds of Blairquhan, but the tower erected on the top of the staircase, with its pyramid, is still pre-, served, and serves the purpose of the town belfry. The pointed and traceried windows of the top storey are peculiar features, and are probably an indication of the Gothic revival which took place in the 17th century.

B

8. Royal Bank of Scotland.

3-storey Italianate building with wide spreading eaves; ashlar, raised rusticated quoins, plinth, 2 moulded bands; sym-

B

		metrical 3 windows facade, coupled round arched windows, centre doorway.	
9.	Nos. 4, 6 and 8 Whitehall.	Circa 1840. Pleasant vernacular row, 2 storeys; No. 4 ashlar, centre panelled pilastered doorway; No. 6 and 8 grey painted.	C
10.	Nos. 1, 3, 5, 7, and 9 Whitehall.	Circa 1840. Vernacular range in stucco; 2 storeys, raised quoins, plinth, band, eave band, and moulded cornice. No. 9 has imposing doorway with coupled flat panelled pilasters, entab-, lature, segmental arched doorway.	C
11.	Nos. 18 and 19 Greenhead.	Pair of houses on west side of Green—No. 18, 3 storeys, 3 sash windows, ashlar, modillioned cornice, centre doorway in recessed painted stone surround. No. 19, 2-storeys, 3 sashes coursed stone blocks patched with cement.	B
12.	Pair of houses known as The Smithy, Greenside.	To right, grey harling, 2 storeys, 3 sashes in cement frames; to left, stucco, 2 storeys, 2 windows,	C

	black painted plinth and dressings.	
13. Welltrees Bar Welltrees Street.	Harled; 2 storeys; 3 small narrow windows in painted stone surrounds; moulded eaves; old doorway to left has shouldered architrave.	C
14. Old Collegiate Church.	The roofless ruin of a 15th century church, built for a small college established here in 1373 by the Kennedies of Dunure. The remains include a rich door in a revived First pointed style, and an Easter Sepulchre which is also an imitation of early work.	A
15. Old graveyard, Kirkwynd.	Disused. Contains some 18th-19th century monuments of interest.	C
16. St. John's Cottage.	Attractive pavilion type small house, circa 1830-40; symmetrical garden facade has centre 2 storey splayed tower flanked by 1 storey supporting wings; ground floor sash windows reach down to floor level and have wooden jalousies; rectangular shaped upper windows; wide spreading	B

eaves; entrance at side.
Interior contains an unusual hall and staircase,
glass domed skylight.

(It will be noted the dates given for some of the buildings (Parish Church, Castle, etc.) do not agree with factual dates but the extract is as printed by the Scottish Development Council).

Chapter 13

CROSSRAGUEL ABBEY

ALTHOUGH Crossraguel Abbey is not within the boundaries of the burgh it has always been looked upon by the townspeople as belonging to Maybole, even if it is in the Parish of Kirkoswald. The meaning of the name cannot be given with any certainty but most agree it means the Abbey of the Royal, or Regal, Cross. The abbey was founded by Duncan, Earl of Carrick, in 1244, in an age when many other monasteries were being built throughout Scotland. Duncan gave land and money to the monks of Paisley Abbey and asked them to build the monastery but they only erected a small chapel in the first instance and held on to quite a considerable balance of cash, which rather displeased the Earl. He went to law on the matter and the Bishop of Glasgow, who was appointed arbiter, found in his favour and ordained that the Paisley monks should build a proper monastery and that monks should be sent from Paisley Abbey to run it.

The said monks were to be free of all interference from the Abbot of Paisley, although he might visit it once a year, and he was to receive a payment of ten merks yearly. The Abbot of Paisley felt that an annual income of ten merks and the right to visit Crossraguel yearly was a poor substitute for the considerable capital he had held on to when the Earl gifted the lands in Carrick to endow the Abbey and he appealed to the Pope in 1265 for redress against the decision by the Bishop of Glasgow. The Pope, however, sustained the Bishop's decision and so Crossraguel became an independent abbey and continued so until after the Reformation.

The abbey, like all Roman Catholic churches, was built so that the worshippers should face the east, where Christ is expected to appear on the day of Judgement. In addition to the choir and nave, it included a sacristy (or vestry) and a chapter house (where the monks met to deal with the business of the church), with a room above which was probably the library. The building also included kitchens, a refectory (or dining room) with the monks' cells grouped over a row of cellars probably used as storehouses for the abbey. Apart from the main buildings an abbot's house was erected above a stream which flowed right under it and probably provided a primitive form of sanitation for the guardrobes, etc. Later another abbot's house (or prior's house) was built and the ruins of this building are in good preserevtaion to this day. One of the interesting ruins is that of the pigeon doocot (or "columbarium") shaped like a beehive, and the monks must have fed well from the many pigeons it held. The cloisters are still easily traceable round a lawn about seventy feet square with a well in the middle of it.

Architecturally Crossraguel could not compete with the great abbeys of Melrose, Jedburgh, Roslin, etc., but it was a homely, couthy, country church, well suited for its purpose and must have had a quiet charm about it when the monks ruled the district for upwards of three hundred years. Billings in his *"Ecclesiastical Antiquities"* describes it as "a half baronial, half ecclesiastical ruin, with a rough square tower frowning over the beautiful remains of some rich and airy specimens of the middle period of Gothic work". It had its fish ponds, its doocot and its cattle grazing on the lands around it and its inhabitants must have found it a pleasant place to live in where they were safe from the feuding of their spirited neighbours in the old Kingdom of Carrick.

The monks were followers of Saint Benedict (their particular branch being that of Clugny) and they wore long woollen robes with cowls, being called "Black Monks" from the colour of their robes. Many interesting incidents took place during the time the abbey was extant but to record even a few would need a book in itself. One of the most famous Abbots was Quintin Kennedy who debated with John Knox in Maybole in 1562 and who still ruled his abbey and worshipped in the old faith until his death in August, 1564, although the Scottish Parliament had passed an Act in 1560 abolishing the Roman Church throughout Scotland.

The interesting point about the ruins of the abbey is their completeness, as they show practically the whole layout of the old monastery whilst other ruined abbeys in Scotland show only a small part of what they once were. It is easy to trace the chapter house, the sacristy, the refectory, the cloisters, the monks' cells, etc., and to build in one's mind a complete picture of the whole abbey when it was peopled by the "Black Monks" going about their daily business. Much of the tracery of windows, carvings, small outhouses and many other things have naturally disappeared but sufficient is still left to make it an interesting place to visit and many people visit the well kept ruins and grounds which are maintained by the Ancient Monuments Departments of the Ministry of Works. It is still possible to see part of the font, the sedilia and the piscina in the nave and choir, while the chapter house is in good preservation. It is strange so much should be left as the abbey was more or less used as a quarry for stones to build some of the houses in Maybole and district after the Reformation when so many lovely old abbeys in Scotland were destroyed or allowed to fall into ruins.

Chapter 14

"ADAM'S ALE"

FROM earliest times great importance was placed on the plentiful supply of good wholesome water from the town wells and all writers specially mentioned that Maybole had a great number of springs and wells which provided the inhabitants with Adam's Ale. Before piped water was commonplace in all communities the existence of good springs was of paramount importance and the Minniebolers were fortunate indeed that throughout the town there were numerous wells where water could be drawn within easy carrying distance of each home. Indeed the abundance of springs must have been one of the main reasons why the earliest inhabitants decided to settle here and for over seven hundred years Minniebolers thrived exceedingly well on the stoups of water they carried to their houses or which were brought to the doors by the town's water carriers, the most famous of whom was "Johnnie Stuffie" who is still remembered for his eccentricities to this day.

One of the main wells was My Lord's Well at the foot of the High Street and it was originally situated within the courtyard of Maybole Castle. An overflow from it ran down the hill (now St. Cuthbert's Road) and the townspeople drew water from the overflow at Market Square before the old buildings at the Castle were removed. When these alterations were made the townspeople had full access to what had formerly been the private well of the Castle and a pump (costing £18) was erected over it, about 1806, to save the labour of hauling up buckets by hand. This old pump was in existence up to 1862 when a new and ornate metal pump, with a gas lamp on top, was fitted and this stood as a local landmark, known to all as "The Pump", until it was removed in the 1930s. When the use of My Lord's Well was common to all, the part of the overflow which had been used by the townspeople was allowed to become derelict but in 1869 when St. Cuthbert's Road was formed the overflow was cleaned out and piped to a trough with an arch over it and this well became known as St. Cuthbert's Well to distinguish it from My Lord's Well further up the hill, which by that time had become known as "The Pump". St. Cuthbert's Well was in use up until the 1930s and proved invaluable at the time the town's reservoir went dry in 1933, and the people had to draw water once again from many of the old town's wells, but finally it was diverted into the town's sewers and the archway built up. Both My Lord's Well and St. Cuthbert's Well were supplied from springs in Kirklandhill Path which originally ran down an open watercourse, being piped at a later date through the lands of the Free Church, the Castle Garden, down St. Cuthbert's Road to Pat's Corner and thence to Tunnoch Burn.

Another well-known well is still in existence in the garden of Wellpark in Culzean Road and this well was an overflow from the Green Well which was in the centre of the Ballgreen. This Green Well was still in use in the latter part of last century and served many of the old houses in Ladyland Road which did not have piped water near at hand, but in 1881 it was built in, and an ornamental granite fountain raised over it. At Gardenrose House (The Bumbee) and in "May Youngs" field there were other draw wells but these have been built in for many years and their water diverted into drains. The Parish Church in Cassillis Road was unfortunately built over the site of the springs which supplied the east end of the town at "Townhead" and these caused endless trouble to the Heritors who were constantly called on to repair damage to the church caused by the rotting of floor timbers, etc., through dampness. There were other springs in "McGeachies Field" where the Roman Catholic School now stands, in the playground of Cairn School and behind the old inn now known as the "Grey Man" and also in the grounds of the old manse (now Swan Court) and the east end of Maybole had an over-abundance of springs which, before they were diverted into drains and built up, sometimes proved troublesome, especially after wet weather.

The west end of the burgh was also amply supplied with springs and the best known was the Welltrees Spout. This, in the old days, was the source of water for the prebend's house at Welltrees, the "Maison Dieu", and other properties built around it and great importance was placed on it being kept clean. In 1807 the council bought a piece of ground around it from John McClure for £4 1s. 8d. so that better access could be formed to it. Later in the nineteenth century a public subscription was raised to build an ornamental wall around it with the words "Ye neir ken the worth o' water till the well gangs dry" inscribed on it to remind the townsfolk to take care of their water supply. This well was calculated to give 10,000 gallons of water per hour and was known and affectionately cherished by all the locals. Unfortunately when new houses were built near it in 1968 the local council found it necessary to build up the well and removed the coping with the inscription which had been known to generations of townspeople. The name of the well was derived from a grove of ash trees which stood around it from time immemorial. The last of these trees was cut down in May, 1939, as it was thought to be in a dangerous condition (although when it was felled it was found to be perfectly sound in heart and would have stood for many years) and a forestry expert calculated the tree was well over 200 years old.

In Coral Glen there was another spring, much smaller in its volume of water and which at times was really only a trickle, but known to all Minniebolers as the "Wee Spout in the Glen", or "Cockydrighty", and nearly all young lads have slaked their thirst at its "stroup" at one time or other. Public subscription in the latter part of last century again met the cost of erecting a wall round it with the inscription "Ye may gang farther and fare waur" and no true Minnieboler ever forgets the advice he was given in his youth when he learned by heart the inscriptions over "The Welltrees" and the "Wee Spout".

A famous well in old days was at the foot of "The Bog Brae" and was known as "My Lady's Well" giving the name to the factory which was built beside it and which became locally famed as "The Ladywell' or "The Bog". It was given its name because it was on lands belonging to the "Auld College" and it also gave an ample supply of water in its day. These were the main wells of Maybole in days gone past but there were many others throughout the town. Traces of some are still to be found but most have been filled in and forgotten. There were many in the yards of the houses in High Street, the best known being behind the shop now occupied by McKay, Butchers, and the shop recently used as a showroom by the South of Scotland Electricity Board at the top of High Street. This well served a public house which once stood there and also the shop at the corner of School Vennal occupied by a grocer locally known as "Hungry Archie". These wells although now disused and supposedly filled in, must still gather water from time to time as often the conduits and manholes for telephones, etc., in High Street are flooded and it would seem the flood water must seep in from the old wells.

Although not within the burgh there are some wells in the district which were well-known to the townspeople who believed their waters had curative powers and who regularly drew water from them if they or their children were sickly.

One was at Ballochmount, a little beyond Slateford Village on Laigh Grange Farm and was known as St. Helen's Well. It was believed to cure ailing children if they drunk its water on Mayday and on this day yearly many mothers used to walk from Maybole to get a jug of water from it if they thought their offsprings weren't thriving as they should. Another medicinal well was on Pennyglen Farm and it was believed sick cattle would be cured if they drank from it and this belief was strongly held by local farmers up until the middle of last century but now both wells are derelict and forgotten and mothers and farmers rely on powders and potions instead of the health giving waters of the wells. Actually the old beliefs were not so fanciful as analysis has shown that both wells have water impregnated with various health giving minerals. Ladycross Well at the foot of the Stey Leas was another which was a favourite spot for townsfolk to rest and slake their thirst on a warm Sunday afternoon when walking round the Cross Roads.

At Tippersweil on the road to Cultizeoun Farm there was another spring, often mentioned in local lore, which stood beside the old road which ran from Whitefaulds Farm to the old road at Abbey Mill and then on to Kirkoswald. It was near a thorn tree on Baltersan Farm where Peden once preached in Covenanting times and which was known as Peden's Thorn, and many a thirsty traveller welcomed the coolness of its water on warm summer days when they stopped to freshen themselves and wash their face and hands before entering the town. A cottage, now gone, used to stand near to it and round by Tippersweil, Cultizeoun and back by Mochrum and the Shore Road was a favourite walk for courting couples for generations. Like the cottage, the well and thorn tree are now gone but the spot is still known to all locals although few now associate it with Peden and the Covenanters but remember it as the birthplace of the "Eastern Princess".

All these wells were of such major importance to the townspeople in days gone by that each year the Magistrates specially appointed committees to inspect and report on them from time to time. They had to ensure that no person presumed to "wash any foul clothes, fishes or entrails of beasts" in them under a penalty of twenty-two shillings Scots, a very considerable sum in those days when a weaver's wage was about 7/- weekly. The people appear to have recognised the necessity of keeping the water supplies pure as there is no reference to any of the inhabitants ever incurring a fine and they were ever ready to subscribe to collections raised for the purpose of building walls, etc., round the wells.

The abundance of water was of course of great importance to the weaving and shoe trades, the weavers needing it to wash their wool (although this was mostly done at the Cairders Burn) and the shoemakers for their tanneries. It was of importance also to the two lemonade works which once were situated in the lower part of the burgh where artesian wells gave a great supply of excellent water.

As time passed the townspeople naturally tired of carrying "gangs" of water in "stoups" when they saw other communities well served with piped water to their doors and even into their houses and they looked around for a source to give them a plentiful supply. Last century a reservoir was first formed at Glenside Farm and then another at Lochspouts Farm (the combined cost being in the region of £11,000) and the Minniebolers not only had gas to cook with but taps that filled their pots, without the heavy task of carrying spring water and the town became really modern and could hold its head up among other burghs. Some progressive citizens immediately installed piped water in their houses, and pumps were placed at strategic points throughout the town to supply houses where the people did not do so, but many of the older inhabitants still persisted for many years to draw water from the Welltrees, the Spout and St. Cuthbert's. As one old worthy was heard to remark, "Lochspouts is a' richt for washing claes, but gie me the Welltrees when I'm drouthy". Through time, however, the old prejudices died and every house in the town came to have its piped supply and the days of the famous old Maybole wells passed away. In

October, 1933, the reservoir at Lochspouts dried up and once again the townsfolk had to draw water from the wells and boys went round the town selling water at fourpence per pail.

As the town spread up the hill it was found there was not supcient pressure not enough water in Lochspouts to give adequate supplies to the houses above the railway line and in the 1940s the town council arranged to connect the upper part of the burgh to the Ayr County Council water main which passed above the town from a break pressure tank on Brockloch Farm. The burgh was responsible for the maintenance of its own water works until 1968 when all the water districts in Ayrshire were combined with the Ayr and Bute District Water Board and now the responsibility of providing Adam's Ale to townsfolk rests with this body.

It is interesting to note how Maybole developed in layers, one on top of the other, entirely due to the sources of the water supplies. The oldest part is at the bottom of the hill where in early days there was a plentiful supply gathered from the springs and burns running down from the higher ground. Later as springs were opened and cleared higher up the hill the town grew round the High Street. When water under pressure was introduced development started along Barns Road, Culzean Road and Greenside and finally the plentiful County supply permitted building up Gardenrose Path, etc., and the town's largest single housing scheme has commenced at Gardenrose Farm, where only twenty years ago water had to be pumped up to the farmhouse by a windmill.

The introduction of piped water naturally led to changes in sanitation and soon the privies, which were formerly installed at the bottom of the house gardens, became obsolete and w.c.'s became commonplace, although many of the present townspeople were well reared without them. This necessitated the installation of drains and a sewage disposal works and the town's first sewage works were built on the lands of Ballony Farm in

1905. These were adequate for a long time but as more houses were built and older houses were fitted with bathrooms the need for larger sewage works became of paramount importance and gave much worry and many headaches to the local councillors for many years until finally a site was found near Littleton Farm, a loan was raised to meet the cost (around £85,000) and a new sewage farm was formed in 1957. When built it was thought it would be sufficient for the town's needs for many years but recently with the growth of housing schemes and the introduction of new factories into the town, there are many who doubt if the sewage works are yet large enough and it may be that very soon they will require to be enlarged.

Chapter 15

MARTIAL MINNIEBOLERS

The men of Carrick were aye "bonnie fechters" and were to be found in the forefront when Scottish armies were in the field of battle. They fought for their freedom at Bannockburn and their faith at Bothwell Brig; they brought home their dead from Flodden and left them among the poppies in Flanders; they waded through blood at Pinkie and mud at Paschendale and Carrick can always be proud of its fighting men.

On the plains of Stirling Bruce proudly spoke of his "ain men from Carrick" guarding him and helping to overthrow the power of Edward at Bannockburn and Sir Walter Scott has him say, "I, with my Carrick spearmen charge" and "Carrick, press on". It was a Carrick man, Sir Hew Kennedy of Ardstinchar, who commanded the Scottish army which fought on the side of Joan of Arc and raised the siege of Orleans in the French war of liberation against the English. At the Battle of Beauge on 22nd March, 1421, he so distinguished himself by his valour that he was granted by the Dauphin the right to wear the Royal livery of France. In 1513 David, Third Lord Kennedy, led the Carrick men at Flodden and died with his King, James VI, as did many other men from the district, and Lord Kennedy's body was brought home to Maybole and buried at the old Collegium. At Langside they fought both for and against their Mary, Queen of Scots, and some went into exile in England with her. At the disaster at Pinkie in 1547 many Carrick men died, among them twelve Lairds or their eldest sons and there was much mourning in the old Kingdom.

The Maybole Covenanters mustered in a field at Whitefaulds (where the house known as "Muster Lea" now stands) and marched to fight for their faith at Bothwell Brig in 1679. Among the 1,200 prisoners taken after the Covenanters fled the field were 257 who, after five months imprisonment in Greyfriars Churchyard, refused to renounce their belief and were shipped as slaves to America but were drowned when their ship, the "Crown", foundered in a storm off the Orkneys in December, 1679. Among these 257 were 21 Carrick men and of these six were Minniebolers. Their names are inscribed on the Covenanters' Memorial on the Cross Roads and they were Mungo Eccles, Thomas Horne, Robert McGarron, John McHarrie, John McWhirter and William Rodger.

At the time of the Bishop's Wars about the middle of the 17th century the Earl of Cassillis commanded a troop of Carrick men who fought for their religion and many Maybole men served under his command. At the Battle of Alford in June, 1645, a Captain John Corrie of Maybole was killed, and his testament, dated April 1645, states he had "been called out to fight for his Kirk and his Kingdom".

When the Carrick men were not united against common foes outside their own district they turned joyously on each other and for generations the old High Street in Maybole was often the scene of strife when the Bargany men and the Cassillis adherents cleared the causeway of the sober burgesses and their wives, who waited patiently until the tumult died down and they could come out from behind their barred doors and bandage up the broken heads. This internecine and intermittent warfare lasted until young Bargany met his death at the skirmish at Ladycross which virtually brought an end to the famous Carrick Feud.

MAYBOLE - CARRICK'S CAPITAL

On 21st December, 1760, there was born in Maybole a man who must have been one of the longest serving soldiers in army history. His epitaph states that Lt. Col. Thomas Aird was born in Maybole, served 56 years in the service of his country, and died in Sunderland on 1st November, 1839, aged 79 years. During his long army service he was 28 years in the Royal Scots Greys and commanded a corps throughout the Peninsular campaign and fought at Waterloo.

It was not until the end of the eighteenth century, however, that the Maybole men were banded together as one fighting unit. In 1797 the Loyal Carrick Volunteers, consisting of 114 men, were formed in the town to give their support, if needed, in beating off the threatened invasion by Napoleon. They would have made better wartime soldiers than back line Home Guards, however, and the only foe they faced were their spouses on the morning after they were disbanded for "drunk and riotous behaviour" on parade in the Town Green the previous evening. This does not reflect on their bravery, however, as any married man will agree it would be easier to meet a Froggie (even if only armed with a spade) than an enraged and affronted wife after she had spent a night nursing her wrath to keep it warm.

Later most of the townsmen with a liking for soldiering enlisted in the local County Regiment, the 21st Foot (later the Royal Scots Fusiliers) and saw service in many lands with this famous regiment. In 1793 the 12th Earl of Cassillis formed, among the local farmers and townsmen, a troop of yeomanry known as "The Earl of Carrick's Own Yeomanry" in honour of their royal feudal superior, the Earl of Carrick and heir to the Crown. This gave rise to the Ayrshire Yeomanry who saw service with their horses in many campaigns until they were finally dismounted during the first World War and attached to the County Regiment as foot soldiers. In the second World War they became a mechanised unit and, although officially now disbanded some loyal and proud troopers still meet for summer camps and exercises and will be ready once again if ever needed by their country. The Minniebolers, however, were not so clannish as only to enlist in their local county regiments and many saw service with the Argylls, the Black Watch and other Scottish units, and Sergeant McAdie, who lived to a ripe old age, is remembered by many townspeople proudly parading on occasion with his breastful of medals which showed he had been on the Kabul to Khandahar march, and in many other campaigns.

It is interesting that the famous Covenanting Regiment, The Cameronians, or 26th Foot Regiment, had great connections with the old town and the first man to enlist, when it was formed at Douglas in 1689, was Richard Slaven who lived at Kildoon, just a mile out of the town. In 1803 when the Cameronians were on route to take up garrison duty in Ireland they camped in the old Sheep Park from the 2nd to the 6th December and the regimental band paraded for the entertainment of the townsfolk. No doubt the sound of "The Black Bear" in the old High Street would stir many of the local youths to keep time to the quick step of this famous Rifle Regiment which bore the black button in memory of the death of Richard Cameron. It must have been a great sight when the tents of the regiment were erected at the Sheep Park, armed sentries were posted and the elders gathered their companies together for communion, which was one of the prized traditions of the regiment. The townspeople so appreciated the visit of the regiment that they raised a subscription "for the purpose of treating the Cameronians on their march through Maybole to Ireland with a glass of spirits and a bake" while the officers were dined by some of the prominent townsfolk at the Kings Arms Hotel the evening before they left. The account for the cost of entertaining the soldiers was faithfully minuted in the Council Records and reads, "$6\frac{1}{4}$ gallons whiskie, £2 6s. 9d; loaves and bakes, £0 10s 10d; balance of subscription given to the poor, £0 15s. 11d; total £3 13s. 6d." (It will be noted that there was not an overdue demand on the "loaves and bakes"). This sum did not include the cost of entertaining the officers which seems to have been paid by their hosts who no doubt would dine and wine them well and there must have been some sore heads when the regiment marched out of the town by the Whitefaulds road to Tippersweil and on towards Girvan, with their rifles at the trail and with the quickstep peculiar to all rifle regiments.

In 1859 once again there were rumours and alarms of an invasion by the "Froggies" across the English Channel and the Maybole men, as their fathers had done in 1797, decided to form a unit to assist in the defence of the country. The Volunteer movement sprang up throughout Britain at this time and General Peel, War Minister of the Government, agreed to accept the services of such men as would equip themselves at their own expense, ask for no pay and fight when needed, and to everyone's astonishment an armed force of over one hundred thousand men was enrolled within a short time, having as their motto "Defence not Defiance". Although the danger from France passed away the Volunteer movement had come to stay and continued to the present day in various forms until in 1968 the Territorial Army was more or less disbanded.

After a great deal of wrangling among the would be officers of the corps, the Minniebolers in January, 1860, subscribed £200 to equip the men and by March of that year the Maybole corps of the Ayrshire Rifle Volunteers was formed. It consisted of eighty men and the officers elected were: David Brown, Writer, Captain; William Murray, Writer, lieutenant; Thomas Austin, ensign; Dr. Girvan, surgeon; Richard Parkinson, bugler; Rev. John Thomson, minister in West Parish Church, chaplain. The officers were dressed in befrogged frock coats and the men in blue tunics and grey drill trousers with pill box caps. These leaders faithfully drilled their men until they were well able to compete with the other companies of the Ayrshire Battalion (which comprised over 1,000 men under the command of the Marquess of Ailsa who had been gazetted Lieutenant-Colonel of the Rifle Volunteers) when shooting matches, etc., were held and indeed the Maybole rifle team won many trophies on the range. By 1879 the Ayrshire Battalion was composed of fifteen companies and the war office in 1880 split them into two battalions, which were in being until 1887 when the 2nd Battalion, which had its headquarters in Ayr, became the 2nd Rifle Volunteer Battalion of the Royal Scots Fusiliers. The Maybole men were formed into "C" company of the 2nd Rifle Volunteer Battalion of the R.S.F. and many of the locals drilled in the Sheep Park or at the Town Green, practised shooting in the old "Armoury" and made a bee line for "Bobby Gerrand's" in the Kildoup when dismissed from their labours. The Minniebolers never were in favour of being connected with the R.S.F. and staunchly adhered to be the old form of "Ayrshire Rifle Volunteers" when speaking about themselves. Many medals earned by these Maybole volunteers must still be in the possession of some of their descendants and the writer has the dress sword and pill box diced cap belonging to his grandfather, together with a long service medal inscribed "Ayrshire Rifle Volunteers; "C" Company 2nd V.B.R.S. Fusiliers", with Britannia crowning a soldier with a laurel wreath on one side, and "Presented to Lieut. H. B. Gray for long service; enrolled 8th March, 1860, retired 22nd May, 1891" on the other.

On 25th August, 1881, the famous "Wet Review" took place when over 40,000 Volunteers from all over Britain paraded before Queen Victoria in Queens Park, Edinburgh. The 2nd Ayrshire Rifles were present, 88 strong, and many Maybole men from "C" Company made up the Ayrshire contingent. They left Maybole by train for Ayr before 5 o'clock that morning, joined up with the Ayr riflemen, then left at 5.30 a.m. by special train for Edinburgh and on arrival there they found the skies dull and overcast but all hoped the rain would keep off until after the review. Unfortunately this was not to be and long before the parade commenced the heavens opened and there was such a deluge that the streets were flooded and Hunters Bog, where the troops were to gather, became a perfect quagmire. It was decided to carry on, however, and the Queen reviewed her citizen army in a steady downpour with spectators and riflemen alike being drenched to the skin. The volunteers, especially, were in a sad state, with the pipeclay from their belts and the dye from their uniforms running in streaks down their grey drill trousers. Notwithstanding the rain the day was a great success and the Maybole men returned to their home town around 6 a.m. the following morning, tired and bedraggled but still in high spirits and able to muster and march behind their band to the Town Hall where they fell out to return to their homes and brag for evermore that they had been present at the "Wet Review". Through time the Volunteers merged into the Territorials in 1908 which always had a good quota of Maybole men until the powers that be decreed in 1968 that the Territorial Army was no longer required.

When the Boer War broke out many of the Volunteers in the town joined fighting units as they wished to see action and the Volunteers were for home defence only, as were the Home Guard of the Second World War. On their return from active service in South Africa they were feted by the townspeople and some, who had especially distinguished themselves, were made Honorary Burgesses. The now commonplace khaki uniform was introduced at this time and some of the soldiers brought back their tunics and wore them at their work and the older people in the town well remember "Khaki" Campbell who worked on a local farm and got his nickname because he wore an old Khaki tunic.

At the outbreak of the First World War in August, 1914, the Minniebolers as usual were eager to get to grips with the enemy and the local Territorials mustered at the Armoury in the town and marched behind their Band to the station where everyone from babes in arms to the oldest townsman turned out to cheer them away. There were crackers placed on the lines, the band blew its loudest, the Territorials waved and cheered and the wives and sweethearts wept as the train steamed out and those left on the platform assured each other the soldiers were only off on a picnic as the war couldn't possible last and they would be home for Christmas. Little did they think that four long weary years would pass before the Maybole men would return, and during these years many more would leave to join the forces and many would never return. In 1919 those who did come back were entertained in the Town Hall, all were given medals from the townspeople with the Town Coat of Arms on one side and inscribed with their names on the other and the men who had won special distinction for their bravery were gifted gold watches. The year 1919 was a hectic year in the old town as the returning soldiery held dances on every possible occasion and everyone made merry for a time until they realised that many of the returning men had no jobs to come back to as trade had fallen away badly in both the shoe factories and in Jacks. This meant many of the men who had left to go to war (some still serving their apprenticeship) could not find work on their return and there was another exodus from the town, much smaller than the 1909 one, but still drastic. In memory of those who died on service the townspeople bought land at Drummurran Farm and formed a Memorial Park, with golf course, tennis courts and bowling green and erected a cenotaph on the hill above the tennis courts inscribed with all the names of the fallen.

Twenty years later another generation of Maybole men were ready to go, as their fathers did, to again stop the mighty Germans when Hitler ran amok in 1939 and the old story of 1914-18 was repeated in the years 1939-45. The Maybole men fought on every front in all branches of the Forces and again some never returned to see the sun rise over Kildoon. The memories of 1914-18 were still sharp and clear and the townsfolk were more sober in their attitude to the second World War and there was no display of enthusiasm as there had been when the Territorials entrained in August, 1914. For the first time in history a foreign foe could also attack the homes of the townsfolk from the air and this brought the harsh realities of war into every household. A Home Guard detachment was formed, Air Raid Wardens appointed, air raid shelters built, the Town Hall doors and windows sandbagged, guards placed on the water works and every possible defensive precaution brought into force. Children from large cities were boarded amongst the townspeople, detachments of the Inniskillens and Scots Guards were stationed for a time in the town and a prisoner of war camp was formed at Ballony and the stay at homes were as much in the battle line as the soldiers who had gone abroad with their fighting units.

For five years the old town survived a period of food and clothes rationing, blackouts, air raid warnings and other alarms until its men returned from the wars in 1945, as they had so often done in centuries past, sadly depleted in numbers and many never fit to walk round the Cross Roads again. A fund was raised by the townsfolk to send parcels to their fighting men during the war and a Welcome Home Fund was incorporated in April, 1944, to collect money to entertain the men on their return when peace was declared. The sum uplifted amounted to £3,518 and this was distributed among the returning soldiers and the relatives of those who had been killed. Scrolls were prepared conveying the thanks of the people of Maybole for the services given to the nation by the serving men and women and each returning combatant was given a scroll with a gift of £4 in cash. In all 747 serving men and women received such scrolls and cash gifts while 29 war widows also received similar scrolls and gifts. The balance of the fund was expended in the purchase of the scrolls (£246) and other expenses and when the fund was cleared a balance of £66 was gifted to the town's Common Good Fund.

The names of the 29 killed in action were inscribed on the cenotaph which had been erected in the Memorial Park after the 1914-18 war. It is indeed proof of the fighting spirit of the Minniebolers when it is realized that nearly 800 men and women joined the Forces in the last war from a small town with a population of around five thousand. It is to be hoped that this spirit will not be called upon again for very many years, as surely the townsfolk deserve to rest on their laurels after hundreds of years of answering the call to arms, but no doubt should it again be necessary the men of Carrick will, as ever, be ready.

Chapter 16

SOCIAL ACTIVITIES

MANY city dwellers have a fixed belief that life in a small rural town must be dull and monotonous and its inhabitants inquisitive busybodies, but nothing could be further from the truth. In a small community everyone knows everyone else and what a stranger might think inquisitiveness is really just interest in each other. This may seem strange to anyone reared in a large city where neighbours can live next door to each other for years and never get beyond passing the time of day when they meet, but it is natural in a close knit small community where, if ancestry is traced back far enough, it is found most of the population are related to each other in some way.

Naturally people with the same interests gather together and societies or clubs are formed where they can meet and indulge in common activities. In a small town all amusements must be organised by the local people and folk will join together to start choirs, drama clubs, guilds and other activities to give them an interest and outlet for their energies. This was more true in days gone past, when small towns were more isolated and more dependent on their own people for entertainment and recreation, but even today it is surprising how small towns and villages still have thriving drama clubs or concert parties and the W.R.I. and church guilds have full memberships of ladies in all country districts.

Maybole has always had many local guilds and clubs where people could meet, especially in winter, to share common interests and while away the dark winter nights, before television became a must in every household, greatly to the detriment of the old social gatherings. Many Minniebolers have happy memories of winter evenings at the socials in the various church halls where happy hours were passed listening to Willie Miller singing *"Ae fond Kiss"* or Bob Strachan and Jeannie Manson rendering *"The Crookit Bawbee"*. Happiness was a simple thing in those uncomplicated days before people were brainwashed and told what they had to accept as entertainment. The kitchen sink was left behind in its proper place and not brought on the stage and folks could dream away an hour or two listening to their ain folk singing the old nostalgic songs which they had known from childhood.

The first societies in Maybole were probably the Guilds of the Masons, the Wrights, the Weavers and the Shoemakers and while these were originally trade guilds they gradually became more social in character. The Shoemakers Guild held its meetings in a house in School Vennal and before it finally became defunct (about the end of last century) it was purely a social club where the soutars of Maybole could spend a few hours away from their wives and weans, much as the more sophisticated men's Clubs in larger cities give refuge to the busy executives today. The Wrights and Weavers Guilds in the town became obsolete much earlier than the Shoemakers but the Masons continued to exist by changing from an operative to a non-operative guild of "Freemasons" and two Lodges flourish exceedingly well in the town to this day.

In 1799 or 1800 (the exact date is not known) the first Orange Lodge in Scotland was founded in Maybole when the soldiers of an Ayrshire Militia Regiment returned from service at the Irish Rebellion of 1798. In 1929 the Grand Orange Lodge of Scotland, in honour of Maybole being the birthplace of Orangism, created a new lodge in the town with the name Loyal Orange Lodge No. 0 and this lodge, as the oldest in Scotland, has the honour of carrying the Union Jack on their parades.

Records show that nearly all organisations in the town up to the present century were all male in character but a change came after the first World War and the Maybole ladies gradually took over and infiltrated into social life to such an extent that the main activities of the town are now to a great extent (if not wholly) petticoat ruled. Bailie Niven would have been horrified if it had been suggested a lady should sit in Council, far less become Provost of the Town, but times have changed and, it must be admitted, much for the better.

In 1922 in the Orange Hall in Dailly Road the first meeting of the L.L.O.L. No. 98 John Knox's Daughters of the Covenant was held and the local Orangemen are now partnered by their womenfolk on the 12th July, whilst the members of the Eastern Star now hold their own meetings as a female branch of the still zealously guarded all male Brotherhood of Freemasons. Ladies now sit in the Council Chamber, the Education Committee, the Juvenile and Magistrate Benches and the only stronghold not yet breached is Kirk eldership and it may not be long until some fine day the bread and wine will be offered by a strapping Hebe instead of a funeral like figure in white bow and black coat.

In 1883 the Boys Brigade movement was founded and it was not long until Maybole had its own company which was formed in 1898 by the Rev. Thomson, ably assisted by Sergeant Stewart, the first drill master. The local company was registered as the 16th Ayr (Maybole) Company and in 1948 was presented with Company Colours by the Women's Guilds of the West Church and Old Church to mark their Golden Jubilee. In 1929 the Junior branch of the Boys Brigade was founded and again

Maybole was not long in forming its own company of Life Boys in 1936.

A year after Baden Powell founded the Boy Scout movement in 1907 four Maybole youths under Patrol Leader John Muir formed the "Kangaroo" Patrol with its meeting place at "Auld Jean's" at the Greenhead. The Troop was registered as the 12th Scottish Troop but undoubtedly would have been given a lower number if there had not been difficulty in getting a Scoutmaster, which delayed application for registration in London, and Maybole can truthfully claim to have one of the oldest Scout Troops in Scotland. In the years before the first World War the Scout movement was very strong in the town and many of the older men can well remember Scoutmaster Simcox teaching them to form a "sheepshank" or how to "brew up" in a billycan over a camp fire with a piece of stick in the "billy" to keep the tea from being "smeeked". In 1922 two packs of Wolf Cubs (a junior branch of the Boy Scouts) were formed in the town and the Scout and Cub movement is still strong and well supported by the youths.

In 1911 Miss Strain, of Cassillis House, formed the first Girl Guide Company in the town and was Captain of the Company for many years. After the formation of the Boy Scouts in 1908 many of the girls wished to become "Girl Scouts" and it was to meet their demands that Miss Strain formed the 1st Company of Maybole Girl Guides which has flourished ever since its formation nearly sixty years ago. In 1926 the Brownies were recruited among the younger girls of 7 to 11 years, being named after the "wee folk" of Orkney with the motto "Lend a hand and play the game" and this junior company of girls proves a fertile source of recruits for the Girl Guides.

There has been for many years a strong Red Cross Detachment in the town and in 1943 a Junior Red Cross Detachment was formed to encourage young girls to train for the Nursing Services and to help the local Detachment in wartime. About the same period a Girls Training Corps, with a senior and junior section, was formed to train girls to share responsibilities in time of National Emergency and also an Air Training Corps to train boys for entry to the R.A.F. but these junior organizations, although well supported in wartime, naturally have not flourished in peacetime as have the Boy Scouts and Girl Guides. In 1933 a Girls' Association was formed under the auspices of the Women's Guild of the Church of Scotland and altogether it can be said the youth of Maybole is well served with various social organizations.

Maybole people have always had an ear for music and enjoy it in all forms from brass bands to male voice choirs. In the latter part of the 19th century a "Christie Minstrel Society" flourished and gave many concerts in "Jack's Hall". It was composed wholly of local men who blackened their faces, wore oversize bow ties and straw hats and delighted their audiences with the *"Campdown Races"* and the quips of their "corner men". It was all the craze at that time to have "nigger minstrel" groups and Maybole was never behind the times. Nowadays such happy bands of minstrels would probably be charged with being anti-racial, would be ordered to wash the burnt cork from their faces and no doubt would be prohibited from singing *"Scots Wha Hae"* and damnation to the English.

At that period there was full employment in the town and many concerts were held in "Jack's" Hall, "Wyllie's" Hall, "Turnbull's" Hall and the Town Hall, where Harry Lauder, J. M. Hamilton, Nellie McNab, W. O. Frame (The Man You Know) and many other famous Scottish artistes appeared and it is said Harry Lauder's fee for his first appearance in "Jack's" Hall was five shillings, from which he paid his own expenses. Many of the townspeople were excellent musicians and singers and got up concerts where local talent filled the bill and few of the older citizens will ever forget "Da" Livingstone bringing the house down with his renderings of *"Brown was paralytic, so was I"*, or *"The Brick came down, we had a half a day"*. During the first World War, Miss Mary Brannan, a local schoolteacher, organized many concerts to raise money for the war effort, where she, like a local Florrie Ford, led the audiences in spirited choruses of old songs and invariably gave her own inimitable rendering of *"The cows are in the clover, they've trampled there since morn, Go and call them Maggie to the old Red Barn"*.

For years there was an excellent Male Voice Choir in the town, which won many trophies in competitions throughout the west of Scotland, and it is said the bass section of the Maybole Choir was unequalled throughout the country. Many of its members were excellent soloists and although the choir no longer exists some of its members still entertain the guests at local Burns' Suppers, etc. Fortunately many of the younger people still show an interest in music and the School Choir at Carrick Academy often bring trophies back from competitions they enter. It may be that in the not too distant future Maybole may once again have choirs to boast about and to listen to with enjoyment in the Town Hall as no doubt people will tire of canned music from the radio and television and wish to hear their ain folk sing the old songs as they did in years gone by.

From the early part of the 19th century Maybole always had a silver or brass band to entertain the local people on a summer evening in the Town Green or on New Year's morning when the bandsmen paraded the streets to the sounds of *"A guid New Year tae ane and a'."* There was a brass band, known firstly as the Maybole Carrick Band, then the Carrick Instrumental Band and finally the Maybole Burgh Band and it was in existence, with short lapses through lack of bandsmen, for well over a hundred years. In 1867 the band instruments were taken from the local bandsmen, because they would not attend practices, and given to the Volunteers who formed a band among its members, and although for a time it was factually a military band it was always considered the Maybole band. About the turn of the century the instruments were returned to the Council and the Maybole Burgh Band came into existence before the first World War. It won many competitions under the leadership of Mr. Shaw, the Bandmaster, and played in the town and district for many years until, again through lack of young people attending practices, in the 1950s the Council took over the instruments and stored them away and the town was left without a band. It was hoped some townsmen interested in band music would come forward and another band be formed but this was not to be and, as the instruments were deteriorating in storage, the council sold them. By coincidence the council purchased scarlet and ermine robes for the Provost and Bailies about the time the instruments were sold and it was the ribald belief of many ratepayers that the council had robbed the band to robe their civic heads and that it was the sale price of the big drum which went to buy the Provost's cocked hat. Whatever be fact or fiction, the fact is Maybole has no band nowadays while it is no fiction that the Provost and Bailies have scarlet robes and cocked hats.

For many years the Orange Lodge had a flute band which delighted to plague the local Roman Catholics with *"Boyne Water"* every twelfth of July but it has also passed away and never again will the Minniebolers be treated to the unforgettable spectacle of "Dickie" in his orange jersey, limping along and banging the big cymbals with unholy delight and absolute disregard for the tune being played by the other members of the band. Once when reproached by the bandmaster, who pointed out the drum should give the beat for the music, he replied, "The drum! Man, it only gangs "Thump-Thump" while I go "Clang-Bang". Let them tak' their time frae me."

Although the brass and flute bands are gone, but not forgotten, the town is still fortunate to have an excellent Pipe Band and long may the hearts of the townspeople beat more quickly as its kilted members swing down the High Street in their bright tartan to the skirl of their pipes. Pipe Major Boyd was the main person responsible for keeping it going for many years and he was personal piper to President Eisenhower whenever he came to reside in his Scottish home at Culzean.

Dancing has always been a favourite activity of the townspeople and every opportunity is taken to indulge in it, especially in wintertime. In days gone past balls were held in the "Dancing Room" in the old Tolbooth above the town gaol and many happy nights must have been spent there with the dancers setting and linking to the lilt of the fiddles. When the Town Hall was built it provided a much larger hall for dancing and the nights of the great Balls of the Yeomanry, the Masons, the Bowlers and Quoiters became annual events. Invitations to these balls were eagerly sought after and the dancing classes of Mr. McQuiston, Mr. Galloway and Mr. McCulloch were alway well attended by the youth of the town preparing themselves to take their place in the Grand March, which always opened a Ball in the old days before the first World War. It was necessary to learn the proper steps of the Lancers, the Petronella, the Waltz Cotillion and other favourite dances and most of the older generation have at some time or other attended "Galloway's Class" to be put through their paces and be rapped by his fiddle bow if they got out of step. Those were the days of dancing pumps and white gloves for the gentlemen and long graceful frocks for the ladies and, of course every man had to take a partner. Little dance cards (with pencils on a silk string) were provided and it was a point of honour that each lady's card be filled with the initials of her partners for the whole programme and there were few, if any, wallflowers, as the Master of Ceremonies made sure that the men did not hang around the hall door but did their duty nobly by dancing with the ladies. A gentleman would give his partner the first dance, the supper dance and the last dance and dance with other partners for the rest of the evening, as it was simply not the "done thing" to dance all night with one partner. The old Town Hall was a festive and happy place when the Yeomanry men led off the Grand March in their dress uniform with burnishers gleaming on their shoulders and everyone eager to be up for every dance until the last waltz at three o'clock in the morning when cups of soup would be served and the gallants would escort their ladies home. After the end of the First World War the returning soldiers held a Ball, which was one of the highlights in the town this century and is still remembered with nostalgia by all who attended it. The days, or rather nights, of the great "Balls" have gone, however, to be replaced with "Saturday Night Hops" where girls go by themselves in many cases, with the hope of finding partners or, if they are unlucky, spend the evening dancing with each other. The older generation may be "squares" in the eyes of youth but the young people of today miss much of the courtesy and pleasure their elders enjoyed.

Naturally with their love for dancing and their ear for music the townsfolk formed many band groups some of which were in great demand to play at dances all over Ayrshire and indeed in some of the Glasgow dance halls. In the days of the "Dancing Room" in the Tolbooth the music was provided by a lone fiddler although often different musicians would take it in turn throughout the night's revels as it was quite common to dance until around five o'clock in the morning, and a solitary "Music Makar" would find it hard to stand up to the strain. Sandy Tannock was the best known fiddler at such functions and it is recorded his fee for playing at a dance was one shilling, which was increased to eighteen pence if he played "till morning". By the end of last century, however, dance bands consisting of violin, flute, cornet and piano had been formed and "Tot" Watson and his partners were in constant demand at dances all over the district. "Kirns", or dances held in farm barns at the end of the harvest time, were common, and lone fiddlers in the town were kept busy in September and October supplying music for the hardy country folks who started with *"Strip the Willow"* about 8 p.m. and would finish with a reel about milking time the following morning. The older folks who have sedately waltzed at a Yeomanry Ball or "hooched" the night away at a "kirn" at Cultizeoun can never hope to understand the modern style of dancing where it seems that everyone stands and gyrates on one part of the dance floor about two yards away from their partners, with mournful expressions and at no time giving the impression that dancing should be a graceful and happy pastime.

Through time the composition of the dance bands changed and saxophones became the predominant instruments and between the two world wars "Jock" Paterson's band was in great favour and played at Turnberry Hotel when any big function was held there. Then accordions took pride of place, in turn giving way to the guitar which seems to be the favourite instrument in all bands at the present time. The Maybole dance band enthusiasts always kept up with the modern trends and were in great demand, and "Mackays" band played throughout the whole of the west country, being noted for its excellent performance and rhythm.

Although the nights of the great balls have passed and the lilt of the violins have given way to the strum of electric guitars there are still groups in the town who keep pace with modern dancing trends and travel afield to play for the enjoyment of the modern youths and it is good to know that the townsfolk still have the love for dancing and music which has been characteristic of Minniebolers for generations. It is of interest to note that a Maybole lad, Tommy McQuater, who started as a young cornet player in the local brass band became a member of a world famous orchestra and he can truly be said to be the town's most noted musician in the dance band world.

Maybole never lagged in introducing new types of entertainment and just before the first World War the cinema was brought to the town by Mr. Biddle who built a wooden hut in "Adam's" yard with entrance to it from the "Back Road". This new fangled entertainment caught on and there were usually full houses every Saturday night, when every seat was taken, from the hard forms in the front rows, where one's head was tilted back at an excruciating angle and the figures on the screen were all out of focus, to the cushioned "tip ups" in the four back rows where the young "mashers" with velvet collars to their coats entertained their girl friends to "a night at the pictures" and a box of chocolates from Miss Dinning's wee shop in the School Vennal. While today the "talkies" are shown on wide screens and in colour it is doubtful if present day cinema patrons ever equal the thrill experienced by the older generation as they watched Pearl White being tied to a railway line or a sawbench and had to wait until the following week's episode to find out whether or not she escaped. In the days of the "Bughut" patrons did not complain about having to wait while "Roddie" changed each reel or repaired breakdowns in the films and were quite content to stamp their feet in time to the *"British Cavalry"* played on the old upright piano by Miss Murray or Miss McNab who could so skilfully fit the piano accompaniment to the type of film being shown. Whilst the entertainment was much less sophisticated in those days the enjoyment was much greater, or seemed so, and everyone heartily laughed at the antics of Mack Sennet or openly and unashamedly cried with Lilian Gish in her misfortunes.

After Mr. Biddle the next owner was Mr. Gilmour and some years later he built a new "Carrick Cinema" at the top of Welltrees Street and the old and original cinema was taken down. The new picture house was much larger and possessed a balcony with "cuddle seats" in the back row and once again there were queues for admission each Saturday night when there were two "houses" and the young couples manoeuvred to get the back seats. When "talkies" came in it was not long before the cinema was converted to sound and the townsfolk tearfully enjoyed "Smiling Through" and other epics, perhaps a little later but every bit as happily as the city dwellers. Cinema business was so good between the two World Wars that another one, "The Ailsa" was built at the bottom of the "Smiddy Brae" and for many years the townspeople had a choice of programme. This interest in "the pictures" died out when television was invented and became as necessary in most homes as the kitchen table and the "Carrick" closed down in the 1950s and became a warehouse and the "Ailsa", although struggling on against the competition of the "goggle box" for some years, finally became a Bingo Hall and now draws large crowds who sit with heads reverently bowed over their Bingo cards listening to the mystic incantations of the "caller" chanting "Kelly's eye" or "Legs eleven" and praying for a certain number to turn up to complete their lines.

Maybole never has boasted of a theatre in the town but last century many strolling players set up "geggies" or wooden booths on the town green and played to large audiences who sat spellbound through the performances. Every other year a famous company of performers, who went by the name of Bostock, would visit the town and they invariably played "Romeo and Juliet". The part of Romeo was always played by one of the Bostock family who was known as "Surly", and Juliet by a lady billed as Miss McGuire who was a married lady of about fifty summers with a grown up family of four sons and two daughters who all took part in the performances. Entrance charges were usually a penny, with twopence being the price of the front seats, being entirely in reverse to the system in the cinema of later days where the front seats were the cheapest and the prices rose the further one sat back from the screen. The townsfolk were sometimes difficult to please and thought nothing of throwing things at the actors if they did not play their parts as the Minniebolers thought they should be played, and indeed on one occasion the audience was so displeased they wrecked the "geggie" which was set on fire by lamps being overturned. Prior to the "penny geggie" period plays were performed by itinerant actors in the old "Dancing Room" in the Tolbooth and records show the rents charged to the strolling players for weekly lets of the hall. Since the Town Hall was built many companies have played in it but with the coming of the cinema the taste for live drama died out in the town and with the exception of local amateur players who occasionally put on a play in winter there have been no "strolling players" walking the boards in Maybole for many years.

In addition to youth organizations, bands, choirs, etc., Maybole has always been well served with other forms of social activities. Most churches have guilds for both men and women and many people are brought to speak or demonstrate to the members on every type of subject. There is a strong Townswomen's Guild and Co-operative Guild and no one need feel lonely on a winter night as everyone is welcomed. The Darby and Joan Club which meets in Carnegie Library weekly caters for the needs of the older generation and the people of the town have organizations to fill the needs of everyone from childhood to retirement age. Evening classes are held each winter in the various schools and there one can be taught anything from country dancing to baking cakes lest anyone should come to visit. The British Legion (which was first mooted when Earl Haig visited the Marquess of Ailsa at Culzean after the end of the first World War) flourished in the town exceedingly well for many years although unfortunately of later years it has not been the force it was formerly. For some years a drama group put on plays annually in the Town Hall and, although in abeyance meantime, it may yet start up again. There have been from time to time clubs of every description, from Photography Clubs to Judo Clubs, and at present there are some Youth Clubs in the town with strong memberships. While often a club is formed, flourishes exceedingly well and then in time dies out no doubt the old town will continue to have its own groups of enthusiasts who band together to amuse and educate themselves, with little regard to what goes on outside its boundaries and, though men may walk on the moon, to a Minnieboler the world will still revolve around the old Capital of Carrick as it has done for so many during the past eight hundred years.

Curiously enough Maybole men have never started a Rotary Club, or a Round Table, or similar organizations so popular in many other towns. This may be due to the influence of their womenfolk who for generations were barred from the various Guilds of Masons, Shoemakers, etc., and who, since their emancipation, are determined the menfolk will never again be free to meet in all male company. As these organizations usually meet for lunch it may be, however, that the Maybole man, when asked to join a Rotary Club, spoke for all when he said, "Na, na. I havna' the time thro' the day and anyway I'm better fed at home." There used to be, however, one all male club which existed in the town for purely social purposes. This was the "High Jinks" club which had its headquarters in a local Inn for many years last century. Its members met once a week for breakfast before they started their work and held a dinner in the evening once a year. Before a member could be admitted he must have been the originator of a successful practical joke against some of his fellow townsmen and it was a strict condition that such jokes must be humorous and not ill intended to its victim. Naturally the club members were all witty and high spirited men and the breakfasts must have been happy starts to a working day and the annual dinners hilarious occasions. At each annual dinner new members were dubbed with imaginary titles, very often characteristic of the member, and it is recorded one foppish member was called "Lord Haw Haw". Another (Dr. Hathon who was said to be a better talker than a practitioner) was named "Lord Humbug" but he objected and was rechristened "The Marquess of Blarney" which title he accepted with equanimity. The club members were nearly all bachelors to begin with but as time went on most of them married and dropped their attendance at breakfast and finally the membership was reduced to three hardened old bachelors, who continued to meet once a year for dinner until one died, another became bedridden and the last one decided the day of the "High Jinks" club was over, and so ended the only really social men's club in the town. In the present times wives would frown on their spouses cheerily setting out for breakfast in a hotel once a week and probably demand that they be taken with them and most husbands would agree this would spoil the whole spirit of the venture. Few wives would understand why it could be possible for their husbands to be live sparks among their fellow men at breakfast on one morning in the week when probably they sat grunting behind a newspaper at home on the other six mornings.

For generations there was a strong Burns Club in the town which met annually for a supper of haggis and neeps in the Kings Arms but this Club died out during the second World War. Other Burns Clubs have started up, however, and probably for generations to come the Bard will be toasted each 25th of January in the old town where his father and mother first met and were married in the church at the Kirkport.

Taking everything into consideration the city dweller need waste no sympathy on the small townsman and feel that he leads a dull and monotonous life as, in the case of Maybole at any rate, the boot is on the other foot and the countryman leads a full and varied life, making his own pleasures among his own folk and does not need strangers in theatres or picture houses to entertain him. The greatest and most glamorous film star can never thrill the city man on the silver screen as does "oor wee Jeannie" when she sings or recites on the Town Hall platform to an audience of locals who have known her since she was born. The greatest elocutionist can never hope to equal "Our Willie" when he throws off his jacket to address the Haggis at a local Burns supper, where everyone is ready to fill in the words should he falter, and certainly to a Minnieboler no story teller could possibly outshine "Jimmy" when he told of his attempt to join the "Council". The social life of a small town, where everyone happily joins in, is a thing to be treasured and preserved and it is hoped it will never really die out.

Chapter 17

SPORT

MAYBOLE has always been a community of sportsmen and in the past, when sport was not the organized financial business it is today, the menfolk keenly contested against each other in games of skill and strength. As years passed by and travel became easier many Maybole men competed as runners and cyclists throughout Scotland and England and their names were known wherever sportsmen gathered to rerun their races, on a winter night with a fire to warm their toes and a dram to enlarge their tales of past victories.

The oldest sport in the district would probably be hawking which was introduced into Scotland in Norman times. As, however, it was once known as "the sport of Kings" few, if any, of the townspeople would be rich enough to indulge in it although the noblemen in Carrick all had their sport with birds of prey and kept their own falconers to train and look after the valuable hawks. At one time men travelled the country selling trained hawks and they were known as "hawkers", while the men who travelled around with the frames, or stands, for the hooded hawks were known as "cadgers". It is strange the same names should still be given to itinerant salesmen to this day and that a "hawker" still considers himself a cut above a "cadger". It is said Marjory, mother of Robert the Bruce, was flying her falcons at Turnberry when she was told by the Lord of Annandale her husband had been killed in Palestine in 1270. Hawking was a favourite sport for generations but the invention of gunpowder was practically its deathknell and it is now only practised by a few enthusiasts, none of whom reside in this district.

The oldest common sport recorded in Maybole was archery and this was practised by all the men who had to turn up for a stipulated number of times each year to shoot at the butts set up in the old Ballgreen. In the 17th century the authorities once complained that the playing of "byasse bowls" was interfering with archery practice and prohibited bowl playing on Sundays. One of the best known archery sports was shooting at the popinjay, which was a model of a bird feathered to resemble a popinjay (or parrot) and suspended from a pole. This was a favourite sport at one time in the town and Sir Walter Scott in *"Old Mortality"* wrote: "The festival of the popinjay is still, I believe, practised at Maybole." After the introduction of gunpowder the ancient game was still practised by the townspeople on the Ballgreen, with firelocks substituted for bows and arrows, but it died out about the end of the eighteenth century.

Bowls have been played in the town for centuries and records show that the "byasse bowls" was a favourite game three hundred years ago when the locals played on a level part of the old Ballgreen. To begin with it was rather crude by today's standards but Minniebolers grew so enamoured of the game they finally formed a proper green in the New Yards and the Maybole Bowling Club opened with a flourish in 1848. The members were strong opponents to meet at any time and often made their mark in the Glasgow-Ayrshire matches, the Gold Bowl and other matches played against clubs in the district. The Club has continued as a private club since it was formed although the members from time to time have found it difficult to carry on. It was recently decided that lady members could join, and with their help it is hoped it will continue for generations to come. After the 1914-18 War when the Memorial Park was formed, the Town Council formed a public bowling green in it, for members of both sexes, and this club has a good membership and can often trounce the older club in the local bowling Derby.

Football is another favourite game which has been played by the young men in the town for generations. In the 18th century the schoolmaster in the small school at the foot of the Ballgreen complained bitterly about the damage caused to the building by the boys kicking balls against it when playing "Futball". (It would seem every game was played at the Ballgreen, even "gowfe", before proper pitches and courses were formed, and there must have been great difficulty in separating the footballers from the bowlers and the archers from the golfers). At the end of the last century a football pitch was formed at Ballony near the "Bog" Shoe Factory and Maybole could field quite a strong team against neighbouring towns. Just before the first World War they were bold enough to enter for the Scottish Cup and drew Glasgow Rangers as opponents. The match took place at Ballony when nearly the whole of the townspeople turned up to cheer on their team and the score was 13-0, (in favour of the visiting team). For many years "Ballony" was the favourite venue on a Saturday afternoon for the menfolk who gathered to watch their team do battle and it was customary at half time for the spectators to adjourn to "Sootie" Boyds in the Masons Row, for a dram to celebrate if the locals were winning or to dull their sorrow if they were being beaten. As time was short and the spectators had to hurry back for the second half "Sootie" would fill out about a hundred pints of beer and have them ready for the rush of customers and naturally the beer was flat before it could be drunk. One Saturday the spectators decided to teach him a lesson and when the half time whistle blew, they rushed from the park and raced past "Sootie's" up the Kildoup to "Bobby Gerrand's" for their half time refreshment, leaving poor "Sootie" with about a hundred pints of flat beer on his counter. This taught him a lesson and he never again drew the pints before the customers arrived.

The pitch at Ballony became disused about the time of the 1914-18 war and for some years there was no proper football ground in the town. Some amateur teams played in the Sheep Park where there was a bowl shaped pitch for the "big yins" and a small pitch at the "Bowsie Brig" for the smaller fry. Many were the fierce encounters against Girvan teams at the Sheep Park when "Jinty", "China", "Killarney" and other football deities showed the "Syboes" that Maybole was the Capital in football as well as other things. Once a team from Dailly came to play at Maybole and when the game was reported in the local paper there were only two surnames (Scobie and Mcginn) among the eleven Dailly players.

Between the two World Wars the old sports ground at Gardenrose was formed into a football pitch and the amateurs played there for many years. After the 1939-45 War a Junior team came into being and still exists. The old playing pitch at Ballony was more or less reformed entirely by voluntary labour in 1945, a clubhouse and covered stand built, and the "Tacketies" are back to where their grandfathers played against Glasgow Rangers.

In recent years football pitches have been formed in the Glebe field and young teams play there and do exceedingly well winning many trophies in competition with other boys' clubs. Before traffic became the problem it now is, the youngsters played football in Kirkland Street, and at the bottom of the Kirkwynd, etc. All that was needed then was a penny ball and jackets for goal posts and many Maybole men who later played for Clyde, Patrick Thistle, Southampton, and other clubs started their football by playing "heid the ba" against the wall of Ramsay's factory. Nowadays football, like "peevers" and "marbles" can find no place on the busy streets but fortunately the local parks still allow the youngsters to perfect their talents and probably football will continue as a favourite game for the townsfolk.

In the 1920s hockey became a popular sport in the town and there was a men's club which played at Whitefaulds and a ladies club whose pitch was at Gardenrose. The game was enthusiastically played for some years by both sexes and the clubs travelled all over Ayrshire and to Glasgow to play matches but enthusiasm dwindled and, after about ten years, the clubs became defunct and hockey is now only played by the school team at Carrick Academy.

At one time cricket was often played in the Sheep Park and Mr. Soutar of the Union Bank, who had been a well-known county cricketer in his day, coached many of the young lads in the art of bat and ball. A team was in existence for some years and matches were played against clubs in Prestwick, Troon, etc., but somehow the game never really caught on in the town and shortly after Mr. Soutar died the club disbanded.

In the last part of the 19th century and for the first decade of the present century the great interest for Maybole men was foot running and cycling. The milestones on the Cross Roads from West Enoch to Cargilstone were carefully set exactly one mile apart and this became known as "The Measured Mile" where all the local athletes trained. An up to date sports track with cambered bends was formed at Gardenrose Farm and many sports meetings were held there and famous runners and cyclists from all over Britain came to compete at them. After the great exodus from the town about 1909 the interest in athletics fell away through lack of young men (it was nearly all young men who emigrated, leaving a population of older men and young children) and the sports ground fell into disuse although the raised camber at one end of the track could, for years, be seen behind the farmhouse at Gardenrose.

One of the earliest, and most famous, of all Maybole pedestrians was Robert McKinstray who was born in Welltrees Street in April, 1837, and who became the greatest runner in Britain in his day, over all distances from 160 yards to 5 miles. His name is known to all townspeople, who speak of him whenever the topic of running is raised, but few today really know much about him and can only vaguely remember "he once beat a Red Indian" as if this was his crowning achievement. A well-known sporting newspaper printed a short article on McKinstray about the end of last century and the following extract from it shows that Maybole can indeed be proud of its fleetfooted son.

"Robert McKinstray was born at Maybole in April, 1837, and stands 5' 6½" in height. When only 15 years old Bob made his debut as a pedestrian at the Culzean sports, when he won half of the races. Soon after this he was apprenticed to a butcher and served his time faithfully. Bob, being indulged by his employer, annually visited the Scotch games and defeated nearly all comers on sprints, long distances and hurdle races; was "King of the Red Hose" at Carnwath for many years; won the 3 mile champion belt at West Calder on July 29, 1863; won the 2 mile championship and £50 at Stonefield Grounds, Glasgow, on October 3rd, 1863, beating J. Murdoch of Stonehouse who received 150 yards start; was defeated by Dan Shannon of Glasgow, on February 6th, 1864 in a 400 yards race for £50 at Stonefield Grounds; beat W. Park for the 2 mile championship and £50 at Stonefield, March 12th, 1864; beat Charlie Mower of Norwich for the 2 mile championship and £50 at Glasgow, June 11th, 1864; won the 5 mile championship at West Calder, July 27th, 1864; beat Dan Shannon April 22nd, 1865, 600 yards for £30; won the half mile sweepstake, £75, at Manchester, May 20th, 1865, beating W. Richards of London and J. Heyward of Rochdale, running the half mile in 1 minute 56½ seconds a performance which stamped McKinstray as the greatest "flier" of the day; beat W. Bell at Newcastle, 2 miles, £40, June 4th, 1865; beat E. Ashworth of Bury 160 yards, £20, July 14th, 1865; won the gold medal at Johnstone, July 15th, 1865 for 3 mile handicap race; defeated W. Richards in a 1 mile race, Richards receiving 15 yards start and staking £30 to Bob's £25 on July 29th, 1865; ran third from scratch on August 19th, 1865 in George

Martin's championship one mile handicap when the time taken was 4 minutes 17 seconds. McKinstray then took up his quarters in England and on February 23rd, 1867, gained the mile and a half challenge cup, value £80 but after winning it 3 times in succession had to yield the trophy to Fleet on May 23rd, 1868, owing entirely to his having been ill for some time and being far from well. During his career on the other side of the border, Sanderson of Whitworth, Lang of Middlesbro', Fleet of Manchester, E. Mills of London and many others of note had all to yield to the Scotchman. His last appearance before the public was at Edinburgh, December 31st, 1869, when he ran a match against an Iroquois Indian named Debeaux Daillebour, alias Redhead, especially brought over from America to race him, 3 miles level, for £30 a side, on which occasion our friend Bob made short work of the Redskin, leaving him so far behind that he gave up the race, leaving McKinstray to walk in at his leisure in a little over 15 minutes". When he retired from running he returned to his home town of Maybole and lived to a ripe old age, respected by all and honoured as the greatest British runner of his day."

Another famous Maybole runner was James Rodger who was Scottish mile champion in 1891 and 1894 and Scottish quarter mile champion in 1895 and 1896. In 1898 at Hampden Park, James Rodger made a new native record for the thousand yards which stood until 1957 when another Maybole man, Jack Boyd, (the present Town Clerk) broke it at Murrayfield Highland Games with a time of 2 minutes 10.9 seconds and it is interesting to note that the Scottish thousand yards record was held by Maybole men for over sixty years. Mr. Boyd was also the Scottish half mile champion in 1959 and although there are no pedestrian championships held by Minniebolers meantime it is hoped someone will again bring a record to the old town which was famous in sporting circles for over a century.

About eighty years ago the Carrick Harriers Club was a thriving body with a large membership, and John Milroy was a member who has also brought much fame to the town as did McKinstray, Rodger and Boyd. Between the two World Wars "Teddy" Maltman was a noted runner and many remember his duels with Andreoli from Ayr who was a well-known pedestrian throughout the country. It seems that the Maybole men were mainly distance runners, as apart from McKinstray (who seemed to be able to win at any distance), there are few records of sprinters in the town. Unfortunately with the dissolution of the Carrick Harriers early this century no other body has been formed, as yet, to replace it and interest in foot running has died out and the "Measured Mile" on the Cross Roads is left for cars to race along and to the few local people who still find pleasure in a walk instead of sitting in a lounge bar or gazing at the television. The trophies belonging to the club were in the town until the second World War when they were sold to raise money for the fund to send comforts to the troops.

Cycle racing also enjoyed great popularity in the town about the same time as the footrunners were bringing fame to Maybole and many townsmen raced the Measured Mile on a summer night with heads down and legs fiercely pedalling, much to the discomfiture of the courting couples who always considered the Cross Roads to be a place where they could stroll in peace without the necessity of keeping one eye on their partner and another on the road to watch for racing cyclists. The greatest of all the cyclists were the members of the Allan family and "Wumphy" Allan is still a name which Minniebolers speak of with pride although few of the younger generation know little of his prowess on a cycle. The Allan brothers were all noted racing cyclists but "Wumphy" was the doyen of the family and he held nearly all the Scottish and British records for distance and time races in his day. Like footracing, cycling lost favour in the town, for much the same reason (no young men to carry on the traditions of their fathers) and there are few, if any, cycle racing enthusiasts left now in the town which at one time provided champions in the sport.

Golf has been played for centuries in Maybole and it is recorded as being played on the town green in the 18th century. It was not until near the end of last century, however, that the first golf course was formed at Kilhenzie and the members of the Maybole Golf Club played there until the outbreak of the first World War when the course was ploughed up for the growing of crops to aid the war effort. After the war a nine hole course was formed in the Memorial Park and the old club was reformed and has flourished ever since. It has a strong enthusiastic membership who fervently hope that in the not too distant future the course can be extended and more holes brought into play. In 1902 the Maybole golfers formed the first Club at the new course at Turnberry and Provost John Marshall of "Jacks" was the first Captain of the Club which is now world famous.

Shooting has always been a favourite sport in the town since the start of the Volunteer movement when the locals were issued with rifles and actually encouraged to use them without fear of a poaching charge being laid against them. The Volunteers had some well-known marksmen in their company who won many medals and trophies in competition against other army units. The old Armoury in Whitehall was used as an indoor rifle range by the Maybole Small Bore Rifle Club (formed in the 1920s) up until recent years and William Murray was a local marksman who could compete with success against anyone on any range in Britain. In 1960 he won the Yates Memorial Competition with a possible score of 300, shooting 30 bulls in 14 minutes, and was the only man ever to win the British Veteran's Championships three times. In his last competition in 1969, he scored 398 out of a possible 400, a great performance for a man of seventy years of age. Some years ago the Club leased the old quarry at St. Murray for use as an open range and, although the local Club is now more or less disbanded, the range is still used by the Ayr Rifle Club and some of the old members of the Maybole Club shoot with that Club. For about sixty years there was a rifle range on How Moor which was in constant use by the Territorials and other army units but at the disbandment of the Territorials in 1968 the military authorities gave up their lease of this open range and it is no longer used.

Curling was always a favourite game of the townsmen and the farmers in the district and the Maybole Curling Society was formed on 26th January, 1829, with a membership of twenty eight, the first President being Mr. James Kennedy of Lochlands. The annual membership fee was 1/- and in 1842 the Club was in dire straits due to members not paying their subscriptions and a special meeting was held and the Club reconstituted but the membership fee remained the same.

The game was played on various lochs around the town for many years, the Heart Loch being the favourite site for bonspiels. In 1842 an artificial pond was formed at Drummurran Farm and was flooded from the Abbey Mill Burn when frost set in and the curlers could take to the ice. The Drummurran Pond proved so unsatisfactory, however, that the curlers again resorted to the Heart Loch and Mochrum Loch until about 1873 when another artificial pond was formed at Barlewan, near Kilhenzie. Once again it did not please the curlers and they returned to their favourite Heart Loch until 1896 when they rented a small piece of ground for £2 per annum on Cultizeoun Farm at the top of Gallow Hill. This was the final home of the curlers, as they purchased the ground for £60 in 1915 and carried out many improvements and made it a first class artificial pond where the townspeople enjoyed skating and curling in the hard winters. At "Gallowhill" Pond the roaring game was enjoyed by all when frost was keen enough to give bearing ice and many stories can be told of the worthies who never missed a bonspiel. On a winter afternoon a huge fire would be lit to heat the large stew-pot, drams would be passed around the rinks and the shouts of "Tunnoch", "High Grange", "Lochlands" and others urging their rinks to "Soop, man, soop" could be heard at Cultizeoun. Many townspeople would gather at the pond at night to skate and, if a late curling match was in progress (lit by byre lamps at each end) it was great sport for the young blades to cut across the rinks and be sworn at by the irate curlers. When the Ice Rink was built in Ayr outdoor curling gradually died out, as the local enthusiasts preferred to play on smoother indoor ice and the Curling Pond fell into disuse. It was sold for £70 in 1944 and the Club, although still nominally in existence, became for all practical purposes defunct, and was finally wound up in September, 1969. Many of the townsfolk and local farmers are still keen on the game, however, and display their skill with "out turn" or "in turn" in the indoor rink at Ayr.

Tennis has never been a favourite game with townspeople although in the 1920s there was a strong Club at the Memorial Park Tennis Courts which played other clubs throughout Carrick and Kyle and which had some fine players among its members. About the same period a private club flourished with its headquarters at Lumsden Home where there was a fine court, but the period of popularity of the game was short and both clubs became defunct about the 1930s. Although a few enthusiasts use the courts at the Memorial Park, the Lumsden court, and three other private courts in the town are now obsolete.

Quoiting was for generations a popular game among Maybole men and the quoiting ground was in Seaton Street where the clay pits were carefully tended and the ring of the quoits was heard nearly every summer evening. There were some good quoiters among the members who could always bring home prizes from matches against other clubs and it used to be as common a sight to see a man carrying a pair of brightly polished quoits as it is now to see a bowler with his pair of bowls in the little round carrying bag setting off to play in the Carrick Cup and other competitions. Quoiting, however, lost favour with the locals and as time went on fewer men took it up until finally about twenty years ago the quoiting ground became derelict and the game is no longer played in the town.

Whilst all types of sport have found favour in the town, one of the games peculiar to Maybole men was marbles. All the old shoemakers were experts at this game and hours were spent at "moshie" when the shoe factories were in full swing and there was full employment. At the dinner break the workers, young and old, would play marbles and loudly object to anyone "hunkering" or breaking the rules. They also played a peculiar game with large marbles (or "jarries") along the street sivors, rather reminiscent of the French game of "boule" in miniature. Once again the closing down of the shoe factories early this century was the deathknell of this game but as the streets seemed to be the favourite venue for it the surge of present day traffic would naturally have put a stop to it.

Whilst their elders were golfing, bowling, curling or playing football the youngsters in the town, like children everywhere, had their own seasonal pastimes. The "girths" were brought out at the proper season of the year, marbles and spinning tops made annual appearances and in the summer the children considered the pavements should be reserved for "peever" beds and not for walking on by their elders. Every lass could chant the appropriate rhymes as she "ca'ed" the skipping ropes and the boys tried to emulate Alan Morton and other football luminaries at "heid the ba'" against a convenient wall. Rounders was a favourite game among the younger children and few elder townsfolk have never played "kick the can" at the "Bumbee" or tip-staff with a piece of stick laid on the edge of the pavement and hit into the air and driven like a baseball with a longer stick. A boy was fortunate indeed if he fell heir to a set of pram wheels when his parents considered (or hoped) there was no further need to store the family perambulator. A board and a piece of rope was then all that was needed to make a bogey which would carry him like the wind from the top of Gallow Hill, past the Station, down the Back Road and Castle Brae, across the main road at McQuistons Corner and down St. Cuthberts Road and past Pat's Corner to the Gasworks. About fifty years ago one bright youth used to harness his spaniel dog to his bogey and the dog would pull it up to the top of the Gallow Hill. The youth would then mount the bogey, and, with kilts flying, race down the hill to the Gasworks Corner at a speed which nearly frightened to death all mothers who saw him and who immediately would confiscate their sons' "bogeys" lest their offspring would try to beat "Kiltie's" speed record.

Nowadays traffic has made it impossible for children to play such games in the streets but perhaps in this modern age the youngsters would not be content with four pram wheels mounted on a board and a rope to steer with but would want a custom built carriage modelled on a Bugatti or a Rolls Royce. In days gone by children worked hard at delivering rolls or milk, being message boys to grocers, or delivering newspapers, but when their work was over they all seemed to find time and energy to gather at the "Bowsie Brig" pitch for a game of football, at the Gasworks Corner to kick the can or to run round the roads with their "girths" (lucky indeed was the boy with an iron "cleek" instead of a stick to "ca" it) and children seemed to enjoy such simple pastimes. To the older folks of today the youngsters seem to spend most of their time in groups round cafe doors listening to pop music on transistor sets or sitting hunched up in an armchair staring at television but this is perhaps unfair as times have changed and children have not the freedom of the streets their elders had. It is true that years ago boys were up to all types of mischief and robbed the fruit trees in the gardens, or pulled the plums in the orchard at Laigh Culzean when they got the chance but somehow there did not seem to be the same amount of vandalism and destruction of property as there is now. Of course in those days the boys had a healthy respect for Inspector Miller and Sergeant Best who were not denied the privilege of cuffing a youngster's ears if they saw him doing wrong. All the schoolteachers lived in the town in days gone past and Miss Duncan, Miss Brannan, "Skin" and "Paddy", if they saw their pupils up to mischief in the evenings were not loth to "belt" them in school the following morning.

While most types of sport were played and enjoyed by the townsfolk without a doubt the favourite pastime was poaching. No town in Scotland could produce men so expert in the use of long net or the gaff as the old soutars of Maybole. The poachers were a race apart, great lovers of nature and wise in the ways of the rabbit, the hare, and the salmon, and the habits of the "patericks" and other birds was an open book to them. No cobbler's pot went empty in times of unemployment as the poachers not only lifted a hare from Tunnoch or Lochland fields for themselves but looked after their neighbours who were less skilful in the art or who were frightened to risk a foray with one of the local gamekeepers. In the 18th and 19th centuries poaching was the most prevalent crime dealt with by the magistrate in the old Tolbooth and at the beginning of the present century the number of poachers in the town was legion. Indeed Inspector Miller, when asked to send a list of the known poachers in the town to the Police Headquarters in Ayr, sent a voter's roll, declaring few, if any, of the names of the menfolk could be deleted. The old poachers, however, were sportsmen in their own way and while they would net a hare or tickle a salmon in a pool on the Doon or the Girvan for their own use, or to sell for the price of a dram, they never wantonly killed by blowing up or poisoning a pool in the river as did their successors of the period after the second World War. For some years the river poachers killed all fish, even minnows, by dynamiting a pool for the sake of a couple of salmon in it but the heavy fines now imposed on anyone found guilty of such a practice have fortunately curbed this deplorable method of poaching. The recent disease in rabbits has so reduced them in number that few now trouble to ferret for them with bag nets and as the taste for hares has gone there are few long nets now hidden in the rafters of the outhouses in the town. Game has become so scarce nowadays that the heyday of the old Maybole poachers has gone, and there will never be again such wonderful old characters as "Jumper" or "Snuffy" to supply an ill gotten hare, which one was well aware had been, not "poached", but merely "lifted" by a gentleman who considered all wild things should be available to all mankind and not kept solely for the use of a few. The old poachers played the game in a sporting manner and never complained or showed violence if caught and it was a common thing to see a worthy who had been fined for poaching in the court in the morning having a dram in the evening in a local inn with the gamekeeper who had caught him and real ill feeling between poacher and gamekeeper was practically unknown. The sport in real poaching was not to get a haul of fur or feather but the battle of wits between the poacher and the gamekeeper and both were good losers when things went against thm.

Pigeon racing has been a favourite sport among the local men for many years and a Racing Pigeon Club has been in existence since 1910 when H. Logan was the first secretary and N. Hinton, R. Scobie and J. Strachan were the leading lights of the society. The club was dormant for some years but in 1925 it was re-formed by keen enthusiasts such as D. Briggs, G. Briggs, A. McCann, J. Gill and others and at the present time it is flourishing with a large membership. Probably the fact that Queen Elizabeth has a loft at Sandringham and is keenly interested in racing pigeons has caused the revival throughout the country of the old sport which dates from the time when the Greeks used pigeons to carry messages warning the people of the approach of invaders. The sport of racing pigeons was really started in Belgium about 1820 shortly after the news of Wellington's victory at Waterloo was brought to England by carrier pigeon two days before Wellington's official despatch arrived. In 1871 some Belgium birds were brought to Britain and this started the interest in racing pigeons which resulted in the National Union being formed in 1896. As usual the Miniebolers, ever keen to take up a new sport, were not long in forming a club and there has been great interest in pigeon racing in the town for the past sixty years.

With so many lochs and streams around Maybole angling has naturally been a favourite sport for generations. There is a strong Angling Club whose members fish a stretch of the River Girvan and few youths have not fished the Smithston Burn with "bramble" worms when it was spate or cycled past Drumyork with hope in their hearts that Glenalla Burn would yield a good basket of sweet brown trout. Mochrum Loch swarms with pike which grow to a great size and take anything from tin spoons to fat bacon rind. It only needs two days rain in summer to bring the local anglers to the bus stop at the "Pump", with fly bedecked disreputable hats, waders turned down below their knees, rods of all sizes, and the all important haversacks to hold reels, fly cases, vacuum flasks and all the fisherman's paraphernalia, there to wait expectantly and ever hopefully for the bus to take them to the Brigend at Crosshill. No one has ever equalled an angler in depicting "HOPE" when awaiting the bus to take him to the river or "DESPAIR" when he returns a few hours later with an empty creel.

Boxing, Judo and wrestling clubs have been formed from time to time but these sports never really caught on, and the clubs would flourish for a time but soon fade away. Rugby has never been a local sport although of recent years it is played by the pupils at Carrick Academy but it has never even been proposed that a senior rugby team be formed. Many other types of sport have had their day in the old town but the old favourites of bowls, golf and football, have survived for generations and will probably still be played for generations to come while newer sports and games will come and go as in the past.

Chapter 18

FAMOUS FOLKS

THE town of Maybole, being the only community in the district for generations, naturally became the focal point for all the people of Carrick and many famous persons have been connected with the old town on the hillside.

Robert the Bruce must often have trod its street, as it is only seven miles distance from his castle at Turnberry. The fight for the independence of Scotland began by Bruce's attack on Turnberry Castle when he landed from Rathlin Island in the bay at Maidens. Local lore has it that when he landed and was told the signal fires had not been lit but that whins had caught fire on the cliff north of Maidens he remarked: "This is a weary neuk to land in" thus giving the present day name of "Wearyneuk" to the spot in the village. The bay he landed in is now shown on the maps as "Port Murray" but its former name was "Port Morrow" believed to be a corruption of "Port of Sorrow" while the headland on which the whins burned is now called "Barwhin Point" but was formerly known as "Burnwhin Point". There can be little doubt but Bruce during his journeys throughout Carrick must often have visited the tcwn. (Some would have Bruce's birthplace at Lochmaben instead of Turnberry but every Carrick man treats such a suggestion with scorn and puts it down to the natural jealousy of Gallovidians).

In early days when Maybole had the families of over twenty noblemen living in it, the Kennedy family, "The Kings of Carrick", looked on the old capital of their kingdom as their home town and many famous members of this family have gone from it to become prominent figures in Scotland's history.

Bishop James Kennedy, who founded St. Salvators College in St. Andrews, was the son of James Kennedy of Dunure and Princess Mary, and was one of the most prominent churchmen of his time. His daughter, Kate Kennedy, is still the central figure in the annual pageant at St. Andrews where she is always impersonated by a young male student. The Bishop was chief adviser to James II and guardian and tutor of James III. At his death it is said the whole Scottish nation went into mourning.

David, 3rd Lord Kennedy, who was created Earl of Cassillis in 1509, took his men from Maybole to fight at Flodden in 1513. He was killed, as was his sovereign, James IV, in that disastrous battle and his body was brought back for burial in the Old College in the Kirkport.

Gilbert, 3rd Earl of Cassillis, was a famous Scottish statesman and he was appointed Lord High Treasurer in 1554. He was one of the Commissioners who went to France to arrange the marriage of Mary, Queen of Scots, with the Dauphin, and, because he refused to agree that the Scottish crown should go to the French heir, he was poisoned at Dieppe and his body was also brought back for burial in the "Auld College".

Gilbert 4th Earl of Cassillis, was a confidant and adviser to Mary, Queen of Scots and was with her when she visited Carrick in August, 1563. Tradition has it that the Maybole people gathered at the Howmoor to see their tall Queen with her retinue pass on her way from Dunure Castle to Ardmillan where she stayed before journeying to Ardstinchar. Queen Mary gave Gilbert a necklace as a keepsake and this necklace is still in the possession of the present Marquess of Ailsa. It was his daughter Jane Kennedy who tied the handkerchief round Queen Mary's eyes before she knelt to be beheaded at Fotheringhay that Wednesday morning on the 8th February, 1587.

Archibald, 11th Earl of Cassillis distinguished himself as a naval commander and raised the seige of Lisbon in 1760 and the people of that city presented him with a handsomely engraved silver platter which is still in the possession of the present Marquess of Ailsa. After he retired from the sea, Archibald, lived in No. 1 Broadway, New York, but, on his refusal to take part in the Boston Tea Party, George Washington evicted him from his home and took possession of it for himself. The Earl married Anne Watts, daughter of John Watts of New York and part of her dowry is said to have been Long Island in New York State but the Earl lost all his American property during the War of Independence.

When Glenlyon's Regiment carried out the massacre at Glencoe in September, 1692, a young ensign in the regiment refused to take part in the slaughter and he was taken back to Fort William and ignominiously discharged. Tradition has it, truth or not, that the name of the young ensign was Archibald Kennedy of Maybole.

Another famous Kennedy was Quintin, Abbot of Crossraguel, and it was he who held the debate in Maybole in 1562 with John Knox. This event was so noteworthy in the history of the town that it is dealt with in another chapter of the book on Maybole.

John Loudon Macadam the famous roadmaker, although born in Ayr, in 1756, was educated at a school in Maybole and he was a frequent visitor to the district until his death in Moffat in 1836. From 1785 to 1798 he lived at Sauchrie a few miles out of the town and on leaving his Carrick home he spent the next sixteen years in studying the conditions of roads, travelling thirty thousand miles and spending £5,000 of his own money on road research. It is locally believed that he first carried out his experiments in 'Macadamising" on the stretch of roadway between where the Station Bridge is now sited in Culzean Road and Whitefaulds Farm and no one will disabuse a Minnieboler of this belief.

In 1749 Gilbert Blane was born at Blanefield at Kirkoswald and he also received his early schooling in Maybole. He became Sir Gilbert Blane and was made a fellow of the Royal Societies of London, Edinburgh and Gottingen, of the Imperial Academy of Sciences of St. Petersburg and of the Royal Academy of Sciences of Paris. He was physician to the fleet in the West Indies during the American War and it was during this period he found a preventative for scurvy which was a plague to all seamen at that time. It is said a ship was captured which had a load of limes as cargo and Sir Gilbert dosed the sailors on his ship with the juice of these fruits and found his seamen did not contract the disease. From then on all British seamen were given lime juice as a preventative for scurvy and this gave them the nickname of "Limejuicers", which is now shortened to "Limey", the name for Englishmen in nearly every foreign country. He was commended in a letter written by Lord Rodney for his "assiduity in preserving the lives of thousands of the fleet". He later became physician to both King George IV and King William IV, afterwards retiring to spend the remainder of his days at Blanefield where he carried on his research in medicine and found a vaccine for smallpox before he died in 1834.

Many Maybole ministers have played a prominent part in church history in Scotland and the Rev. James Bonar was one of the most famous. He was parish minister from 1608 and was elected Moderator of the General Assembly in 1644. He was a rich man and built an aisle to the Parish Church at his own expense and also gave a donation of 150 marks to the Glasgow College Library.

In the early part of the nineteenth century James Smith of Monkwood Grove at Minishant was one of Scotland's greatest botanists. He gave much valuable information on botanical subjects to Sir William Hooker which Sir William incorporated in his famous books on botany. James Smith died in 1848 and was buried in Ayr old churchyard where his friends erected a tombstone with the following inscription: "Erected by his friends and admirers in memory of James Smith, Botanist, Monkwood Grove, who died 1st January, 1848, aged 88 years. This simple monument to the Father of Scottish Botany will direct the many students who profited by his kind gratuitous instructions in the science of Botany, where the tear of fond remembrance may mingle with the dust of a real and true friend". He was the tenant of the gardens and orchard at Monkwood and was a simple and unworldly man but his knowledge of botany was unsurpassed by any in the whole of Scotland at that time and people came from many countries to listen and learn from him and many old gardens throughout Scotland today owe their beauty to the humble Minishant gardener who advised on what should be be planted in them.

During the second World War many local people played their part as they have always done in time of need, and one who has become a legendary figure was Lt. Col. Bernard Fergusson, D.S.O., O.B.E., of Kilkerran. He gained world fame for his daring exploits with the Chindits and later became Governor General of New Zealand, a position his father, Sir Charles Fergusson, had held many years previously.

When the Marquess of Ailsa gifted Culzean Castle to the National Trust for Scotland he made a stipulation that General Dwight Eisenhower, the Supreme Commander of the Allied Forces be gifted the top flat for his use as a Scottish home during his lifetime. On many occasions the General, who later became President of America, spent holidays at Culzean with his family and friends and enjoyed a rest when he could shoot and golf and be free from the cares of his busy life. He was a frequent visitor to the town which he always considered, as he said, "his Scottish hometown", and on Saturday, 5th October, 1946, the Freedom of the Burgh was conferred on him by the townspeople. This was the first instance of such an honour being granted to anyone and President Eisenhower, in his remarks after the ceremony, said he would "always consider himself a true Minnieboler, if not by birth, at least by adoption". This sentiment is echoed by all townsfolk who proudly claim fellow citizenship with the first King of Scotland and a President of America. The Freedom Scroll presented to the President was encased in a beautifully carved oak miniature chest designed and made by Mr. James Jeff, the Kirkcudbright artist who also carved the Town Staff which is carried before all Council processions by the Town Officer.

Maybole has also produced some fine artists and undoubtedly the most famous one was Robert McBride, who was born in the town in 1913 and schooled at Carrick Academy before studying at the Glasgow School of Art in the 1930s. He, with another Ayrshire artist, Robert Colquhoun of Kilmarnock, mostly lived and worked in England and Ireland and they were both featured in a B.B.C. production on "Living Artists" some years ago. McBride's paintings are exhibited in galleries throughout the world and some have a prominent place in the museum of Modern Art in New York and the Gallery of Modern Art in Edinburgh. After Robert Colquhoun died in the early 1960s, Robert McBride went to live with A. J. Cronin in Dublin where he was killed by a bus in 1967. Dylan Thomas, the famous Welsh poet, exchanged some of his manuscripts of his poetry for some pictures by McBride but unfortunately these valuable manuscripts have been lost.

There have been many other local people who have gained fame outwith the bounds of the burgh and surrounding district but these few notes on some of them prove that the quiet old "village on the hill" has been the hometown of men who have played an important part in much of Scotland's history.

Chapter 19

PERSONALITIES

ACCORDING to some dictionaries a "personality" is defined as "a person of distinctive character, outstanding among his fellow men". If this be so Maybole has always had "personalities" among its citizens, men who were outstanding for their ready wit, their distinctiveness in dress, their eccentricities and that indefinable "something" which sets a "personality" apart from the ordinary mortal who is born, lives, dies and is soon forgotten. In the old town most "personalities" are usually spoken of as "worthies" and what better word can be used for persons whose memories are worth handing down through the years. One of the greatest of the old worthies were John McLymont, known to all as "Johnnie Stuffie" who lived about two hundred years ago, and his droll sayings and queer manners have been retold from generation to generation until even today there are few townspeople who do not immediately visualise "The queer wee man wi' the simple air" when his name is mentioned. So many tales have been handed down about him that he deserves a chapter to himself in this story of Maybole.

The most prominent townsman in days gone past was Bailie Niven and when dealing with the town's history about a hundred and fifty years ago it is practically impossible to turn up any notes on matters relating to the town and district where the bold

Bailie's name does not appear. He was undoubtedly at that time "Lord God of Maybole and Master of all the Lime Kilns in sight" as his manservant once described him. He was a schoolfriend of Robert Burns, a banker and merchant in the town, "Leader" of the council for many years, Laird of Kirkbride, the only townsman to have a vote before the Reform Bill of 1832 and at his unmourned death left over £100,000. As his coffin was lifted on to the shoulders of the pall bearers one of the few spectators remarked: "Hoist him up, he'll never be nearer heaven." He was a great miser and on the occasions he was forced to have guests for a meal at Kirkbride or in the Bank House in Maybole he would often be heard to say: "Wha's for cheese, I'm for nane. Pit it bye Maggie." It is unfortunate that a man who was a genius in business and undoubtedly did a tremendous amount of good for the town by his far sighted, if ruthless, policies in Council should only be remembered for his meanness and his pompous manners, but his success in business made him many enemies and it is true that "the evil that men do lives after them, the good is oft interred with their bones."

The town crier and court officer about the time that Bailie Niven ruled from the bench in the old Tolbooth was William Gordon and he was a well-known character with a great sense of his own importance. One day he was going round with the "Deid Bell" when he passed his son riding a donkey. "Weel, Jock," he said as he passed. "I see ye're riding your brither." "Man, faither," replied Jock, "I didna ken he was yin o' yours tae." He had a full sense of the importance of his office and once when going about his business met Sir David Hunter Blair who, in the passing, asked where he was off to on such a fine day. "Sir David," was the dignified reply, "If I was to ask you where you were going you would say I was ill bred." He was sent to Ayr on town business one summer day, and, having walked to Ayr and back by the High Road, decided to slake his thirst in an alehouse which was then in Slateford village. Having no money he sold his boots to the publican, drank the proceeds, then starting home again was heard to remark to himself. "Step forrit, Gordon, if it's no' on ye, it's in ye."

Rab Bryce is still remembered in the town although it is over a hundred years ago since he lived in a house at the foot of Coral Glen and gave his name to the spot still known locally as "Bryce's Corner". He was a carter of enormous size and great strength and loved to take part in any quarrel which developed into fisticuffs, caring naught whose side he was on but purely for the fun of it. He always wore a broad Kilmarnock bonnet and a grey jacket and knee breeches and acted as a carrier for many of the local merchants. His horse was always poorly fed and its harness old and rotten but Rab continually boasted of its strength and prowess and once contracted to draw a caravan from Maybole to Girvan. He harnessed his nag to the caravan, stepped to its head and urged it on but as soon as the animal put strain on the harness it broke and Rab marched off gaily leading the horse and leaving the caravan behind. When the bystanders drew his attention to what had happened he remarked: "I tellt ye ma horse was strong. It only needs a tinkers powney tae pu' that contraption."

A well-known clockmaker (whose clocks are now much sought after) had a shop in High Street and was known to all as "Watchie Logan" early last century. He travelled the district repairing clocks in the farmhouses and was fond of a dram after he had done his work. On one occasion he was at West Enoch attending to a clock when the farmer was over generous with his bottle and "Watchie" left for home in a happy, but rather sleepy, condition. On reaching the "Beggars Rest" he sat down and fell asleep and some of the weavers who had been for a walk round the "Cross Roads" found him snoring away completely oblivious to everything. For a ploy they put him into a sack (he was a very small man) and carried him down to the back shop of a local butchers where they told the butcher they had poached a deer on Mochrum Hill and would let him have it for ten shillings. The butcher, anxious for a bargain, paid over the money and the weavers made themselves scare as quickly as possible, before the sack was opened. When the butcher untied the sack the cat (or rather "Watchie") was out of the bag and the fun started, as "Watchie" had sobered up and was indignant at his treatment while the butcher felt that someone should repay him his outlay for the poached "deer". They both set off in search of the weavers and finally ran them to earth in "Jimmie Edgar's" well-known howff in Weaver Vennal, where they were celebrating their windfall. The upshot of the matter was the appearance of "Watchie" and two of the weavers in court the following morning on a charge of insobriety. The ten shillings (a large amount in those days) had been spent while the question of its repayment was discussed and the innkeeper was the only one who benefitted by the trick played by the weavers on poor "Watchie". For years afterwards the local wags delighted to walk into the butcher's shop when customers were being served and loudly ask the owner if he would like to buy a deer.

About the beginning of the 19th century one of the kenspeckle figures in the town was Dr. Hathon or "The Marquess of Blarney" as he was commonly called by all. He was a skilful doctor but inclined, like many men of his time, to take a little too much to drink, until some of his friends finally persuaded him to be a little more temperate. He made a resolution never to drink before noon and managed to keep to this for some weeks until one day about 11 a.m. he met the farmer from Attiquin on the street at the door of the Kings Arms Hotel. The farmer was due him a fee for his attendance on a sick member of his family and took the chance to pay the doctor and to invite him into the Kings Arms for a dram. The bold doctor hestitated for only a moment and then looking up at the town clock declared, "Weel, it's hardly my time yet, but I'll mak' up for it the morn". Once he attended a woman in childbirth when he was rather unsteady and the husband remonstrated with him and told him he should not drink when he had patients to attend and the doctor excused himself with the retort: "I've had a dram, aye, but I'm no' fu'. My Goad, man, naebody could face a job like this cauld sober."

Another well-known practitioner was Dr. McCann, an itinerant Irish quack who settled in Maybole and boasted he could cure every ill but "the rale die". He was attending a woman in Kirkoswald one December day and the patient railed and moaned there was no cure for her. "Deed, I canna cure ye," said the Doctor, "but I think I can cobble ye up 'till March comes in." He would never admit that any patient died when being treated by him but protested that he had either been called in too late or the patient hadn't followed his instructions. After examining a patient his invariable remark was: "Ye're no' in a guid way but gie me sixpence and a bottle and I'll mak' up something tae pit ye on your feet." A young man consulted him and was told: "Ye're in a bad state but I can cure you. It'll cost you ninepence though." Dr. McCann travelled all over the district with his quack medicines and begged lifts from anyone going his way. On one occasion he returned to town on the front seat of a hearse which was returning from a funeral in Kirkoswald and on being twitted about this pointed out he was a suitable man for the front of a hearse, "For," as he said, "I'm gey watery eyed." He made up all his own medicines from dandelions, dockens, and other weeds and herbs and although it is doubtful that he was entitled to be called "Doctor" the local people had great faith in his cures and swore by his "sixpenny bottles" which he maintained could cure anything from cholera to consumption. In later life he was not able to gather his herbs to make his potions and consequently his practice fell away and he died in the "Poors House" about 1865.

Last century in Sinclair's Close there was a butcher's shop owned by a Thomas McCall, who was a noted character, and some of his sayings have become byewords in the town. He was in the shop one day when a lady brought him the news that an heir had been born to him. "Dae ye tell me, noo," he asked. "It is a man-child or a boy?" He had two daughters and he was wont to describe them as "the biggest is the wee-est" which translated merely meant the oldest was the smallest. He was in the habit of buying sheep in preference to cattle, which were much dearer, and when asked for a joint or a bit of pork he would lean over the counter and confidentially ask the customer: "Wud ye no' hae a bit mutton insteed, wummin? It's a gran' thing tae pit beef intae a man."

Old Attie Hughes, who was the town scavenger and who pronounced Bailie Niven's epitaph "with the consent of the whole parish", was extremely proud of his position as a "burgh man" working for the Council and considered no one could equal him with brush and shovel in clearing up the streets. As he grew older the Council engaged an assistant scavenger and Attie was grieved at the imputation he was no longer fit for his work and held his assistant in bitter contempt. "Ye see him" he would declare, "Weel he micht dae for plain work, but for ornamental work like sweeping roon a lamppost or afore Bailie Niven's door,—why it's simply no' in him." He was the bitter enemy of an old townsman named Kirkwood who used to be given cast off clothes and occasional alms by a man who lived in Whitehall. When Kirkwood died, Attie was sweeping the street in Whitehall when the gentleman passed and asked about Kirkwood, mentioning he hadn't seen him for some time, and he had some clothes to give him. "He's deid," replied Attie. "Dead!" said the gentleman. "Aye, deid," crowed Attie, "there's your great favourite for ye. Awa' an' never let ye ken".

"Burke" Morrow was a carrier in the town and with his horse and cart had a steady business hauling fish from Ballantrae to Ayr station where they were despatched by train to Glasgow. Many were the rumours that his loads often consisted of more than fish but no evidence could be found until one night "Burke" was late with his load from Ballantrae and decided to put his cart in the yard of "Pat O'Hara" until the following morning. Later that night a man, McLelland, who had been carousing in "Pats" (a public house at the foot of Kirkland Street) felt the journey to his home was rather much for him, and seeing Morrow's cart with a large sheet over it, crept under the sheet and slept soundly for an hour or two. On wakening he realised his bed was a cart of fish and thinking he would like a fresh herring or two for breakfast he climbed out and started to fill his pockets. As he put his hand under the sheet to search for a nice big fish he gripped the foot of a dead body which had been hidden under the mass of herring. This quickly sobered him up and he immediately made off to look for the town constable to whom he told his tale, but by the time they both got back to Pat's Corner, the bold "Burke" was on the High Road to Ayr. He was caught up with about the head of Lovers' Lane but on being searched no body could be found and it was decided McLelland had not fully recovered from his spree and had been "seeing things". Although the truth of this story could not be vouched for the townsfolk decided there was never smoke without fire and Morrow was ever after known as "Burke", as it was commonly believed he was a bodysnatcher, and there are many points which lead one to think there may have been some truth in the rumour. At this time it was common for the kin of those recently buried to watch at night over the fresh graves in case the corpse was stolen and sold to a doctor for dissection and a sentry box was erected in the old cemetery to shelter the watchers. The backyard of "Pat O'Hara's" inn was next to the old cemetery (the St. Cuthberts Road not being in existence at that time) and it would have been easy to slip a corpse over the wall and quickly store it under the fish in Morrow's cart. It was at this period the local sexton was fined by the Council for digging up new graves and selling the coffins although no reference was made as to the disposal of their contents. Rumour had it that the doctor who lived at Redbrae (now Lumsdon Home) was keenly interested in the dissection of bodies and before Morrow's cart was searched at the top of Lovers Lane it had already passed Redbrae house where a body could have been quickly dropped into one of the outhouses of the doctor's home. The townsfolk must have turned those facts over in their minds and felt prevention was better than cure and if one examines the graves in the old Kirkport cemetery it will be found that "thruch" stones and iron cages which fully covered the lairs were greatly the fashion at this period. At any rate Morrow ever afterwards rejoiced in the name of "Burke" and was considered an authority on all matters pertaining to the disposal of the dead. Mr. Galloway, who had an inn in Weaver Vennal, once erected a sign outside his hostelry which read "Funerals attended to. Shrouds lent". Few knew what a shroud was and Burke was asked to explain. "Shrouds," said he. "Why, these are the cloths the hearse drivers tie round their hats at funerals."

"Lunnan" Jimmy, a shoemaker in the Dangartland (Drummellan Street) received his nickname through the fact that in his youth he had travelled afar, and had even once been in London, a fact which gave him a subject for conversation for the rest of his life. He had gone by sea from Leith and as the ship was sailing down the east coast of England a strange ship approached, and the captain of Jimmy's ship came to the conclusion it was either a pirate or a French ship, and he made preparations for a possible attack by it on his own vessel. The passengers as well as the crew were given guns and swords but "Lunnan" Jimmy refused them as he swore he was against bloodshed, being what was more recently known as a "conchie". He was willing to help though and offered to "go down below and hand up the ammunition". The two ships passed on their way, however, without engagement and Jimmy came home to relate his experiences in the ship and in the city of London. In those days a visitor to such a distant place received as much adulation on his return as the men who now walk the surface of the moon.

"Sturdy" Bain lived in Whitehall and was a merry shoemaker who spent more time in the alehouse than on the cobbling bench. He was a great maker of rhymes and once made a bet with Sandy Tannock, the fiddler, that he could make a better verse about nothing than Sandy, who also prided himself on his turn of poetic speech. The couple adjourned with some friends to the Red Lion Inn and finally the judges agreed that "Sturdy" had won with the verse:

> "On naething I'm compelled tae write,
> I see't as plain's winnock,
> The merest naething ere I saw,
> Was Fiddler Sandy Tannock."

The farmer in Laigh Grange, like all good Carrick men, held family worship every morning and evening, to which all the farm workers and any visitors to the farm were invited. Laigh Grange seldom, if ever, changed his form of prayer and many who attended the services could have taken the old man's place at the big "ha' Bible". His opening lines of the evening prayer were invariably: "Guid Lord, as the muckle black craw flees high but dirties laigh doon on the stanes by the sea shore, whilk the tides wash away every twenty four hours, so do Thee wash away our sins by Thy grace. Watch ower oor Belle that's awa' in service, Guid Lord, and keep her frae harm, but as for Jenny, that's at hame here, dinna bother aboot her as I'll mind her mysel." There was no vagueness in his requests as he asked for protection for his lass who was away from home nor hestitation in his own responsibility to look after the daughter still under his care and he was supremely confident he could "mind her himsel."

At the curling matches on the Heart Loch in the long hard winters of last century many of the town and district worthies gathered to enjoy the game, the rich stew which always simmered in the pot at the side of the loch and of course the dram which is as necessary to a curler as the whin brooms which were used at one time to "soop" the stones over the "hog". Many stories are told of "Lochlands", "High Grange", "Attiquin", and many others who enjoyed the roaring game and the companionship of their fellows when heavy frost made it impossible to work the land or carry out other outdoor work. On one occasion the "Eglinton" match was being played at Maybole when the Earl of Eglinton took part and skipped his rink against a Maybole rink which included the worthy but hard swearing farmer from High Grange. Before the match this enthusiast was warned by the club secretary to tone down his language, as not only was the Earl playing against his rink, but the local minister was also playing with him, and this he managed fairly well for a few ends. The Earl was playing extremely well that day and High Grange grew more and more excited until, on the Earl delivering a fine shot which took out a stone played by the Minister, he could contain himself no longer and he threw his broom in the air and yelled at the top of his voice: "Weel dune, by Goad, my Lord, ye're awa' tae Hell wi' the minister". On another occasion a game was in session when the Marquess of Ailsa was skipping a rink and one of his players imbibed rather freely so his Lordship decided to hide the whisky bottle. The worthy curler on searching for it between ends was told the whisky was finished whereupon he indignantly threw down his broom and declared, "My Lord, whisky and curling gang thegether. If there's nae whisky there's nae curling" and marched off the ice.

Hughie Nocher, an Irish gangrel settled in the town and lived for years by selling crockery from a barrow from door to door, at the same time collecting rabbit skins and he always described himself as a "fur and china merchant". Falling on hard times, when he once took ill, he was forced to spend some time in the Poorhouse, but on his recovery he left it and again started up in business. On being asked how he fared during his sojourn in the Poorhouse he bitterly complained that he was fed on porridge and ale and someone protested that surely he got bread and tea also. "Tay," he retorted. "Did ye say tay? Why you may as well look for holy water in an Orange Lodge." Hughie was a strict Catholic and the deadly enemy of the leader of the Orangemen, one James Kirkwood, who was nicknamed "King William" until a large scab grew on his nose when he was rechristened

"Lord Limpet". This worthy always took a prominent part in Orange parades and at one such parade Hughie turned to a bystander and spluttered. "Look at him. There he gangs wi' the Bible in his loof and he canna even read it—an' if he could he wadna'."

About the middle of last century one of the townspeople who was a joiner by trade also carried out the duties of undertaker and sexton, and it would seem the latter employments paid him best, as in his own words, he had "nae materials tae buy". He seldom attended church but invariably sat on "Jack's" dyke waiting on the kirk to skale when he would eagerly ask "Onybody prayed for the day?" If the answer was in the affirmative he would anxiously enquire: "Nigh unto daith?" and if the answer was to his pleasing, he would produce his snuff box and reward his informer with a pinch. He always presented his bill the day after the funeral as he maintained it was easier to get payment from the bereaved "when the tears were in their een." If trade was slack he would often lament: "I dinna ken what things are coming tae. I hav'na turned a sod for weeks." On one occasion he was speaking to an acquaintance about a person who was so ill his life was despaired when he said: "Ah weel, it matters naething tae me. Hir burial grun' is in Kirkmichael." His interest in the funeral side of his business became so much of an obsession with him that on one occasion when his son met with a bad accident and was thought to be dying he was heard to mutter: "Dear me, dear me! Oor Adam deeing—an' I'll get naething for burying him." Fortunately the son recovered and joined his father's business so in all probability the position would be reversed and Adam would "get naething" for burying his father.

The farmer in Daltammie (now Dalchomie) once advertised grazing to let for cattle on the "Naps of Daltammie" and an applicant called at the farm to look over the land before making an offer for the season's grazing. The grazier was not impressed by the area to be let and remarked there was little grazing for cattle on it, to get the reply: "There's maybe no' muckle grass for the beasts but, man, they'll ha'e plenty o' water an' a gran' view." The farmers in the district were all of ready wit and had a pawky humour which can only be really appreciated when the stories about them are told in the local vernacular. There are many tales of the kenspeckle figures of High Grange, Attiquin, Trees, etc., who were all well-known personalities in the town and district and the farmers were always called by the name of their farm and seldom, if ever, were addressed by their proper surnames. One well-known farmer was a great attender of local funerals and always wore an old fashioned high tile hat with "weepers" tied round it. One day a local lawyer twitted him on his old fashioned headgear and asked where he had got it. "Man, Fiscal," was the reply, "It was a' that was left o' ma faither's estate yince ye had dealt wi' it."

When the town had two companies of Volunteers one was commanded by a Captain Shaw and the other by a Major Logan, both retired regular army officers and both a little jealous of each other. Once the Major dined with Captain Shaw and his family and on being asked by an acquaintance what he had for dinner he replied: "There were new shore potatoes but I couldn't get at them for the *Shaws*." The bold Major quarrelled with a local dignitary over a verbal bargain they had made and which the dignitary did not keep, excusing his withdrawal from the bargain by pointing out it was not binding because it had not been written on stamped paper. A short time afterwards both parties were in a company in the Kings Arms Hotel when the defaulter happened to mention he was troubled with dysentery and did not know what to take for it. "Take stamped paper, my man," instantly observed the Major. "You know yourself there's nothing more binding." The company commanded by the Major had the reputation of having the best marksmen in the regiment and on being asked why this should be he pointed out that all the men were noted poachers. Major Logan was a keen musician and a fine violinist but was very aggrieved when an acquaintance one day asked if the letter W.L.F. (West Lowland Fencibles) on his uniform stood for William Logan Fiddler.

Funerals last century seemed to be rather convivial gatherings where the whisky flowed more freely than the tears but near the end of the century they became more sober occasions as is evidenced by a conversation the Rev. Mr. Moir had with a mourner one day. By way of conversation he remarked to the mourner that the old heavy drinking customs at funerals seemed to be dying out. "Deed aye," was the answer, "a funeral's no' worth going tae nooadays." Once the Rev. R. Lawson approached a parishioner and asked a small favour, supporting his plea by mentioning he had officiated at three weddings in his family. "Three weddings," replied the parishioner, "that's nothing. Ye've been at three funerals tae." A story is told of a woman going into a shop in the town and ordering two pounds of "biled ham and two bottles of whisky." The shopkeeper's immediate reaction was to ask: "Wha's deid?" as invariably the mourners were regaled with a dram and a plate of cold ham at the tea always held after the funeral. Many townsmen made a habit of attending all funerals in the surrounding villages, as they knew they would get a refreshment and something to eat afterwards to refresh them before they started homewards, and Crosshill funerals especially were a favourite with the local worthies. A local minister noted this favouritism towards Crosshill interments and on asking why from one of the regular "mourners" received the reply: "Man a Crosshill funeral's better than a Kirkmichael wadding."

It was not only last century, however, that personalities were commonplace in the town and many have cropped up since the start of the 20th century and are remembered by the townsfolk who will probably pass on tales of them to be recounted in the years to come whenever Maybole people gather together to crack about their hometown. Many remember "Ruggy Duggy" who was a great walker and who once bet he could walk from

"Stumpy" in Girvan to Maybole Town Hall in two hours. He left "Stumpy" one day at two o'clock and on reaching the Town Hall the clock in the belfry showed the time as 4.35p.m. "Ruggy" looked up at it and swore: "It's a damned lee. Templeton's pit it forrit on purpose," thus maligning the poor clock-keeper whom he swore was in "cahoots agin him". The youths of the town were the bane of poor "Ruggy's" existence, and tormented him unmercifully, but their elders always looked well after him and saw he did not want until his death in the 1920s.

"Wullie" McJanet was an able and skilful joiner whose great distinction seemed to be that he was the most unkempt and unwashed man in the town. He shuffled around in summer and winter, wearing a long coat fastened at the neck with a safety pin, and his boots never knew laces. He was always in demand, however, when a skilful piece of joinerywork was required and he was always most temperate, never known to use bad language and his manners were always impeccable. He was a bit of a recluse. But when he could be presuaded to enter into conversation his listeners were invariably surprised that such a disreputable looking man could converse with such fluency and knowledge on practically any subject. Few townspeople were aware of the tragedy in his life which made him lose heart and become what he was in later life. He was born in the district and had been well educated, and became engaged to be married to a girl in Edinburgh. His fiancee took ill a week before the wedding and died and was buried in her bridal gown on the day and at the hour the marriage was to take place. "Wullie" was so heartbroken he gave up everything, took to drink and tramped the country for a time. Finally he pulled himself together, gave up drinking, learned the trade of joinery and came to settle in Maybole where he lived until he died. He was buried in a pauper's grave and when his effects were gone over by the Rev. D. Swan it was found he had a beautifully made cedarwood chest in which were stored his wedding clothes together with white flannels, blazers, etc., that he had worn when he played cricket in his happier days. His was certainly a case where people are inclined to judge harshly when facts are not truly known.

One of the outstanding personalities in the first half of the present century was undoubtedly the genial host of the Kings Arms Hotel, the redoubtable John G. McCubbin, known to all as "the Provost" and to his intimates as "John G.". He became owner of the Kings Arms Hotel after the death of his father, Thomas McCubbin, who had taken over the hotel in 1881. It was then a small country inn but Mr. McCubbin added an upper storey, built a hall and stables and opened up an entrance to the "Back Road" to give easy access to the railway station. On a sunny summer afternoon "John G." was a kenspeckle figure leaning against the highly polished brass rail which used to protect the window at the side of the hotel entrance, with his thumbs in the armholes of his yellow waistcoat, his hat tilted down to shade his eyes and a large cigar tilted at a Churchillian angle and placed dead centre between his lips. He knew everyone, as everyone knew him, and his usual reply when anyone halted to enquire how he was keeping was: "I'm no' complaining." His great hobbies were breeding collie dogs and horses and he was often successful in showing both all over the country. In his later years he devoted his energies to training racehorses and his greatest success was when his horse "Craigenelder" won the Adamhill cup at Bogside. He was fond of foxhunting and had many good hunters which he often raced at point-to-points and in steeplechases at Bogside, Carlisle, Perth, Kelso, etc. He had a ready wit and often scored in an argument with his pawky repartee and delighted in telling stories, many against himself. One of his favourites was about the time he bought a horse from one of the local farmers after a long tussle as to its price. After the bargain was sealed by the usual handshake the farmer remarked the horse had two faults which he thought the purchaser should know. "Two faults," quoth

John G. "I'll soon cure them, what are they?" "Well," said the seller, "It's difficult to catch when it's running loose in a field." "I'll keep a head stall on it," was the reply. "That'll make it easier to catch. What's its other fault?" The farmer looked at him and said: "It's no' worth a damn yince it's caught," and John G. ruefully concluded his story by admitting the farmer was right about both points. One day a local remarked on how well he was looking and enquired as to his age when John G. proudly owned up to being over seventy. "Man, but ye're fresh for your age," said the enquirer, adding "but of course ye should be. Ye've never done any work in your life." John looked along his cigar at his inquisitor and replied: "Weel you've naething tae greet aboot. I never kept you oot o' a job." He took a prominent part in the affairs of the town and district and was Provost from 1927 to 1936, during which period he was undoubtedly the "Leader" of the council as Bailie Niven had been a hundred years previously. He was always genial and unruffled, but firm in his convictions and cared not a jot for any man. His ready wit was ever appreciated by even his antagonists (and what Provost ever lived who did not have detractors) and "John G." will always be remembered with affection by Minniebolers.

The medical men of Maybole have produced many characters who are affectionately remembered by the townsfolk. Dr. Hugh Girvan will always be remembered for his pawky and dry humour as will his father who was known as "The Old Doctor" to distinguish him from "Young Doctor Hugh". He was a well known figure on his two barred bicycle, with his little black bag strapped on the carrier, as he travelled around the district on his old machine. For a time he had a motor cycle with a basket woven sidecar but he returned to his push cycle in his latter years. At one time he was troubled by boys pulling his house bell at nights and he spoke to his friend, Inspector Miller, about it who promised he would see it was put a stop to. About a week later the Inspector met him and enquired if he was still troubled by the bell being rung by the boys and Dr. Hugh told him he had not been bothered for a few nights. The Inspector promptly claimed honour for his constables in putting a stop to the nuisance so quickly but was rather taken aback when the Doctor quietly remarked: "You see, the night after I spoke to you about it, the boys pulled the whole bell out by the roots and it won't ring at all now!"

His father, "old Dr. Robert" once became greatly interested in mesmerism and, on being twitted by a brother physician on the subject, wagered a gill of whisky he could mesmerise the doubter. They both adjourned to the Kings Arms, a gill was put on the table and Dr. Robert proceeded to make passes which soon seemed to put his subject to sleep. The Doctor was delighted with his success and went out to get some fellow townsmen to witness the sleeping man, but as soon as he left the room the "victim" sat up and quaffed the gill of whisky. This so incensed the mesmerist that never again did he practise the art.

Dr. McTyer and Dr. MacFarlane were fellow practitioners in the town and one day "Dr. Robert" swallowed some poison by mistake and Dr. MacFarlane was immediately sent for, but on arrival he was so upset he could do nothing and Dr. McTyer was speedily summoned. As Dr. McTyer entered the bedroom where the poisoned patient was lying he found Dr. MacFarlane sitting on a chair at the bedside being soothed by Dr. Girvan who looked up and said: "McTyer, whether do you think it's MacFarlane or me has been pushoned."

Dr. Cowan and Dr. Valentine who both lived in the New Yards, were also typical old fashioned and worthy country doctors, beloved by their patients and "skeely" at curing all common ills, although Dr. Cowan, who was a brilliant man of medicine, unfortunately died at an early age just before the first World War. Dr. Inglis and Dr. Sandilands are still remembered by many of the older generation who placed great faith in them and many are the tales told of them, especially about the "wee Doctor" who was a notable figure in his long scarf and raincoat driving around the countryside in his T Ford, with invariably a Borzoi or a spaniel dog sticking its nose out of the back seat. He was a keen shot and loved a day with the ferrets and a gun at the rabbits. One day he went shooting with some friends at Burncrooks when one of his companions shot at a rabbit which bolted down a hole. Thinking he had wounded it the sportsman knelt down and put his hand into the burrow to try and pull it out. The Doctor, unaware of what had happened, and being a little shortsighted, saw something moving amongst the whins where the burrows were and let fly, with the result that his companion was pelleted in the part which was most prominent as he was bending down. The rest of the party were then treated to the spectacle of the doctor sitting on a stone puffing at a cigar, with the wounded and indignant rabbiter over his knees, picking out the shot with an old penknife and treating the scars with liberal doses from his whisky flask, between times steadying his own nerves with sips from the same flask. When the job was done the Doctor stood up and remarked to his aggrieved companion: "There noo Willie you'll maybe no' sit easy for a time, but you're aye fleeing about anyway so it'll make nae difference." On one occasion in the Town Council, of which he was a prominent member for many years, he crossed swords with a young councillor who grew more choleric as the argument raged until finally the Doctor ended matters by declaring: "Sit down, man. I brought you into the world and if you don't calm down I'm likely to see you out of it."

The practitioners of old knew every patient practically from birth, and were relied upon to cure everything from wee Jeannie's cough to Grandpa's hoast. They were advisers, arbiters, father confessors, and confidants to all, travelling long distances in their dogcarts or boneshaker cars and bicycles and very often were paid in kind with a dozen eggs or a fowl or a pair of rabbits, and indeed very often not paid at all, but they were a dedicated body of men and respected throughout the community. Their successors are every bit as dedicated and respected today but somehow in these modern times the demands of the National Health Services seem to place a greater burden on them and some patients feel they are reduced to cyphers on cards stored in surgeries instead of personal friends of their doctors to whom they can unburden their woes. This is rather unfair to the modern medical men who wish they could spend more time with their patients but they are besieged every night, when surgery opens, with many who in the old days would keep a cold until it was better but now feel that free health services entitle them to full medical services for every minor ailment. No doubt many a present day doctor sighs for the old days when life was at a slower pace and "the doctor" had time to have a crack with his patient, soothe the relatives and lift his half crown fee from the corner of the mantleshelf as he went out.

At the latter end of last century and the beginning of this century one of the great and powerful personalities in the town was the Rev. Roderick Lawson, minister of the "Glen Kirk" for many years. He took a great interest in local affairs, wrote many articles and poems on the town and district and was the power behind the throne in local politics. He persuaded the council to change many of the old street names unfortunately and it was he who was responsible for the loss of century old names like Dangartland, Smithy Brae, New Yards and Kildoup which became humdrum and commonplace streets now known as Drummellan Street, St. Cuthbert's Street, Cassillis Road and Welltrees Street. He was really the last of the old style parochial ministers and ruled his flock with a rod of iron and if any were absent from kirk on Sunday morning they had to have a very good excuse ready for him when he called on Monday to inquire as to the cause of their absence. When he started his ministry in the town many of the older generation had been married by the Scots style of proclaiming they were husband and wife and had settled down to rear their families fully confident of their marital status. This practice was not acceptable to the Rev. Roderick Lawson and he persuaded most of the old couples to be married again with the blessings of the church, and often boasted afterwards that he had "married half of Maybole". One old lady in Weaver Vennal rather flummoxed him, however, when he pointed out to her that although she was legally married in Scots style she was not married "in the eyes of God", and that he would be glad to marry her and her husband again. "Get married again," she said. "Na, na, I'd rather gat rid o' him. Onyway I'd look a fule getting married at ma' time o' life an' me wi' seven o' my ain and nine grandweans." This was one of the few occasions he did not get what he had set his heart on and had to admit defeat.

Another well-known minister was the Rev. David Swan who came to the town as assistant to the Rev. Mr. Porteus and stayed as minister in the Auld Kirk until his death some years ago. He was a great walker and visited all his country parishioners on foot and was often met on country roads tramping along with his flat crowned hat, his ministerial coat, strong leather leggings above his heavy leather boots and a heavy stick in his hand. He always enjoyed telling of the time he first preached a sermon in church and afterwards, keen to know how he had fared, asked the beadle how he had enjoyed it. "Weel," replied that worthy, "There was no' much pith in it, but man, ye had a fine genteel way o' setting it aff." He was noted for his liking for good food and his ability to "clean his plate" and once he was visiting a farm where he sat down to tea when a large "clootie" dumpling was set on the table. One of the children sitting opposite complained: "Mither, I canna see the minister ower the dumpling." "Gie him time," replied the farmer's wife, "He'll shune empty the plate an' ye'll see him then."

Many other townsfolk have been outstanding in their wit, their style of dress or their individual habits which set them apart from ordinary folks but they are too numerous to mention, as Maybole seems to have been a town which produced kenspeckle figures in every generation. They will live long in the memories of those who knew them, however, and in years to come will become household names as Johnnie Stuffie is still remembered. Few who saw "The Gentle Shepherd" bowling along the New Yards in his high wheeled gig behind the "humpy backit" pony will ever forget him. "Wee Davie" McCulloch will be spoken of by those who never saw him but have heard the numerous stories about him told by the older folks. "Smiley", who used to take off his jacket as he came out of "T.I's" every Saturday night and challenged everyone to fight and Hughie Watson who tramped the country, enlisted in seven regiments, deserted from six of them and was drummed out of the seventh one, will live on in local lore. One well remembered townsman attended all public meetings and usually had much to say on nearly every topic under discussion. He once attended the annual meeting of a local society and in a heated exchange with the chairman accused the society's committee of "fugeling the books". The society took umbrage at this as they thought they knew what their accuser meant and they approached a local lawyer on the matter and asked that he be charged with slander. The lawyer (being a local man) also thought he knew what was meant by the accusation and agreed to take proceedings but when he got down to drafting the charge he discovered no dictionary gave the meaning of the word "fugeling" and the matter was dropped much to the merriment of all Minniebolers who have their own interpretation of the word which is unknown, it seems, to compilers of dictionaries.

"Tam" Tennant, in his half tile hat, and "Wee Tam" from the "Grain Store", Inspector Miller, the stalwart-and beloved Inspector of Police, and "Kill the Pig" one of his predecessors were all men of great personality. They gave a sparkle to life in the town in the days before Burton's or John Collier forced on menfolk a standardised style of dress which makes all men equal from a sartorial point of view but somehow seems to kill any personality they may have hidden under their narrow lapelled jackets. In bygone days a yellow waistcoat, a half tile, a cut away coat, or a velvet or astrakhan collar to a top coat seemed to give the wearers that little touch of individuality which is so sadly missing among the men of today.

One of the peculiarities of Minniebolers is the giving of nicknames to fellow townsmen and invariably anyone who is outstanding in anything, from sport to poaching, is rechristened, but never in a manner which is hurtful or derogatory and many townsmen answer to their nickname as readily as to their Christian name. Thus instead of the ordinary Toms, Dicks and Harrys many rejoice in such names as Jumper, Snuffie, Killarney, Jinty, China, Lord Limpet, The Crigger, Wumphy, The Doodler, Shirty, Sooty, The Sheik, Teerie, Soda, Haddy, The Daisy, La-di-dah and other fanciful appellations. No person who is disliked or unworthy of notice is ever given a nickname and the "personalities" who are thought worthy of being thus singled out should indeed consider themselves above the ordinary run of men. A "Jimmy" or "Johnny" usually requires the addition of a surname to identify the person spoken of, but there is never any doubt who is referred to when "Beau" or "Boss" are mentioned.

Chapter 20

"JOHNNIE STUFFIE"

"A queer wee man, wi' simple air"

THE opening line of the poem by the Rev. Roderick Lawson gives an apt description of "Johnnie Stuffie" one of the best known "characters" in the long history of Maybole which, throughout the centuries, has produced many noteworthy and loveable personalities.

John McLymont was born in Maybole in 1763 and lived for most of his 84 years in the town. He was a very small man with a large head and, unfortunately, was of simple intellect or "had a want" as the local expression has it for those who do not altogether measure up to modern I.Q. standards. Like all simple people he had a knack of being embarrassingly honest in his outlook, often much to the discomfort of his more able fellow townsmen who tried to make fun of him, but who, more often than not, found the tables turned against them.

He was eccentric in his dress, invariably wearing a high crowned top hat and a tail coat which was far too large for him and the tails of which usually trailed on the ground. He had a great love for clothes and local people gave him their cast-offs, which he hoarded carefully and in time he accumulated dozens of coats and hats of every style and size. As he was a great snuff addict his clothes were badly stained with it and he always carried a large coloured handkerchief with which he would loudly blow his nose and wave about like a banner when in a heated argument with his tormentors

He never learned a trade and throughout his whole life he ran errands and carried water from the various wells in the town for the housewives who paid him an odd copper for this service. He never used the ordinary shoulder yoke to carry his two wooden pails but devised a sort of oval wooden hoop which he laced through the handles of his "luggies" and which encircled him like the bumpers of the small electric cars seen in present day fairgrounds.

From his youth he was known as "Johnnie Stuffie" because he was a great glutton and was always "stuffing" himself. He became so used to his nickname that he invariably answered to it and on many occasions did not realise he was being spoken to if addressed as Johnnie McLymont. After the death of his mother he lived by himself and would let no one into his house to tidy it up or interfere with his hoard of coats and hats. He used to say "Women are a' richt in their place but my place is no' for them." For years he lived in a house in Whitehall which stood on the site where the Carrick Hotel now stands, latterly moving to a small house behind what is now known as Greenhead and finally to a house in Buchanan Street, or Inches Close as it was commonly named. About 1846 he was no longer able to stay by himself and a kindly relative took him to his home in Crosshill and looked after him until he died the following year. On his death a kindly Minnieboler met the cost of his funeral and he was buried in the old cemetery at the foot of the Kirkwynd where his gravestone still stands near the entrance gate with the inscription: "Here rests until the Resurrection, John McLymont, the Maybole Natural, who died 18th May, 1847. Take heed that ye despise not one of these little ones."

Many tales of Johnnie have been handed down over the years since he was a kenspeckle figure on the High Street with his lum hat and luggies. He was always the butt of the younger people, as his queer style of dress and odd physical appearance, together with the fact that he was simple minded, gave great scope for the youngsters to play tricks on him. Even their elders sometimes tried to belittle him but in their case Johnnie invariably came out best with his honest and simple approach to all problems.

One day he stopped the Rev. Dr. Paul, the Parish Minister, and put to him a problem which had been bothering Johnnie for some time. He wanted the Minister to tell him whether or not certain situations called for a lie to be told and on being answered that lies should never be told he asked: "Whether is it better to tell a lee and keep the peace or tell the truth and kick up a Hell o' a row." Such a problem has puzzled many wiser men than Johnnie and no doubt the simple wee man would go blythely and happily through life telling a lie or the truth according as to what he thought was the better thing to do.

He was always a willing and eager messenger and water carrier but would hardly have fitted into modern life where so much is governed by the clock. He was asked one Saturday night to bring a pail of water to a certain householder and replied: "Man, I'm unco' busy the nicht, but if you pit it ower tae Monday I'll make sure ye get it then." Sunday being a day of rest Johnnie never ran errands or carried water but religiously attended church where he sat on the top step of the pulpit stair next the Minister from where he could watch the congregation and loudly report to the preacher if any of the flock appeared to nod off to sleep during the lengthy, and often dreary, sermons. One of the elders in the church was reproached one day by Johnnie for never visiting him and the elder excused himself by pointing out he was not in his "district" for visitations. The excuse was not acceptable to poor Johnnie, however, who wanted to know if there were "special districts in Heaven."

He was a great glutton and ate enormous quantities of food when any kindly person offered him a meal after he had run an errand or carried water for them. If he was given a bowl of soup and a scone he always contrived that one outlasted the other and would need another scone to finish the soup or a drop more soup to go with the bit of scone that was left. Once he rather overplayed his hand when he was attending communion in a local church and had been asked to have a meal in the minister's kitchen after the service. During the meal he had managed to hide some extra food in what he thought was his top hat so that he could take it home with him. Unfortunately when the meal was over and everyone ready to make home it was discovered Johnnie had filled the beadle's hat instead of his own and the outcome was that poor Johnnie was forbidden ever to enter the manse again.

He was well aware of his shortcomings and once when a young girl jeered at him and asked if he knew he was a fool he replied: "Aye, but I'm a fool of God's making and your one of your aim making." On the whole he was kindly treated by the townsfolk who believed in looking after their own "naturals" rather than shutting them up in institutions and someone would always see that he never wanted for food or clothing. He was a bit of a miser and saved every odd penny he could put aside, banking it with Mr. Niven in the Royal Bank of Scotland. On being asked one day how much money he had he replied: "Naebody kens but God Almighty and Mr. Niven."

The Rev. R. Lawson wrote the following poem about him which immortalises one of the town's best loved worthies and it gives a word picture which will never be bettered.

JOHNNIE STUFFIE

A queer wee man, wi' simple air,
    Was Johnnie Stuffie,
Well kenn'd alike by rich and puir
    Was Johnnie Stuffie,
The water-carrier o' the toon,
The Messenger to a' aroun',
And the butt o' every idle loon
    Was Johnnie Stuffie.

Nae common bonnet croon'd the heid
    O' Johnnie Stuffie,
But auld lum-hat was there instead
    On Johnnie Stuffie;
A lang great-coat, ance thocht genteel,
Ay wrapped him roun' frae neck to heel,
Which only did the feet reveal
    O' Johnnie Stuffie.

On Sabbath days, first in the kirk
    Was Johnnie Stuffie,
Wi' well brushed hat and well washed sark
    Cam' Johnnie Stuffie;
But no amang the rest sat he,
But on the pulpit steps sae hie,
The congregation a' could see
    Bauld Johnnie Stuffie.

But a' folks dee, and 'mang the lave
    Maun Johnnie Stuffie,
He rests noo in his quiet grave,
    Wee Johnnie Stuffie;
Nae mair he'll stand the idle jeer,
Nor answer gie baith quaint and queer:
Though girr and water-stoups are here
    Whaur's Johnnie Stuffie?

Chapter 21

HUMOUR IN COURT AND COUNCIL

FOR hundreds of years justice has been dispensed from the bench in the old Tolbooth and all manners of crimes, from poaching to murder, have been faithfully dealt with and the law of the country upheld. In bygone days the presiding magistrates were a law unto themselves and their findings and penalties would raise an outcry and demands for a "stated case" nowadays when the law would appear to be on the side of the offender and the offended is offered little consideration, or so it seems to the ordinary layman. Naturally, through the centuries many serious cases were considered in the old courtroom and duly recorded, but there were also many humorous incidents which, although not formally minuted, have been gleefully handed down from generation to generation and have become part of local lore.

There are few stories of repartee between the bench and the accused until the beginning of the nineteenth century when the worthy Bailie Niven was the presiding deity and many stories are told of his stern attitude to anyone who was brought before him. Bailie Niven (or Squire Niven as he liked to be called) was the most prominent townsman of his day and he was very despotic and ruled the town with an iron hand which was not even encased in a velvet glove. Being a Justice of the Peace as well as the Municipal Magistrate he was often on "The Bench" and some strange scenes occurred in court during his reign when he delivered his judgements with great pomposity. His overbearing attitude, however, so incensed the townsfolk that a riot actually ensued in which the windows of his house in High Street were all smashed, and after this his power waned and the Bailie, who used to boast he could clear the street with one stamp of his foot, seldom appeared in the town and spent most of his time on his estate at Kirkbride. When he died Attie Hughes, the town scavenger, preached his requiem when he said, on hearing of his death: "Weel, weel, he's awa', and gane wi' the consent o' the hail parish."

On one occasion Bailie Niven was presiding in the case of McGuigan versus McMillan when McGuigan, the pursuer, stated he had sold McMillan a breeding sow and McMillan had asked him to keep it until he built a sty for it and he, McMillan, would give McGuigan a young pig for his trouble when the sow farrowed. "Weel, your honour," stated the pursuer, "I kept the sow for a fortnight and then McMillan took it away but he wouldn't give me the young pig he promised me." An argument broke out in court between the pursuer and defendant and finally Bailie Niven sternly said to McGuigan: "Sit down, Sir, and I'll see you get justice." "But, your Honour," said the plaintiff, "it's not justice I want—I want my pig."

On another occasion a young man was brought to court charged with breaking the window of a shop in the town. The town constable swore he was the guilty party but no witness could be produced to substantiate the charge. This did not deter the bold Bailie from giving judgement however. "Sir," he said sternly to the accused, "I have heard the charge, and I see by your face you are guilty and I sentence you to seven days in the town gaol." Such was justice in Bailie Niven's day.

A poaching case was being heard by him one day when one, Gavin Hill, was called as a witness. Wull Gordon, the town officer, formally called the witness in the usual way—"Gavin

Hill aince, Gavin Hill twice, Gavin Hill three times," and then in even louder terms, "Man, are ye in the court?" Hill who had been standing behind Gordon quietly said: "Here" and the town officer indignantly said: "Damn ye then step forrit." Hill stepped up to the bench and audibly asked Gordon: "Wha's he that's sitting on the kist?" "Silence," shouted Bailie Niven. "Don't you know who I am?" "Aye," responded Hill, "Ye're the mannie my wife buys her black soap frae." This did nothing to soothe the Bailie's temper and he harangued the witness for so long that finally Hill turned to the Clerk of the Court and said: "Sit roun', man, it's no' for the likes o' you tae be sitting and me stan'ing, wha's been working a' day in a sheugh up tae the headban' o' ma breeks in water." It's impossible to describe the Bailie's indignation at this affrontery to his dignity in court but when he finally calmed down he cried to the town officer: "Gordon, seize the scoundrel and take him down to the cells." This hastily ended the case but Hill got in the last words as he was led out struggling with the town officer, crying: "Canny, Gordon, canny for Goad's sake man, you've torn the lapel of ma guid new waistcoat an' the Bailie will charge me plenty for a new one."

One night an Irish labourer, with drink taken, took a "loan" of the knocker from Bailie Niven's door, to waken, as he said, Mr. Gray across the street. The Bailie naturally was annoyed and during the quarrel which ensued, the Irishman facetiously referred to the colour of the Bailie's chin which invariably turned bluish after shaving. The affronted Bailie charged the labourer with theft and the following day on the bench read him a lecture and fined him for the misdemeanour. The fine was paid and for the rest of the day the Irish labourer paraded up and down the High Street remarking to himself in loud tones audible to all: "The man's beard may be green or blue for all I care—sure I've no call to interfere with the man's blue beard." The fuming Bailie approached the police to have the man again apprehended but wisdom prevailed and the Irishman was allowed to talk to himself until he tired and went off to drown his sorrow in the Red Lion.

Although he was entirely despotic, at times the Bailie's judgement was reminiscent of the wisdom of Solomon. He once dealt with a case where a Maybole man had sold a pair of cart wheels to a Crosshill man. At the time of the bargain the Maybole man had only shown the purchaser one wheel but had sworn the other wheel was in as good condition. When the wheels were delivered to Crosshill it was found the one which had not been shown was in very bad condition and naturally the purchaser felt aggrieved and finally the matter came to court. Bailie Niven gravely considered the matter and finally decided that the Maybole man should repay half the cost of the pair of wheels and the Crosshill man would then choose which wheel he wanted and take it home with him and leave the other with the Maybole man. Few would dispute the wisdom of the judgement but one wonders what each man did with one cart wheel.

About the end of the nineteenth century when Provost Ramsay was a magistrate he had occasion to fine a local farmer for assaulting a well-known poacher whom the farmer had found taking a hare from one of his fields. Not only had the farmer thrashed the poacher but he had confiscated the hare and the poacher, feeling this was an injustice (as he felt he deserved to retain the hare as spoils of war) charged the farmer with assault. Provost Ramsay duly heard the case and fined the farmer Ten Shillings which was promptly paid and the farmer left the court. At the door of the courtroom the poacher jeered at the farmer and gleefully crowed at getting his own back. Without saying a word the farmer hit him and stretched him on the pavement, then turned on his heel, walked back into the courtroom, plumped a gold half sovereign down on the bench in front of Provost Ramsay and said: "I've hit him again, Jimmy" and walked out, leaving the magistrate and clerk speechless.

About the end of last century an individual who rejoiced in the royal name of Bruce occasionally indulged rather freely and was a constant customer in court. One morning he appeared before the magistrate (Mr. Smith) on the usual charge of drunkeness and after being severely told off for his constant bad behaviour was fined half-a-crown. As he had no money to pay his fine he was accordingly committed to prison for a few days and as he was being taken out by the policeman he turned to the bench and, drawing himself up to his full height, announced "Oh aye, ye may be a big man and sit on the Bench in Maybole but a Smith never sat on the throne in Scotland" and so made a dignified exit, as a descendant of Kings should.

On one occasion in the 1950s a local worthy was charged with a breach of the peace and the magistrate found him guilty, read him a lecture and fined him Ten Shillings and Six Pence. The accused produced a pound note to pay the fine, but the Clerk could not give the right change and asked if the accused had sixpence when he would get Ten Shillings change. The accused searched his pockets without finding a sixpence and then, quite naturally and with all the confidence in the world, turned to the magistrate who had just fined him, held out his hand and said, to the amusement of all in court: "Lend me a tanner, Sanny." Surely there can be no greater proof that a Minnieboler can always turn to a fellow townsman in time of need.

During the second World War many units of the armed forces were stationed around the district and among them were some members of the Polish Army. One of the Poles appeared before the court one morning after he had been imbibing unwisely on the potent Scotch "wine" and was charged with being "drunk and incapable". When the Fiscal prepared to read out the charge another official in the Court pointed out that the accused, being a Pole, would probably not understand what was being said if he was spoken to in English. As, however, the official had been studying the Polish language he offered to translate for the Fiscal and his offer was gladly accepted. Very slowly and clearly the official spoke in his brand of Polish to the accused who stared at him unblinkingly and with a glazed look during the whole time the charge was being translated. When the official finished his speech the Pole continued to stare at him with a bemused look for a short time and then turned to the magistrates and said in perfect English: "I'm afraid I do not understand what the gentleman has said. Can he speak English?" Collapse of the Bench, who after composing themselves, duly found the accused not guilty, probably as a token of appreciation for the bright shaft of unconscious humour on his part.

On one occasion a few years ago a magistrate who often sat on the Bench was in his office when a well-known local worthy burst in on him in an excited state and, without any preamble whatsoever, blurted out: "Sure you'll no' send me to prison this time?" After calming him down the magistrate discovered that once again the worthy was to appear before him the following day on a charge of beating his wife, a charge which was very commonplace with the said accused who appeared with monotonous regularity and to whom the magistrate had threatened dire punishment if he appeared again on a similar charge. The Fiscal had told him that as the same magistrate would be on the Bench to take the case, in all probability he would be sent to gaol and the bold worthy thought he would see the Magistrate and plead his case out of court. On being asked what had happened the worthy explained he had too much to drink on the Saturday night and on going home his wife had rather displeased him in some manner and he had chastised her. The magistrate pointed out that he should not beat his wife no matter how much she displeased him to which the worthy replied: "Maybe so, but they're nane the waur o' a licking at times. Ye maun ken that ye're ain wife wad be the better o' ane occasionally." The magistrate must have given much thought to the worthy's words of wisdom as the following day he read him a lecture but discharged him without fining him, much to the delight of the wife who had been beaten and who was in court to hear the case and plead for her lord and master. The couple left the court arm in arm and proved there is much truth in the old saying that a wife would rather be beaten than ignored.

For many years the court had a regular customer in a lady well-known to all as "Sunshine Annie". She had no fixed abode and would get gloriously drunk on every possible occasion on anything from "Red Biddy" to methylated spirits. When "under the influence" her language would have shamed the proverbial trooper but whenever she appeared before the bench her manners and speech was irreproachable. As she never had any money it was useless fining her and the magistrate invariably discharged her after giving her a lecture to which she would gravely listen attentively, fervently promise to mend her ways, and leave the court like a dowager sailing out of a drawing room, to appear a short time later on the same charge. One of the magistrates grew so tired of her regular appearances that he finally sentenced her to thirty days imprisonment. "Sunshine Annie" was stunned for a moment but quickly recovered and, bowing to the Bench, said: "I thank you, your Honour, you're the only gentleman who has ever thought a lady might need a rest from a busy life. A month's retirement, where I can be looked after, will just set me up for the winter." Needless to say "Annie" returned from her rest cure livelier than ever and again was a frequent visitor to court but no one ever plucked up courage to send her for another holiday at the ratepayer's expense.

While the laws of the state were often dealt with in the old Tolbooth in a humorous manner, the councillors who made the law for the town were often unconscious wits at their meetings in the Council Chambers. Many tales are told of battle royals in Council where members had to be forcibly restrained from fisticuffs or harangued their opponents in most ungentlemanly language. Often what appeared at the time to be of immense importance, on reflection turned out to have a humorous side and what seemed to be deadly and unforgiveable insults were gleefully retold later as shafts of wit which won the day for one side or the other. Fortunately Maybole men are clannish and seldom hold spite against each other and deadly enemies across the Council table would join at the door of the chamber and daunder down together to the King's Arms if the Provost could control the meeting sufficiently well to ensure it finished before "closing time".

Once when Provost McCubbin was in the chair, with Dr. Sandilands sitting next to him, a member sitting at the other end of the table rose and protested he could not make out a word the Doctor had said in a motion he was putting forward. "You can't hear him," said the Provost, "then all I can say is you're damned lucky. I hear every word he says and it's not worth listening to."

The bold "Wee Doctor", as he was affectionately known by the local people, invariably sat in Council with a long knitted scarf wound two or three times round his neck with ends reaching down to his knees. One night he and the Provost disagreed vehemently on some subject and "John G." grabbed the ends of the scarf and pulled them so tight he nearly strangled the Doctor. By the end of the meeting, however, they were the best of friends again and sojourned together to the back room in the King's Arms where "John G." produced his own private bottle and the two cronies drowned their differences.

One evening the Council members found themselves enveloped in acrid smoke reminiscent of old rags burning and it was discovered the Doctor had lit up a cigar without removing the cellophane paper round it. His attention was drawn to this but he calmly continued to puff away remarking: "I like it better this way." The Council indeed lost one of its most kenspeckle figures when he retired from public life.

At the time the town reservoir at Lochspouts ran dry (October 1933) a public meeting was held in the Town Hall, with Provost "John G." presiding, to discuss what should be done to remedy matters. During the meeting a member of the audience interrupted from time to time with the bald remark: "Mr. Provost, there's springs in Lochspouts". He did not vouchsafe any further information about the springs but sat down again each time he had his say. After about the fourth interruption the Chairman looked over his spectacles at him and sternly said: "There's springs in your backside, sit doon and haud your tongue." The meeting adjourned without further interruption and it is not known to this day where the springs actually were.

At another public meeting, when housing was being discussed, the same ratepayer who had insisted there were springs in Lochspouts rose to speak against the suggestion that the burgh needed more and better homes. "New houses will no' help folk," he explained. "I've a dochter that's a nurse an' she's aye oot nursing folks in big new hooses. An' ye ken why? Because they're aye no' weel." His profound argument was of little avail, however, and it was decided more new houses should be built.

The poor water supply was often a subject for discussion at election meetings and one candidate for the Council spoke strongly in support of a better supply being brought to the town. He was slightly carried away with his argument and finished his election speech with the advice: "Housewives, until we get a better supply, you all must conserve your water!" As it was some years before the supply was improved it is hoped none of the ladies took the advice too literally.

Many other stories are told of the unconscious shafts of humour which occasionally brightened up the usually dull business in court and Council and it is hoped the wit with which Minniebolers have been fortunately blessed in the past will not die out in this era when everything seems to need to be reduced to a formula and fed into a computer.

Chapter 22

MAYBOLE MINSTRELSY

THROUGHOUT the centuries many songs and poems have been written about Maybole and district, many humorous, some sad, some good and many bad, but unfortunately most have been forgotten and few townsfolk could today quote a line of any poem relating to their home town. In the distant past Maybole was synonymous with the whole district of Carrick, as it was the only place of any size in it, and naturally many people when speaking of Carrick really meant Maybole although perhaps not mentioning it by name. There are therefore many jingles and poems which are now taken to be about Carrick as a whole but when first written were connected with the old town. The focal point of the whole area was the town with its Old College and two castles in its midst with Crossraguel Abbey on the outskirts and the people from the country districts gathered in the town whenever local or national matters were to be discussed. Thus when Sir Walter Scott wrote his "Auchendrane, or the Ayrshire Tragedy" while he broadly placed the story in Carrick, its principals, Sir Thomas Kennedy, William Dalrymple, etc., were more truly Minniebolers than just men of Carrick. When he also had Bruce say at Bannockburn: "I, with my Carrick spearmen charge, now forward to the shock", it can be fairly surmised that most of his "Carrick men" came from the small township which in those days had a greater population than the whole of the rest of Carrick put together. It is only about two hundred years ago that this was emphasised in the old jingle which is still often quoted.

> "When Girvan was a sandy knowe
> And Crosshill lay beneath the plough,
> And Dailly stood—no one knows how—
> Stood the auld toon o' Maybole."

Before the advent of radio and canned music, and before television became a menace to social evenings, the townsfolk often gathered in each other's houses and passed a winter's evening in telling stories or singing the old songs which would be passed down by word of mouth, as these were seldom written. On such occasions the youngsters heard the old poems and songs from their elders and stored them away in their minds to recount them in turn to their children. It is impossible to give all jingles, poems and songs in a book on Maybole and district as they would fill a volume by themselves but the following short collection may be of interest to Minniebolers who love their old town and have an ear for the lilt of their home tongue when speaking of "Cockydrighty", "The Spoot o' Lumling", the "Capenoch" and other well remembered landmarks. There are many short jingles which are so old no one can tell when they were first written or who wrote them but they have lived for generations and, it is hoped, will still continue for many years to be quoted when Maybole men think of their old town. The most common are the following old rhymes:

> "Minniebole's a dirty hole,
> It sits abune a mire,
> But to me and hundreds like me
> It's the finest in the shire."

"Minniebole's a dirty hole,
  Ayr is fou o' clashes,
  Girvan is a bonnie toon
  Wi' bonnie lads and lassies."

  *   *   *

"Minniebole's a gran wee place,
  It sits langside a hill,
  'Tis there ye get the finest claith
  An' mutchkins o' guid yill."

  *   *   *

"If ye should gae tae Maybole toon,
  Your jaunt will no' be wasted,
  Gin ye should buy a pair o' shoon
  They're the finest ever lasted."

  *   *   *

"Carrick for a man,
  Kyle for a coo,
  Cunningham for butter and cheese
  And Galloway for woo'."

  *   *   *

"Twixt Wigton and the toon o' Ayr
  Portpatrick and the cruives o' Cree
  You shall not get a lodging there,
  Except ye court a Kennedy."

  *   *   *

"Johnnie Smith o' Minniebole
  Can ye shoe a wee foal?
  Yes, indeed, and that I can,
  Just as weel as any man."

"In Maybole toon thae leeved a man,
They ca'd him Bailie Niven,
Wha gathered muckle gear and lan'
But never got tae Heaven."

The first two rhymes, whilst taken as being derogatory to the town by strangers (especially Girvanites) should be read in an etymological sense and not in a sanitary one as, of course, they refer to the town being built above a mire. The fifth one is often the subject of hot debate, as folk from Kyle sometimes think their province should be commended for their men, but surely Bruce six hundred years ago could not be wrong when he praised his Carrick men. The sixth rhyme refers to the famous Kings of Carrick who reigned over their Kingdom for generations and whose town house was the old Castle of Maybole. The smith referred to in the seventh jingle is said to have had a smithy at the Ballgreen which was latterly known as "Granny Hunter's Smiddy" until it finally became disused and now forms the back premises of the "Greenside Bar". The last rhyme was about the much maligned Bailie Niven whose wealth and power made him an outcast among his fellow townsmen although his work in improving streets, etc., did much to improve the lot of the townsfolk.

One of the best known Maybole poets was Mitchelson Porteous who was a printer and bookseller in the town last century. Although born in Ayr 1796 he settled in Maybole where he lived until his death in 1872. He was a Town Councillor, Magistrate and Justice of the Peace and took a prominent part in the town's affairs. A keen student of astronomy he built himself the largest telescope in the district at that time and spent hours studying the stars from an attic window of his shop. For nearly fifty years he can be truly said to have been the town's Poet Laureate and wrote numerous poems in English and in the Doric. His collection of poems was published under the title *"Carrickiana"* and are mostly in broad Scots and describe local incidents and characters of his day. He also wrote a *"History of Joseph"* in verse and a metrical version of the Book of Job and translated *"The King's Quair"* into modern English. Altogether he was a man of many parts and few townsfolk have reached his level in the literary world. His Elegy on *"Booler Jamie"* was written on the death of James Gray a well-known Maybole bowler on the old green in New Yards and is a lengthy poem of which the following are some extracts:

>Ohon! Ye boolers o' Maybole!
>What can your bubbly grief console!
>Maun the auld toon wi' you condole
>>An' greet and grane;
>An' gar her bell gae jow an' tell
>>For Jamie gane?

>* * *

>When youngsters braggit at a rink,
>He teuk them up just in a blink,
>For jaws o' onie kin' o' drink,
>>Yill to champaing:
>Fegs! he sune eas'd them o' their clink,
>>Bauld Jamie gane!

>* * *

>Whan winter's win' blew snell an' dour,
>An' froze the lochs in dale an' moor,
>Wi' shother'd broom-kow, steeve an' stoor,
>>An' curlin-stane,
>The first that trod the icy floor
>>Was Jamie gane.

>* * *

>Now, Boolers, Curlers! I hae dun
>My best to keep your hearts abune:
>>Get some Mustioner to tune
>>>Frae it a strain,
>Whilk at your meetins ye may croon:
>>>O' Jamie gane!

The Rev. Roderick Lawson was born in Girvan in 1831, and after studying for the ministry came to Maybole and was ordained minister of the "Glen Kirk" in 1864, where a memorial tablet records he laboured for thirty four years until his death in 1907. During his lifetime in the old town he came to love it, and he wrote many poems and songs and also many books on the town and district. He collected ballads and rhymes of local interest and published them under the title of "Ballads and Songs of Carrick". Only a few of these can be given here but his books are well worth reading today, although unfortunately they are now very scarce and difficult to come by.

"COCKYDRIGHTY"
or
"THE SPOUT IN THE GLEN"

In this drouthy warld there's nocht to compare
   Wi' the water that comes frae the sky,
For washing your face, or making your tea,
   Or slockening your drouth when you're
But of a' the waters that cheerily flow
   To bless bairns, women and men,
There's nane in this toon that's at a' to compare
   Wi' the wee tranklin' Spoot in the Glen.

The Welltrees is sweet, and it never rins dry,
   But it disna dae to be keepit owre lang;
And the auld Castle Well's refreshing to drink,
   But it gangs gey an' aft oot o' fang.
And the Pipe-water — weel, the less that is said
   About that the better, we ken;
But for a gude drink to cule your dry mou,
   Commend me to the Spoot in the Glen.

MAYBOLE - CARRICK'S CAPITAL

It's no vera big — it's jist a wee spoot
    That comes oot o' the breist o' the brae,
But it's sweet, and it's cule, and it's pure as the snaw
    That comes frae the clouds far away.
And it's free to a' comers — the bairns wi' their cans
    And a' folks aboot the West en';
Even the rouch carter lads will pu' up their carts
    And tak a gude swig at the Glen.

There's a great deal o' drink that's no vera gude,
    And brings meikle sorrow and shame,
It steals awa health, and your money to buit,
    And lea's ye a sair ruined name.
But the Drink that I praise has nae siccan fauts;
    It'll no land ye in the prison's dark den,
And ye'll no hae your heid sair, or your jaiket in rags,
    If you stick by the Spoot at the Glen.

There's mony a ane in a far distant land
    Wha minds hoo, in youth's sunny day,
They gaed wi' their stoups, and ca'd their bit crack,
    At the place whaur the wee Spoot's today.
And there's mony a ane's gane farther awa',
    Wha asked on his deathbed to sen'
For a jug o' the cule, cule water that rins
    Frae the wee trinklin' Spoot in the Glen.

And the wee Spoot aye rins, year in and year oot,
    And it asks neither fame nor a fee,
Content if it slockens the drouth o' the weans,
    And mak's your drap parritch or tea.
And the lesson it teaches to young and to auld,
    Frae childhood to threescore and ten,
Is, "Do what ye can, and ne'er think o' reward,"
    Jist like the wee Spoot in the Glen.

MAYBOLE - CARRICK'S CAPITAL

"THE WELLTREES SPOUT"

The Welltrees Spout comes bursting out
    From its bed of silent stone,
Like the Smitten Rock of old that flowed
    In Horeb's desert lone.
And its waters cool from their bubbling pool
    Leap up to the light of day,
As glad to look on the face of man
    And cheer him on his way.

Full many a scene of the Past, I ween,
    Is linked with that quiet spot,
And many a face once knew that place
    Whom earth now knoweth not.
Yet still the big Ash lifts its head,
    And sings to the passing breeze,
While the children gay shout at their play
    Round the steps of the old Welltrees.

O Welltrees Spout, that gushest out
    With waters clear and cold,
I give thee the praise of useful days,
    And the thanks of young and old.
I wish that my life were with good as rife,
    And my heart from stains as free,
As the waters that rise to my gladdened eyes
    From the root of the old Ash tree.

"THE AULD SCHULE"

(in Greenside)

O the Auld Schule, the Auld Schule,
    What though the place was wee!
O happy hearts were gathered there
    When life was fu' o' glee.
Thy playground is deserted noo,
    Thy wa's are silent a',
But mony a happy memory
    Does that Auld Schule reca'.

O the Auld Schule, the Auld Schule!
    Thy forms were gettin' frail,
Thy desks were rough and shaky too,
    Thy floor was like to fail.
But richt gude wark was done in thee,
    And lessons taught wi' skill,
And clever men and women bright
    Were trained in that Auld Schule.

O the New Schule, the New Schule!
    Ye're unco fine and crouse,
Ye're a great credit to the toon,
    Oor ain new, grand Schulehoose.
But the Auld Schule, the Auld Schule!
    Forsaken though ye be,
There ne'er will be a New Schule
    Will seem the same to me.

MAYBOLE - CARRICK'S CAPITAL

"THE CARGILL CONVENTICLE"

The news has come to Maybole toon
    And spread on every hand,
That Donald Cargill is coming to preach
    In spite o' the King's command.
He's coming to preach to the Carrick men
    In the lone sequestered dell,
Where the big stone stands beside the path
    That leads to Ladycross Well.

Oh, dark are the days of the Covenant now
    And few the preachers be
Who lift their voice like a trumpet loud
    And claim their liberty
But God has yet seven thousand left
    To stand for His holy will
And Chief of them all at this testing time
    Is the dauntless good Cargill.

So the folks have come, and the watch been set
    And the preacher grey stands forth
To plead for that Crown and Covenant
    Most banished from the earth.
And he bade them keep their conscience pure
    Let Kings say what they may,
And cited the hills as witnesses
    'Gainst the coming Judgement Day.

The meeting's o'er — the folk's gone home —
    The preacher's gone his way,
To meet his fate on the gallows high
    And be laid 'mongst felons' clay.
But still the green hills cluster round
    That spot so still and lone
Where the daisies spring and the laverocks sing
    Around brave Cargill's stone.

The Maybole folk shall ne'er forget
    The day Cargill was there
When they listened to his preachings
    And bowed their heads in prayer.
And to mark this great occasion
    A monument was raised
In memory of their men who died
    Because their Lord they praised.

"THE LOVERS' LOANIN'"

O, cheery is the morn when the day is newly born,
And not a breath o' wind is moanin';
But sweeter far the cheer, when the licht is no sae clear,
Wi' the lass that ye lo'e in the Loanin'.

Chorus

Then gang alang wi' me, my bonnie Maggie Lee,
Ye promised me to come in the gloamin'.
Noo the day is wearin' past, an' the mirk is comin' fast,
O, come to the bonnie Lovers' Loanin'.

O, merry is the day when every thing is gay,
And the hinney-laden bee gangs dronin';
But sweeter far the hour when the nicht begins to lour,
To walk wi' your lass in the Loanin'.

O lichtsome is the time when youth is in its prime,
And nae thocht o' sighin' or groanin';
To dauner by your sel', wi' the lass you lo'e so well,
In the bonnie quiet lanesome Lovers' Loanin'.

"THE LAZY CORNER"
or
"THE CASTLE CORNER"

There is a place in ilka toon,
Weel kenn'd by a' the country roun',
Whaur gathers every idle loon,
        And it's ca'd the Lazy Corner.

The tippler comin' aff the spree,
The tradesman glad his wark to flee,
And the man wha has naething else to dae,
        Gang to the Lazy Corner.

It's wonnerfu' the things they hear
Of a' that's happen'd, far and near—
Whether they're true's a sma' affair
        T' the folks at the Lazy Corner.

The corner wi' ill news is rife—
Wha's sent to jail—wha's threshed his wife—
Wha's focht and nearly took a life—
        Is food for the Lazy Corner.

The clishmaclaivers o' the toon,
The gossip o' the country roun',
Tittle-tattle—that's the soun'
        Has charms for the Lazy Corner.

Then, ilka body that gangs by
Maun stan' remarks—be't lass or boy
While winks, and nods, and glances sly
        Mak' fun for the Lazy Corner.

Of course it's richt that folk should talk—
But better, surely, tak' a walk,
Or by the fireside ca the crack,
    Than stan' at the Lazy Corner.

For in this busy life o' man,
Whase length can hardly reach a span,
It's surely wrang to idly stan'
    Doon by the Lazy Corner.

"THE TOON STEEPLE"

Our steeple is old, our steeple is grey,
It has served us well for many a day,
For more than two centuries it has stood
And faced the rain, and storm, and flood.
It has watched the growth of this town of ours,
And measured the march of the passing hours,
And laughed with our smiles, and wept with our tears,
This steeple of more than two hundred years.

It has relics to show of the bygone Past:
The "Jouggs" which bound the culprits fast,
And the "Stocks" which bound him faster still,
When nought could tame his stubborn will;
And the old tinkling Bell which the Frenchman made,
Whose voice has gladdened both man and maid;
And the quaint old door looking down the street
To the "Lazy Corner" where idlers meet.

MAYBOLE - CARRICK'S CAPITAL

One winter night the wind blew high,
And bore disaster far and nigh;
The townsfolk rose with morning light
To see the damage of the night;
When lo! the Steeple-top was seen
A comic spectacle, I ween;
It looked athwart the morning sky
Like tippler's hat put on awry.

The top was doom'd: it must come doon;
It was a danger to the toon;
The very Cock that turn'd about
To show the way the wind was out,
Had now to bow to Fate's decree
And yield its post of dignity;
And so, with ropes securely bound,
'Twas brought all safely to the ground.

But now our Steeple look'd so bare
Expos'd thus to the wintry air,
That every townsman, Scot and Pat,
Wish'd well our Steeple a new hat,
But what sort of Hat should now be got
Was next the subject of deep thought—
"A Dome" cries one—"a Hat like those
Worn now-a-days by all the beaux."

"No hat at all," cries some mad wag,
"But Flagstaff tall to support a flag":
Whilst the most, to compliment the town,
Would only have an "Iron Crown".
So the Crown was bought and perched upon it,
Just like a small Glengarry bonnet,
And the weather-beaten Steeple grey
Was flouted by the crown so gay.

But had they asked the Steeple bare
What sort of a hat it wished to wear,
Its answer, I wean, could only be—
"Just give me the hat I used to see—
The old cocked-hat, with its cozy air,
And the Weather-cock above it there;
For an old-fashioned hat suits old-fashioned people,
And that's just the case with your old Town Steeple."

Thomas Ferguson was born in Maybole in 1833, his father being Superintendent of the Poor, and after his schooling in the town he went first to Glasgow, then as a foreign correspondent to London and later to Dumbarton where he became a partner in a rope spinning works. He finally retired to his native town where he was a kenspeckle figure until his death in March, 1918. In 1898 he published a book of verse which included many nostalgic pieces on the district in which he spent his boyhood and later he wrote many poems which unfortunately were not set down in print and are now lost and forgotten.

"THE TOON O' MINNIBOLE"

My blessing on thee, auld Maybole,
  The toon where I was born;
Beside the Wee Spout in the Glen
    The rare auld toon,
    The fair auld toon,
      The toon o' Minniebole.

A tear slid silent doon my cheek
  When I frae thee did part:
Where'er I gae I carry thee,
  Auld Maybole, in my heart:
    Thou dear auld toon,
    Thou queer auld toon,
      The toon o' Minnibole.

And like the swallow, I hie back
   Ilk year to the auld toon;
Wi' what a joy I see again
   The green slopes o' Kildoon
      And wander roun'
        The guid auld toon,
            The toon o' Minniebole.

From Mochrum to the Straiton hills,
   The haill expanse seems mine;
On nae sic bonnie scene as that
   The happy sun doth shine;
      Frae Dailly hills
        To Patna kilns,
            Unmatched auld Minniebole.

Come back, far days, when for the sea
   We started fu' o' splore:
How lonesome to me now the hush
   Upon Culzean's dear shore,
      Where ance we sang,
        And lap, and flang,
            Nor thocht o' Minniebole.

Crossraguel's haunted wa's wi' dread
   Our boyish hearts did fill,
By auld Baltersan for lang hours
   We ginelled at the Mill,
      Then hirpled hame
        Barefit and lame,
            To scones in Minnibole.

The Auld Green Schule! where at the ba'
  We played till oot o' breath,
And where our wee bit quarrels whiles
  We settled up the Peth!
    I fear us boys
    Had tricks and ploys
      Unkenn'd in Minnibole.

The Auld Schule brought us lear enough;
  And when we won our prize,
And to the auld folk took it hame,
  What joy danced in their eyes!
    They thocht, nae doot,
    We'd a' turn oot
      Great folks in Minnibole.

But time has swept us far apart;
  Some, posts wi' credit fill,
While some sleep soun' at the Kirkport,
  Some at the Clachan hill,
    And a' maun gae,
    Nae distant day,
      Far, far frae Minnibole.

Williams Shaw was another native of Maybole who wrote many songs in praise of his native town in which he lived until his death in the 1930s. He was schooled by John Wyllie in the old Parish School at the foot of the Town Green and his schoolmaster took a keen interest in him and prophesied he would make his mark in the world. Mr. Shaw, however, could not bear to leave his beloved Maybole and spent his life as a trusted clerk to Mr. James Gibson in the Royal Bank. He was a phenomenal mathematician and the compiler of *"Shaw's Mathematical Tables"* which was used in all banks throughout Scotland. He wrote much verse for newspapers and evangelical magazines and varied his themes considerably. During the first World War he wrote many poems urging peace between nations and his stanzas on Nurse Cavell who was shot by the Germans for helping British soldiers to escape from Belgium is well-known.

"WE ARE COMING, NURSE CAVELL"

A woman's voice is calling,
  It is borne upon the breeze,
To ev'ry land and ev'ry strand,
  Of all the Seven Seas.

And Freedom's sons are rising,
  A stern and mighty host;
They are coming, they are coming
  They are counting not the cost.

Above the din of battle,
  And the roar of giant guns,
Above the braggart shouting
  Of the lewd and murderous Huns.

The tramp of untold legions
  Is rising loud and clear,
And 'mid the tempest of their wrath
  These words I seem to hear—

"We are coming, we are coming,
  From city, mount and shore,
To avenge this latest infamy,
  And twice ten thousand more.

"And not one heart shall falter,
  And not one hand shall fail;
Now tremble, all ye murdering hordes,
  For Right shall sure prevail.

"Our way may oft be dreary,
    Nurse Cavell,
Our feet will oft be weary,
    Nurse Cavell,
We know not what's in store,
Some shall return no more,
They shall reach the 'silent shore',
    Like thyself, Nurse Cavell.

"But this we know—we're coming,
    To speed the Reckoning Day,
And swell the conquering millions
    Already on the way.

"Let unborn ages hear it,
    Let our children's children tell
How swift we sent the answer—
    We are coming, Nurse Cavell."

"SUNSET ON CARRICK SHORE"

The sea was calm, the setting sun
    In splendour all untold
Had thrown a bridge across the deep
    That shone like burnished gold.

"Oh, this," I said, "must be the path
    That angel feet have trod;
Oh, this must be the shining way
    That leadeth up to God!"

Thus soared my childhood's fancy
　　Above the silent sea;
'Twas long ago, as you must know,
　　When Time was young with me.

But now once more, from Arran shore,
　　There gleams that shaft of light
Which met my gaze in bygone days,
　　And held my raptured sight.

And when my latest sun goes down
　　Beyond life's fitful sea,
May mine, through grace abounding,
　　A golden sunset be.

Then, oh, how near shall be the path
　　That angel feet have trod,
And bright as day the shining way
　　That leadeth up to God.

　　A well-known local poetaster was William Davidson who was born in 1885 and spent his whole life in the town, taking a prominent part in the local Council and the town's affairs. He was a great lover of nature and wrote on a variety of subjects and two of his best known poems illustrate his depth of feeling for his beloved calf country and the bitterness he felt when it was proposed during the 1914-18 war that sparrows be exterminated as they were thought to eat too much of the grain grown by the farmers.

"TAIRLAW LINN"

There is a spot, a calm retreat
Where earth and heaven seem to meet,
Where pleasures are for ever sweet,
      'Tis Tairlaw.

Where rugged hill-tops towering high
In mystic splendour cleave the sky,
And summer breezes gently sigh
      Round Tairlaw.

Far, far removed from man and sin
And from the workshop's awful din,
The rushing waters leap the linn
      At Tairlaw.

And foaming, pausing down below,
Then rushing on in ceaseless flow
Down through the glen where bluebells grow
      At Tairlaw.

'Twould seem as if some magic wand
Borne by a little fairy hand
Enchanted that fair sun-kissed land
      At Tairlaw.

With raptures sweet my heart would swell,
If I could but for ever dwell
Amid these scenes I love so well
      At Tairlaw.

MAYBOLE - CARRICK'S CAPITAL

"A SPEUG'S LAMENT"

Vile sinfu' man, O hoo I yearn
That better laws ye a' should learn
    In hames sae snug
Plotting there, tae dae me harm,
    A puir wee speug.
Why coont me noo ane o' your foes?
Why aim at me your cruel blows?
    Am I to blame?
A man will reap just what he sows
    Honour or shame.

Man canna sin and suffer nane,
The Master makes that unco plain
    Tae ane and a'.
And if His laws they lang disdain
    Some day they'll fa'.
Noo, why you men should in your rage
Dark war against wee sparrows wage
    I fail to see
That you should in sic work engage
    Is strange tae me.

Your accusation is na fair
That sparrows eat mair than their share
    O' precious grain.
Tae mak your barns in war mair bare
    I wad disdain.
I like a pick o' corn 'tis true,
When grubs are rare and worms are few
    In faugh or lea,
But what it taks tae fill me fu'
    You'd hardly see.

But what aboot the barley bree,
You men are drinking day by day
    Frae frothy jugs,
Destroying grain mair than wid dae
    Ten million speugs?
Reflect ower jist what gangs for drink,
Then honestly, frail man, I think
    Your laws you'll mend,
And waste nae grain or hard earned chink
    On sic a blend.

But hae a care, for He wha sees
Each sparrow that aroun' ye flees
    Hoo'ever sma',
At hame or far ayont the seas
    Will mark its fa'.
But I hae got four youngsters sma',
Tae feed them noo I maun awa
    And luik for grub.
Tak my advice, don't harm ava
    A puir wee speug.

    At the beginning of the 20th century when work was scarce many townspeople emigrated to Canada and elsewhere in search of employment. Among them was William Stewart, a local shoemaker, who was forced to leave his hometown in 1907. The evening before he left the town he took a walk over the Clachan Brae to Lochlands and, sitting on a stone at the "Runnel", pencilled his farewell to his native town. He also wrote on his memories of the Cairders Burn and both his poems are nostalgic to the older generation who knows so well the landmarks he mentions. Nowadays, with the younger generation using cars to go everywhere, they do not walk round the "Whinny Knowes", or to "Capenoch" or the "Cross Roads" as their forefathers did when courting their mothers in days gone past and the names of local landmarks may soon be forgotten.

MAYBOLE - CARRICK'S CAPITAL

"FAREWELL TO MAYBOLE"

I'm leaving the land of my birth today
To seek a new home in the land far away,
And now when the time comes to say goodbye
The gathering tears bedim mine eye,
And a feeling of sadness my bosom fills
As I bid adieu to the Carrick Hills.

I stand neath the Runnel's leafy shade
Where oft in boyhood days I've played,
To take one last long look around
At the straggling form of Maybole town,
The woods so green and the valleys wide
Shut in by the hills on every side.

The birds are singing their morning song
Down by Kilhenzie's wood and home,
And green is each wood, each glen and mire,
Twixt the Burning Hills and Culdoon's lone spire
And past the shoulder of Knockbrake
Is seen Baltersan's ruined shape.

There Mochrum rears his head with pride
And looks far o'er the Firth of Clyde,
Above the town the broad Howmoor,
Sees the fishermen sail out from Dunure,
Brown Carrick, rising from the Banks o' Doon,
Commands a view o' Ayr auld toon.

We've searched the woods, the glens and braes,
To find the berries, scribes and slaes
And many a pillowslip we'd fill
Twixt Crawfordston glen and Guiltreehill,
And when the night in darkness set
We drew the leafields with partridge net.

257

MAYBOLE - CARRICK'S CAPITAL

Over Benquhat in the eastern sky,
The summer sun is mounting high,
The morning mist his beams have spent,
Which hang around Straiton monument,
Raised to the memory of Blairquhan
Who fought and fell at Inkerman.

There, standing in front is Glenalla Fells,
Those sheep clad slopes I love so well,
Behind where the burn winds in and out
I've spent happy days with the wily trout,
Or searching the meadows of Balbeg,
In quest of whap and peesie's egg.

Through yonder pass with noisy din,
The Girvan comes rushing from Tairlaw Lynn,
Loch Lure, Loch Braden and Girvan Eye
  His clear and limpid streams supply,
Those lovely lochs lie calm and still
Reflecting back each heather hill.

Shalloch on Minnoch, Carrick's King,
From his broad base the rivers spring,
The Doon, the Cree, and the Girvan fair,
Each in his narrow streamlets share,
And the Stinchar starts on its lonely way
And seeks the sea at Ballantrae.

Those lonely hills have heard the chant
Of the men who stood for the Covenant,
In those stirring times of religious strife
When to own your faith was to risk your life,
Those haunted men did refuge seek
  Beneath the hills so wild and bleak.

Farewell, my native hills, farewell,
I'll still remain beneath thy spell,
Tho' I should lie on a foreign shore
And hear Niagra's thunder roar,
Each wooded vale and hillside steep
Is planted in my memory deep.

"THE CAIRDERS BURN"

As I wander in the morning,
O'er romantic Allan's Hill,
When the trees are clothed in beauty,
And the air is calm and still,
Scenes of Childhood pass before me,
As mine eyes with fondness turn,
To the rustic bridge at Fordhouse,
And the dear old Cairders Burn.

There I paddled late and early,
When my heart was young and free,
And this tiny little river,
Seemed to me a mighty sea,
Here I captured baggy minnows,
In a bottle or an urn,
With a playmate girl beside me,
At the sweet old Cairder's Burn.

Yonder Kildoon stands before me,
As it stood in days of yore,
And Knockbrake still faces bravely,
Shower and blizzard from the shore,
But the place that charms my bosom,
On this tranquil summer morn,
Is the rustic bridge at Fordhouse,
And the hallowed Cairder's Burn.

Here I list the flowing water,
And I catch its sweet refrain,
'Tis the same glad song of childhood,
It is singing once again,
Broken by a note of sadness,
As it ripples round each rock,
For the absent chums who guddled,
Further up near Thornbrock.

As I leave the bridge behind me,
And the water flowing fast,
On my mind are deeply graven,
Scenes and memories of the past,
And no matter where I wander,
Still my thoughts still fondly turn,
To the rustic bridge at Fordhouse,
And the charming Cairder's Burn.

John Fulton was another emigrant from the old town in the early part of this century and like many of his fellow exiles he settled in Hamilton, Ontario, where a Maybole Association was formed among the people who had been forced to go abroad in search of work when the "Bog" failed and half the townsmen were thrown idle. This association is still going strong and its members (mostly now the sons or daughters of the emigrants) are to this day keenly interested in the affairs of the old town on the hillside which is a Mecca for all when they visit Scotland on holiday. John Fulton became the Bard of the Hamilton Burns Club and wrote many poems about Scotland's Poet and about Maybole and district and a book of his poems was published in Canada entitled *"Poems by John Fulton, the Scotch Canadian Bard"*. The following poems are examples of his work which show his love for his birthplace. His poem on "Clockie Tam" tells of the old tale of "Watchie" Logan and the time he was sold as a poached deer to a local butcher although he disguises the victim under another name.

MAYBOLE TOWN

Far up amongst auld Carrick hills
'Mongst crystal springs and glittering rills,
'Mongst shady trees and scented thorn,
Whaur wild birds' song wakes early morn,
Stands Maybole Toon, o' ancient glory
Famed in romance, in song and story,
Whose sons for freedom always fought,
And with their blood new glory bought,
On monys a gory field.

There castles grim tell of a day
When martial lairds then held the sway;
Each hill or dell, where'er you turn,
Bespeaks the Wallace, Bruce or Burns.
Up on the hill stands Peden's tree
And Cargill Stane doon in the lea,
Baith men who stood for conscience sake
Were hunted down by moor or brake,
By Claver's bloody band.

The scene's now changed, no more resound
The noise of steed or Claver's hounds;
The peaceful traveller wends his way,
Where'er he choose he now may pray;
The tyrant now witholds his hand
For justice now pervades the land.
The ploughman now from bondage free
Goes whistling homeward o'er the lea
To cottage hame and wife.

Whilst in the toon wi' joke and sang
The Souter lads still ply the Whang
As hearty as in days of yore
When Souter Johnnie sang and splored;
And bricht eyed bairnies fresh frae schule
The streets and lanes wi lauchter fill;
And Maybole still majestic stands—
A bullwark o' auld Scotia's land—
Up 'mongst auld Carrick hills.

AULD CLOCKIE TAM

Nae doot auld folks o' Maybole Toun
Weel minds a man wha' aince went roun'
And cleaned auld clocks and made then soun'
   When they gae'd wrong;
A man weel kent by a' aroun'
   As Clockie Tam.

Noo, tho' his richt name I'll no' tell,
I'll tell yous what him aince befell
Yae nicht when he was unco' snell
   Wi' barley bree,
And sleepin' soun' in Enoch's dell
   Beneath a tree.

And sleepin' soun', nae care or fear,
O' danger him a-drawin' near,
Was ended nearly his career
   Wi' poachin' hauns
Wha' thocht they saw a way there clear
   Tae mauk a dram.

MAYBOLE - CARRICK'S CAPITAL

Noo, poachers, whiles are awesum folk,
But, as a rule, they like a joke;
So they pap't Clockie in a poke
   And wander'd hame
And took him tae a dealer's shop
   Wha' dealt in game.

Noo, this dealer that they took him to,
Year in, year oot, was always fou—
A fact the poachers brawly knew,
   So laid their plans.
So, in they marched, bold men and true,
   An' spun their yarn.

They said they'd got a deer at last,
As Clockie on the flure they cast,
And asked to get the money fast
   For they had fears
The keepers had them tracked, alas,
   And were then near.

And so the dealer, wi' the din,
Forgot tae look what was within
The pock the poachers had brocht in
   and see his deer,
And handed owre tae them the tin
   Wi' conscience clear.

Noo, just as oot the door they got,
Auld Clockie frae his slumbers woke
And wrestled hard within the poke
   For tae get free,
For, whaur the de'il he noo had got
   He could na' see.

Till lo' abune him something flash'd
And Clockie's brains were nearly dash'd
  Oot on the flure,
And noo, for aince himsel' he fash'd
  About a prayer.

"Oh, Lord, wouldst crush these murderous foes
Wha's dinging me such kick and blows,
And in thy ways I'll always go,
  Aye, evermore;
And never mair whaurs drinks I'll go,
  O, never more. Amen."

Noo, when the dealer heard this prayer
He stopp'd his blows just then and there
And whumled Tam oot on the flure,
  And sent him clear,
Determined that he would nae mair
  Buy in sic deer.

But, as for Clockie, puir old man,
His pious vows went far awrang,
For noo he swore he took the dram
  His nerves tae richt,
For they were shatter'd and knock'd wrang
  Wi' that nicht's fricht.

And, noo the moral tae the tale—
If, in life's fight you would prevail,
Remember Clockie in the Dell.
  From drink abstain,
For men gaes down 'neath wine and ale
  And fuddled brains.

John Russell was born in Bathgate and on being appointed County Sanitary Inspector for the Carrick District in 1900 he took up residence in Maybole. He was an enthusiastic Territorial and became Major of the 5th Battalion, The Royal Scots Fusiliers, going on service with them at the outbreak of the first World War and being killed in action in Gallipoli in 1915. For some years he was secretary for the local Burns Club and in 1913 he wrote a poem commemorating the visit of Robert Burns to Maybole in August, 1786, when he collected £1. 1s. 0d. for the sale of seven copies of his Kilmarnock edition of poems and held carousal afterwards in the Kings Arms Hotel with some of his cronies. This poem was read to the members of the Burns Club at their supper in the same Kings Arms Hotel on the night of 25th January, 1913.

"BURNS' VISIT TO MAYBOLE"

Lang syne beneath this self-same roof
Was laid within the poet's loof
A jinglin' purse, the welcome proof
    O' luck's renewal;
(Ev'n bards maun hae their feedin'stuff
    And claes and fuel).

The billies, rigged in hodden claith,
Wha met that jovial nicht beneath
This auld inn's roof-tree, sleep in death;
    Rab's coins are dust.
Image and superscription baith
    Alike are lost.

Nae longer stands the Bard in need
O' sic like help as Carrick gied
When for his poverty, wi' speed
    She toomed her sporran;
Frae want and care lang syne he's freed—
    Lendin' or borrowin'.

Yet as the Janwar chills
Weave snow-wreaths round the Ayrshire hills
The heart o' loyal Carrick thrills
    In rapture throbbin',
And love her purse to burstin' fills
    Wi' gowd for Robin.

Archibald Crawford, although an Ayr man, was interested in the legends of Carrick and wrote about many of them. In 1825 he published a book *"Tales of my Grandmother"* which was founded mainly on the traditions of south west Scotland, and many other Carrick subjects. Although born north of the Doon he certainly believed that Carrick bred men and Kyle was a dairying province as his following poem shows.

"CARRICK FOR A MAN"

When auld Robert Bruce
Lived at Turnberry House,
He was the prince o' the people, the frien' o' the lan';
Then to Kyle for your cow,
Gallowa' for your woo,
But Carrick, my billies, when ye want a man.

At the stream o' auld bannocks,
   There was cracking o' crummocks
It was a hard tulzie, lang fought han' to han';
   Then to Kyle for your cow,
   Gallowa' for your woo,
But Carrick, my billies, that day proved the man.

Then why should we not be crouse,
   When we think o' auld Robin Bruce,
Whose blood it still flows, and whose progeny reigns?
   Then to Kyle for your cow,
   Gallowa' for your woo,
But Carrick, my billies, gives Britain her Queens!

In 1876 William Kissock was born at Kilkerran and was schooled at Dailly. On leaving school he tried his hand at sketching but grew tired of art in a few years and turned to writing poetry and plays. For a few years he lived as a recluse in remote parts of Carrick and devoted himself to writing. In 1913 he published a volume of *"Scottish and English Poems"* and in 1917 produced another book of verse entitled *"The Carrick Shore and other Poems"*. Both publications dealt with a great variety of subjects and were of considerable merit. The following is a short extract from "The Carrick Shore" and two of his other better known poems.

"THE CARRICK SHORE"

And here's Goat's Green, where fairies dance,
All clad in green in moonlight's glance,
   To music of the sea;
They trip along from out the Cove
To dance as Graces danced to Jove
   When Pan played harmony;

And round that rocky point so near,
    The headless horseman rode;
And once a year you still may hear
    Clink of his courser's shod,
As, dashing and splashing,
    The gallant charger bore
The cold wight the whole night
    To his dear lady's door.

The Carrick witches held their ploys
In this sweet place, the brae o' Croy,
    The hill of mystery;
Where water rises, and every rill
Goes flowing backward up the hill,
    As flying from the sea.
Magic's deep heart is beating warm,
    As in the days of yore;
The place has never lost the charm
    Of elvin and wizard lore,
With bell chime and hell rhyme,
    The witch dance moves along,
With mad cry and glad eye,
    Chanting their midnight song.

"THE POET"

'Mong people passin' on life's road
    A poet aince I saw;
An' wonderin' asked a woman there
    If she kent him ava.
"O, that's a daft, half-witted fellow,
    Wha makes great screeds o' rhyme,
Wha sits a' nicht wi' candle licht
    An' lies tae dinner-time.

A trouble in the body's bad,
    But waur when in the brain;
O, he stravaigs the country wide
    In storms o' win' an' rain.

He's come o' decent folk, ye ken,
    Lang natives o' the place,
Tae a' his friends a rale heart breck,
    A mither's sair disgrace.

An' then I asked about his warks,
    The meanin' o' his lays;
"There's ne'er a meanin' in his warks,
    But foolish rhyme", she says.
"A lot o' bosh about here-after,
    An' hoo the soul may fare,
An' sangs o' lassies' een sae blue,
    Wi' luve for evermair.

"He says we'll think o' him when deid,
    I'm share we wull, says I,
For ye'll come on the Parish rates,
    An' in the Puirhoose lie."

"THE GUIDMAN"

A woman's wark is never dune,
    Frae morning on till dark
Altho' there's mony a feckless yin
    That canna wash her sark.
It's little guid tae sit an' greet—
    It's better far tae try;
Tho' unco ill tae gar en's meet,
    Whan nithin's lyin' bye.

Whan I put on my first lang goon,
  Ma hert was fu' an' free,
As glaiket as the thistledown
  On autumn winds that flee,
As daft as yett on win'y day
  Frae early on till late;
For men I didna care a strae,
  Till Rab cam' in ma gate.

Noo, Rab sits in the inn ilk nicht,
  Wi' yill-stoup at his nose;
Tho' no for wark, his han's aye richt
  For draughts and dominoes.
An' while he laughs wi' drunken men,
  I dowie bide alane;
An', while he plays at catch-the-ten,
  I tend a fractious wean.

Whan drink comes in, the gumption gangs,
  Tho Rab's no' ill tae me;
It's unco hard tae eat the tangs
  Tae gi'e yer man the spree.
O' sleep I never ken a wink—
  Rab sits the hale nicht thro',
For he's a thowless coof in drink,
  An' essert as a soo.

I kin'le the fire at brek o' day,
  An' bundle up his piece;
But he wad just—as I may say—
  As shin set out for Greece.
I'll no compleen, but thole awa,
  As jist a woman can,
Tho' fashious, oolin' ills befa',
  For luve o' ma guidman.

MAYBOLE - CARRICK'S CAPITAL

Before the 1914-18 War David McKie worked for some years in the Estates Office of the Marquess of Ailsa. He had a great love of the country life of the old town and district and he wrote many poems on various subjects which were published from time to time in the *"Evening News"* and the *"Edinburgh Dispatch"* as well as the local weekly newspapers. He joined the Ayrshire Yeomanry at the outbreak of war and after being badly wounded and discharged as unfit for further service he returned to his home town of Tarbolton and published a book of verse entitled *"Songs of an Ayrshire Yeoman"*. Most of the poems deal with his life in the army but many are about the old Kingdom of Carrick and people of Maybole.

"THE EARL OF CARRICK'S OWN"

I've listed in the County Horse,
    A trooper, don't you know;
With spurs of steel upon my heel,
    Full swagger now I go.
I've sworn an oath to serve the King,
    And to defend his Throne;
I'm proud to be a trooper in
    "The Earl of Carrick's Own".

The call of bugles in my ear
    Is sweeter than a song;
With rifle and with bandolier
    I gaily ride along.
Our Colonel is a soldier true,
    As Afric's plains have shown—
We're proud of such a leader, in
    "The Earl of Carrick's Own".

MAYBOLE - CARRICK'S CAPITAL

The pretty girls all glance at me,
    Or maybe 'tis my clothes;
No dull aesthetic soul is mine,
    I quaff life as it flows,
Let hoary wisdom prate of fields
    Where youth's wild oats are sown—
I scorn him like a trooper in
    "The Earl of Carrick's Own".

Those sleek, thin-fingered laddie-daws
    Who strut like bantam cocks,
May smile disdainfully and say,
    "They're only soor-milk Jocks;"
But should Invasion's scourging breath
    Across our hills be blown,
They'll find we still have valour in
    "The Earl of Carrick's Own".

"CARRICK"

You have never been to Carrick,
    Never crossed the classic Doon,
Never heard the Girvan singing
    To her olden magic tune:
Never seen the hills of Straiton
    By the lips of morning kissed,
Never looked on hoary Arran?
    Then a glory you have missed.

"What", you ask, "is lovely Carrick?"
　　But you ask in vain of me,
For my song could ne'er interpret
　　Half her charm and mystery;
But if you will deign to listen,
　　Then my muse will strive to tell
Just the shadow of her beauty,
　　And a whisper of her spell.

'Tis a land of wonder, Carrick,
　　Wheresoe'er you choose to roam,
O'er her mountains, through her woodlands,
　　By her rivers and her foam;
Nature with a special favour
　　Bids the seasons lavish there
All their beautiful abundance,
　　Just to make old Carrick fair.

There are pleasant towns in Carrick,
　　Villages and hamlets too;
There are happy hearts in Carrick,
　　Rich in kindness, warm and true:
There's a cantie, couthie quaintness
　　In the spirit of her folk,
And there's still a laughing welcome
　　For the simple fashioned joke.

And the past is near, in Carrick,
　　For it seems but yesterday
Since the Kennedys went riding
　　Through the moonlight to the fray;
And Crossraguel priest was roasted,
　　And the Countess, like a bird,
Tempted from her keep of Cassillis
　　By a gipsy's luring word.

Vain my song to picture Carrick,
    You must cross the classic Doon,
You must hear the Girvan singing
    To her olden magic tune:
You must meet her men and women
    By their hearths' inviting glow—
Only then you'll cease to wonder
    Why we love old Carrick so.

"BROCKLOCH GLEN"

There's a bonnie wee bit den
    Jist a mile abune the toon,
In the bosom o' the glen,
    Whaur there's ne'er a jarrin' soun';
Whaur the bells are bloomin' sweet
    And there's wealth o' wavin' fern,
And the buddin' branches meet
    High abune the singin' burn.

Ower the rocks the water fa's
    In a clear, melodious stream,
And when mornin' gilds the wa's
    It is bonnie as a dream;
Or when gloamin' twines the grove
    Then it seems beneath the glow,
Such a den as Eve would love
    In her Eden long ago.

One forgets his peck o' care
   Listening to the burnie's flow,
And the mair you wander there,
   Still the sweeter does it grow;
For it charms the finer strings
   That sae oft forgotten lie,
And it opes the sacred springs
   With their spiritual supply.

There's a silence like a prayer
   Underneath each gracefu' tree,
And if you could only share
   All the peace it brings to me,
You would bless the Gracious One
   For his gift of such a boon
As yon glen at set o' sun,
   Jist a mile abune the toon.

"MADAME"
(To Mrs. C———, Maybole)

No lady of the distant, sunny South is she,
   Nor dame high born,
   Whom pearls adorn,
And at whose feet the courtiers bend obedient knee.
Yet I would claim for her as rare a royalty
   As theirs, who wear a crown,
   And trail the purple gown
With stately stride and mien of majesty;
   For she possesses this, the real nobility
   Of life, and more than art,
   The deep and queenly heart,
The giving hands, the broad and tender sympathy.
And now I give salute, as would a knight with spur,
To all the regal ways that I have found in her.

"THE CAIRDER'S BRIDGE"

We linger on the little bridge
    Whene'er we pass along,
We linger there and listen
    To the water and its song;
And if we didn't linger
    There would seem a something wrong,
A tender admonition
    In the water and its song.

We linger on the little bridge,
    We love to linger there,
For sure the starlit water
    Seems to wash away our care;
And, though 'tis time to hurry
    Still we find a spell to spare,
To linger and to listen
    And to hold each other there.

We linger on the little bridge,
    The reason may be this,
Before the time of parting
    We would steal another kiss;
And if we didn't linger,
    Then I'm sure that we would miss
The music of the water,
    And the wonder of the kiss.

Carrick and its men have been the subject of much poetry since John Barbour, Archdeacon of Aberdeen, in the 14th century wrote his long and vivid story of "The Brus" in which he describes the adventures of Robert the Bruce over a period of forty years until his death. This poem was written about

1376 and present day readers find it difficult to translate to modern English but King Robert II thought so greatly of it he gifted Barbour £10 and a perpetual pension of £1 yearly. Blind Harry, the 15th century minstrel, also mentions Carrick in his epic on Sir William Wallace, and Walter Kennedy, one of the principals in the famous "Flyting of Dunbar and Kennedy" was born at Cassillis about 1460 and must have often trod the streets of the old town. The famous Boyd cousins, Mark, Robert and Zachary, were all Carrick men from Penkill and Trochrague and were among the most noted 16th century Scottish poets. Robert Burns found much of his subject matter in Carrick, the story of Tam o' Shanter being founded on a Maidens farmer and his Soutar crony. Hew Ainslie and Hamilton Paul, both noted, if now neglected, poets, were born in Dailly parish at the end of the 18th century. Both wrote many lyrics on the beauties of Carrick and it has been said Ainslie was second only to Burns as the poet of Ayrshire. John Keats stayed in the Kings Arms Hotel in Maybole for some time during his visit to Carrick and the same hotel also sheltered Shelley, Wordsworth and R. L. Stevenson during their visits to the ancient Kingdom. Dante Gabriel Rossetti the Italian poet and painter stayed at Penkill Castle in 1868 and there wrote his long poem "The Stream's Secret" in a little cave at Penwhapple Burn. In one of his black moods he visited Tairlaw Lynn and attempted to commit suicide by throwing himself over it and to this day the lynn is often called Rossetti's Lyn. From 1865 to 1868 William Bell Scott, poet and painter and friend of Rossetti, also stayed at Penkill Castle where he painted scenes from "The King's Quair" on the walls of the circular staircase and wrote his poem "The Old Scotch House" or "Penkill Castle". Many other lesser known poets such as James Dow, who was reared at Kirkoswald in the early 19th century, William Lennox, Superintendent of Poor in Ayr and who fought as a private soldier at Waterloo, John McSkimming of Barr and Elizabeth Ramsay, a cottar's daughter on Dunduff Farm have all found the legends of Carrick excellent subjects for their poems, many of which are now unfortunately forgotten but all of which are well worth reading by those who have a love of the old and forgotten things which made Carrick one of the most interesting and historical parts of Scotland.

Chapter 23

FREEMASONRY IN MAYBOLE

MAYBOLE has long been a stronghold of Freemasonry and the two Lodges in the town are still viable although they have had many vicissitudes throughout their history. Lodge St. John No. 11 is the older body being affiliated to Grand Lodge in 1737, the second Lodge, Royal Arch No. 198, being formed about seventy years later. In 1811 it was proposed that a third Lodge be formed in the town as at this time Maybole was a thriving burgh and it was thought at that time a third lodge would also flourish but Grand Lodge refused the application and, in light of the later downward trend in trade and population, this proved to be a wise decision.

Masons' guilds, from which Freemasonry developed, were in existence hundreds of years ago and trade guilds of operative masons were spread all over Europe. How these guilds of purely operative masons came to be associated with "free and speculative" masons and with religion is a long story, especially the connection with Saint John, and it is impossible to deal with the subject in a short article on the two Maybole Lodges, but a few notes on the development of masonry in Scotland may be helpful in showing how it developed in important centres and proves that at one time Maybole was a town of some standing. The earliest mention of masonry in Scotland is in 1147 when there was an existing Lodge of operative masons in Stirling, and its members were engaged at that time in building Cambuskenneth Abbey. There must have been many similar lodges throughout Scotland at that period when many abbeys were being built and it is almost certain there would be one in Maybole when Crossraguel Abbey was built.

In 1729 the first Scottish Lodge of purely "Free" masons was founded in Edinburgh and named Edinburgh Kilwinning and all members were non-operative. The Capital of Carrick, not to be outdone by Scotland's Capital, also showed great interest in masonry about this time and although a definite date can not be confirmed there seems to have been a thriving lodge of freemasons in the town in 1726, about three years prior to the founding of Edinburgh Kilwinning. The Maybole Lodge was originally called Lodge Kilwinning, but later the name was changed to Lodge Maybole and finally to Lodge Saint John.

In 1736 the Grand Lodge of Scotland was formed in Edinburgh and Maybole was not long in applying for recognition and their charter was confirmed in 1737. The signatures to the confirmation of the charter were the Earl of Cromartie, G.M., William Congalton, S.G.W., Charles Alston and John Dougall, Secretary to the Grand Lodge. The witnesses were Archibald Govan of Greenock, J. Robertson of Hamilton, both members of Lodge Kilwinning, and Archibald Kennedy, an Edinburgh lawyer who was a member of Lodge Maybole. It is interesting to note the name of Archibald Kennedy as he would probably be a member of the Culzean family who have always shown great interest in Freemasonry and the Fourth Marquess of Ailsa, of Culzean, was one of the most prominent members of Freemasonry in Scotland. In 1737 when the Maybole Lodge was granted their charter the Right Worshipful Master was John Fletcher, a joiner in the town and his Depute was Archibald Kennedy, the Edinburgh lawyer previously mentioned, while the Senior and Junior Wardens were William Guthrie and

James Maxwell, both local councillors and very important men in the town.

The first number granted to Maybole was No. 14 but this was changed to No. 10 at a later date and then finally to No. 11 which is its number today. It is a curious point that Lodge St. John No. 11 was one of the sponsors of Lodge Glasgow No. 4 and this is an example of an older lodge having a greater number than a lodge very much its junior in Masonic history and points to the confusion in numbering lodges throughout Scotland.

In 1797 a second lodge was formed in the town, its sponsor being Lodge Royal Arch in Ayr and it was given the number 264 and named Lodge Royal Arch, probably in gratitude to its sponsor in Ayr. Its first R.W.M. was John Andrew whose Depute was John McLure and the Senior Warden was Robert Ramsay with another John McLure as Junior Warden. At a later date the number of this Lodge was changed to 197 and later to its present number of 198. It is interesting to note that at this period Culzean Castle was being built and it is probable many of the operative masons employed on the work, and who lodged in Maybole, would combine to form the new lodge. Lodge No. 198 has always had a greater number of operative members in its roll than No. 11 and even in recent years operative masons and builders have been more predominant in the younger lodge.

It would appear there was little harmony, and definitely no brotherly love, between the two lodges in the town as before a year had passed a complaint was made to Grand Lodge in 1798 by two members of the older lodge, the Rev. William Wright and James Ferguson, that Lodge Royal Arch No. 264 was guilty of the "most heinous irregularities and carried out their ceremonies in a manner alien to the craft." No action was taken by Grand Lodge, however, and No. 264 blythely carried on for two years until 1800 when the R.W.M. of No. 11, Quintin McAdam, again lodged a similar objection to the workings of the junior lodge. The Grand Lodge then seem to have felt there was some justification for the complaint as they issued a stern warning to the Master of No. 264 who must have obeyed orders as there was no further complaint regarding the behaviour of the members or the method of carrying out their ceremonies. Masonic ritual was not standardised then as it is today and probably No. 264 members carried out their ceremonies in a different manner to those of No. 11, who being the older lodge, would feel that the young upstart lodge should fall into line and do as their elders and betters did.

Freemasonry in Maybole has flourished since these days and both lodges are still strong with a good membership roll of fellows of the craft. During the nineteenth century, however, it can be truly said that masons took more part in the public life of the town than they do today. This was a century when trade and wealth increased in Scotland and many public buildings were built throughout the land and nearly all foundation stones for such buildings were laid with full masonic honours, when the members of the craft attended in full regalia with, invariably, bands to lead them. One of the first ceremonies fully detailed was the laying of the foundation stone of the new Parish Church in Cassillis Road, or New Yards as it was then named. On 4th April, 1807, both local lodges marched to the site of the church with bands playing and ensured that the foundation stone was well and truly laid. Each lodge marched separately from their own meeting place and met at the site and after the ceremony again separated and marched back to their own lodges. St. Andrew's Lodge from Girvan marched with the members of St. John's Lodge, Maybole, while Ayr St. Paul's Lodge marched with Lodge Royal Arch No. 198. Both parties remained apart during the whole ceremony and it would seem the bitterness of seven years standing was still strong between the different lodges.

On 19th March, 1834, the laying of the foundation stone of Maybole Gas Works was a great highlight in the town's affairs and once again the two lodges were in the forefront of the proceedings although at the rear of the procession. A procession started from the Town Green and it is minuted that it consisted of "the Friendly Societies, the Town Council, Shoemakers, Tailors and other Craftsmen in their robes of office, with insignia displayed, banners flying and music playing." A mounted horseman led off the procession, followed by the Weavers, who were then the most prominent craftsmen in the town, carrying the emblems of their trade. After them came eight members of the Maybole Carrick Band, the members of the Shoemakers' Guild in full robes, then Wrights with their insignia, followed by the contractors responsible for the building of the new Gas Works. Next in the procession came the Magistrates and members of the Town Council and immediately behind them the remaining nine members of the seventeen strong local band. The rear of the procession consisted of the Masonic Lodges, in full regalia with banners flying, in the order of two Girvan Lodges, Ayr Lodge, Maybole Royal Lodge No. 198 and finally Maybole St. John's No. 11. It must have been a colourful sight to the local townspeople (with the Magistrates and Councillors without robes or insignia feeling rather out of it) and it is said the whole population turned out to view the proceedings and make merry afterwards. History does not record details of the masonic harmonies after the ceremony but it is interesting to note that the Secretary of No. 198 reported to the brethren at the next meeting after the harmony that only nine whisky glasses remained in the lodge from a stock which originally cost £5 19s. 1¾d. after discount was taken off on payment of same.

About the end of the nineteenth century the masons again met in full regalia to lay the foundation stone of a house built in New Yards across from the Bowling Green and this must be the only private house in the town where such a ceremony was held but it is believed the owner of the house was the then R.W.M. of No. 11 and this would be the reason for this unusual occurrence. In 1887 when the new Town Hall was built on the site of the old jail the members of both lodges in the town were again out in full strength to ensure that the operative masons laid the foundations to the satisfaction of their speculative brethren and no doubt the "founding pints" would be issued freely at the harmonies which always followed such outings. In 1905 the foundation stone of the Carnegie Library was laid with full masonic honours in the presence of the Magistrates and Town Council before a large gathering of townsfolk and this was the last occasion when such a ceremony was carried out in the town, but it may be that at some future date a building worthy of recognition will be erected in the old burgh when once again the craftsmen can take their rightful place and ensure the foundations are truly laid.

Although Freemasonry flourished exceedingly well last century the two lodges were not without difficulties from time to time. In 1848 Lodge St. John was cashiered and not shown in the roll of Grand Lodge for that year, for the simple reason it had not paid its annual dues. The membership fees were 2s. 6d. yearly and lodges were granted two years to pay same to Grand Lodge, but any lodge in arrears for five years was struck off the Roll and therefore No. 11 must have been in arrears from 1843. It should be remembered that at this period trade was extremely bad and this decade became known as the "Hungry Forties" and no doubt the members simply could not afford their half crowns which was a considerable sum to them in those days. It was found that if £5 was paid this would put the lodge in good standing again and James Rennie called a meeting of the members who gathered up the necessary sum between them which was remitted to Grand Lodge and on 15th February, 1859, Lodge St. John was again admitted to the roll of Grand Lodge. On the following evening, 16th February, the resuscitated lodge met and elected James Rennie as R.W.M. with William Hannay as his Depute. At this meeting William Hannay, John McMillan, James McMillan and John Kennedy, all members of Lodge Royal Arch No. 198 were affiliated to Lodge St. John No. 11 and it is interesting to note William

Hannay was elected Deputy Master, James McMillan, Senior Warden and John Kennedy was made Junior Warden. It would seem therefore that while the fortunes of No. 11 at this time had waned, No. 198 was in full strength and the old rivalries of 1798 had been forgotten or forgiven and the Junior Lodge members were willing to help their brothers in distress. In recognition of this bond between the two lodges the members of No. 11 invited the members of No. 198 to dine with them on the evening of 28th April, 1859, and the invitation stated that No. 11 members wished to entertain their fellow brethren of No. 198 "with the greatest possible conviviality and to harmonise in the light." It would no doubt be a memorable evening but the memories of those attending seem to have been rather hazy as no reference is made in the Lodge Minute as to how the evening passed.

Finance seems to have been a problem with No. 198 as well as No. 11 and the minute book of the younger lodge often refers to the difficulty in lifting payment of dues from its members. In 1809 Grand Lodge proposed that a Temple be built in the town to house both lodges in the one building and offered financial help in the building of it. A joint meeting was held and on 25th August of that year both lodges sent letters to Grand Lodge regretfully turning down the proposal "due to the exhausted state of the funds in the lodges." In 1864 once again the two lodges considered the possibility of building a Temple for their joint use but after long consideration this project fell through due to "the exhausted state of funds." The "exhausted state of funds" is a phrase often found in the minute books of both lodges, and on 14th January, 1811, the treasurer of No. 11 reported there was only 19s. 9½d., in the funds to carry on the working of the lodge. This is not too surprising when we read that in 1812 on the death of John McAdam, the treasurer of No. 11, his trustees refused to hand back his apron and jewel, which were lodge property, or to pay back £1 11s 6d. of lodge funds which he had in his possession when he died. In the balance of accounts presented on 13th January, 1814, the lodge was in debt to the sum of £3 10s. 2½d., quite a considerable amount in those days when the cost of whisky and ale for a night's harmony among the brethren seldom exceeded five shillings in all.

In early days the lodge members met in various places, mostly local hostelries, but finally for many years they settled on the Commercial Hotel (or Wyllies Hall at it was called) as the home for No. 11 and the Kings Arms Hotel for No. 198. When the Commercial Hotel Hall was put up for sale the members of No. 11 purchased it and formed an attractive Temple by closing up the access to the hotel and fitting it with masonic furnishings. In the 1940s further alterations were carried out and now it would seem to be the settled abode of the brethren. In the 1950s an old former inn in Castle Street, (known as "De Bunk" locally) was acquired by No. 198 and altered to form a compact and suitable place for the carrying out of their ceremonies. It is perhaps a pity the offer by Grand Lodge in 1809 to help in building one Temple for both lodges could not be accepted but perhaps the brethren in the town will yet combine to build a Temple with rooms for harmonies, etc., and this would be a splendid opportunity to bring back the colourful days when the members would "process with full regalia, banners flying, and music to lead them" to lay the foundation stone and thereafter join in an evening of harmony and conviviality. Should this ever happen it would be interesting to note if the treasurers would again have to report on the dearth of glasses remaining in stock as was recorded in 1834.

During the nineteenth century both lodges flourished exceedingly well, even if in debt occasionally, and it was not until the first decade of the present century that a marked decline became apparent in their membership. In that period the Ladywell shoe factory, which had been a great source for new members, failed and trade on a whole was in the doldrums and very few initiates joined the Craft. The first World War, however, brought much needed new blood into both lodges and many airmen stationed at Turnberry joined both No. 11 and No. 198 as well as many townsmen who were leaving to join the forces. During World War Two there were again a great number of airmen from the Turnberry R.A.F. Station who joined the lodges and there must be many brethren spread throughout Britain who claim either No. 11 or No. 198 as their Mother Lodge. At the present time there is great enthusiasm being shown among the younger members of the lodges and in December, 1968, the members of No. 11 elected twenty-seven year old James Davis as R.W.M. and it is probable that he is the youngest master mason ever elected to this position in the whole history of this ancient lodge. No doubt the rise and fall in the fortunes of Maybole Freemasons will be repeated in the years to come but it is to be hoped that such an old established fraternity will continue to thrive in the ancient Capital of Carrick.

Chapter 24

ROBERT BURNS' ASSOCIATION WITH MAYBOLE

"THERE is a purpose of marriage between William Burnes, Bachelor, residing at Alloway, in the Parish of Ayr, and Agnes Brown, Spinster, residing in Maybole, in the Parish of Maybole, of which proclamation is made . . ."

When these banns were "cried" in the old church at the foot of the Kirkwynd in November, 1757, by the Rev. James McKnight (who in 1769 was Moderator of the General Assembly) none of the douce Minniebolers in the congregation that day could possibly know they were listening to the opening lines of a drama which would take its place in Scottish history. The menfolk in the congregation would, as usual, listen to the proclamation without actually hearing it and the bonnets of the goodwives would nod together as much as to say "A' well, she's got a man at last," it being common knowledge that Agnes Brown had broken off a seven years' engagement with a local ploughman, William Nelson, only a year earlier and now, at the age of twenty six, she was about to be married to an older man of thirty six from the neighbouring parish.

It was in Maybole that the parents of Robert Burns met, courted and married and therefore the old town can claim a connection with him. Much has been written about his birthplace at Alloway, his father, William Burnes, originally from Kircardineshire (Clockenhill in the Mearns district) and his life from birth at Alloway to death in Dumfries but little has been mentioned about his connections with the old Capital of Carrick. Burns' mother lived in Maybole for most of her unmarried life and one of his greatest schoolboy friends, William Niven, lived in Maybole where Burns often visited him.

Early in the eighteenth century a William Rennie (or Rainy), who was a baker in Ayr, decided to start a business in Maybole and he and his wife set up a small bakery in the town. On 7th May, 1731, their daughter Agnes married Gilbert Brown (born 1708) who was the son of John Brown, a farmer in Craigenton near Kirkoswald and a tenant of the Earl of Cassillis. At the time of his marriage Gilbert Brown was working as a forester on the estates of the Earl of Cassillis and it is said he set up house with his bride at Whitestone at Culzean and local tradition has it that their daughter Agnes was born there on 17th March, 1732. Whitestone was situated about two hundred yards south of Balchriston Gate Lodge at the entrance to the former Main Avenue to Culzean Castle. The gate lodge has completely gone now and only part of the gable of Whitestone stands in the woodland at the south end of where the highway was straightened in 1965 to improve an awkward corner near the entrance to the Wrack Road which leads to Maybole shore. Shortly afterwards Gilbert Brown became joint tenant with his father in Craigenton Farm and Agnes Brown lived on the farm until she was about 12 years of age. She was the eldest of the family and had four brothers and three sisters when her mother died in 1742. Although then only ten years of age she took over the running of her father's house and she was helped in this difficult task by another girl, Ann Gillespie, who was only a year older than her and who became the wife of John Davidson, the immortal "Soutar Johnnie". Her mother on her deathbed had remarked to her sister, who had come to visit her as she lay dying, that she was not sorry to be going from the trials of this world and she was leaving her children to the care of God as her husband Gilbert would soon get another wife. This prophecy was soon fulfilled for two years after his first wife's death, Gilbert Brown married again, and indeed after the death of his second wife married for the third time.

On the marriage of her father to his second wife, Agnes, who had worked so hard to keep the family together, was no longer needed at Craigenton and she left and went to stay with her grandmother, Mrs. Rennie, in Maybole, which became her hometown for the next thirteen years. Prior to her mother's death Agnes had been taught to read a little by a weaver in Kirkoswald but never received any tuition in the other two R's and knew nothing about arithmetic and could never write even her own name. This accounts for the fact there are no relics of any letter by Burns' mother but it is strange that such an inveterate writer as her son should never have written to her (at least there are no records of any such letters) or written a single line of poetry mentioning her. Neither is there any record of Burns ever visiting his maternal grandfather at Craigenton Farm although he lived in Kirkoswald for a time when he went to school there in his seventeenth year and Craigenton is only about two miles from the village. Probably the fact that his grandfather married again, and his mother was more or less cast out to live with her grandmother in Maybole, embittered Burns against the Browns. Differences between members of families were as common in his day as they are nowadays.

When Agnes Brown moved to Maybole in 1744 she lived with her grandmother for some years and then became housekeeper to her paternal uncle, William Brown, who was a widower and who also lived in the town. Her grandfather, as well as being a baker, worked a small piece of ground near Maybole, (which was a common practice at that time) and had a man, William Nelson, to do the ploughing and odd work on the land. Agnes became acquainted with William Nelson and in 1749 they became engaged to be married. The engagement dragged on for seven years, which was an unusually long time in those days, but possibly Agnes did not wish to leave her widowed uncle to fend for himself. The seven years' engagement proved too much of a strain on William and in 1756 he became involved with another local girl who had his child and Agnes broke off her engagement. Shortly afterwards at the annual fair in Maybole she met her future husband William Burnes and the traditional site of this meeting is marked by a bust of the poet over a building near the bottom of Maybole High Street where it is said the fair booth stood at which they met. At this time William Burnes had been paying court to a girl at Alloway Mill and it is believed he had written a letter to her proposing marriage but had not plucked up enough courage to send it to her. After meeting Agnes Brown he transferred his affection to her and burned the letter to the Alloway Mill lass. After a few months' courtship, when no doubt William paid many visits to Maybole, the couple became engaged and were married on the 15th December, 1757, the bride being twenty six years old and the groom ten years older.

After the marriage the couple took up home at Alloway and from thereon their life has been an open book to all, but few have mentioned that very probably many visits were paid by them and their children to Maybole to visit Agnes' grandmother with whom she had lived for so much of her unmarried life. It is understandable she would not often visit her father's home where a stepmother would probably not be too welcoming, but as Alloway is only five miles from Maybole no doubt the proud mother would visit her granny and childhood friends to show off her children, as all mothers do, and it can be assumed that Robert Burns in his very youthful years was often brought to the old town.

When Robert Burns was seventeen years old his parents decided to send him to a well-known school in Kirkoswald where the headmaster, Hugh Rodgers, was noted as a teacher of trigonometry, land-mensuration and sun-dialling. Robert had shown a great liking for education and his father was anxious that every opportunity should be given him. The fact that he could send his son at the age of seventeen years to a school to learn mensuration, etc., should surely explode the myth that Robert Burns was a poor ploughman and his folks were in straitened circumstances. At that time country boys usually started work about ten or twelve years of age and whatever schooling they may have had was finished, and probably forgotten, by the time they were seventeen.

During his son's formative years William Burns did everything possible to see he was given as good a schooling as possible and indeed in May, 1765, along with four neighbours started a school in Alloway, bringing a young lad of 18 years to tutor their children. Robert Burns did not attend this school long enough to gain much knowledge but undoubtedly he got his love of books and desire to further his education from his first tutor. This love of learning came to Burns not only from his father but from his father's father as he (Robert Burness) joined with some neighbours to build a school and employ a tutor on the farm of Clockenhill which is thought to have been the first school built in the Mearns district. It is not surprising therefore, with such a father and grandfather, that in the middle of the second half of the eighteenth century, when schooling in country districts was practically negligible, that Robert Burns should be sent to board at Kirkoswald and attend a school where such persons as the famous physician Sir Gilbert Blane (who discovered the cure for scurvy) and Sir Andrew Cathcart of Carlton were taught. The boarding of the poet at Kirkoswald was not a difficult matter as his mother's brother, Samuel Brown, lived at Ballochneil about a mile south of Kirkoswald Village and it was arranged Burns should stay there during the summer of 1775 when attending Hugh Rodger's school. The cottage in which Burns lodged is now a ruin with only part of the gables standing at the rear of Ballochneil Farm Cottages, on the farm of Park, about a mile south of Kirkoswald on the road to Turnberry.

MAYBOLE - CARRICK'S CAPITAL

On the same day that Burns entered the school at Kirkoswald another pupil also enrolled and a friendship sprang up between the two youths. The other pupil was William Niven, who was born in Maybole in February, 1759, (a month after Burns' birth) and he was the son of David Niven a well to do merchant and Magistrate of the town. William Niven had just completed a course of classical studies in one of the schools in Maybole (of which there were quite a few at that time) but his father felt he should learn more about arithmetic, etc., to help him when be became a partner in his father's business in Maybole.

During his schooling at Kirkoswald it is believed that Burns went nearly every weekend with Niven to his home in Maybole and stayed there from Saturday till Monday morning when they would both walk the four miles to Kirkoswald before school began. Burns therefore must have known Maybole well at this period of his life but naturally the townsfolk would never dream that the young lad who was such a constant friend of Bailie Niven's son, and who would be in many ploys in the town, as all young men were in these days as well as nowadays, would after his death, a short 20 years later, be immortalised as Scotland's National Poet.

After Burns left the school at Kirkoswald he corresponded with his schoolmate for the rest of his short life. Indeed it is said that his "Epistle to a Young Friend" was originally addressed to William Niven but as the Poet had become aware that "his early companion was pervaded with the single idea of how to become rich (or rather remain rich and become richer) he changed his original intention of connecting the effusion with the name of Niven." The two men were so opposite in nature it is understandable that, although Burns always retained a certain amount of friendship for his schoolmate, in later years he had certainly no deep affection for him and undoubtedly Niven's love of wealth was the cause of their drifting apart.

The Poet and William Niven, however, regularly corresponded after their schooldays and when the first edition of Burns' poems was printed by John Wilson in Kilmarnock in 1786 Niven undertook to sell some copies among his Maybole friends. The cost of a copy (3/-) was quite a lot to pay for a book of poetry in those days (about half a week's wages) but Niven managed to sell seven copies, presumably to some townspeople, and it is unfortunate for the descendants of the purchasers that none of the copies seem to have survived as they would fetch a great price today. Perhaps some fortunate Minnieboler may yet unearth a copy among the old and forgotten things so often stored away in the attics of the older houses in the town. In August, 1786, Burns came to Maybole from Mossgiel to collect the money for the seven copies of his poems and stayed the night with Niven's parents. A party of the poet's admirers (probably the purchasers of the books, among them being Hugh Rodger his old Kirkoswald schoolmaster) met in the Kings Arms Hotel that evening and spent a most convivial night.

The following morning Burns hired a riding horse to take him back to Mossgiel and it would seem he had arrived in Maybole the previous day on foot or had begged a lift from some carrier taking goods to the town. As William Niven's father had carriers bringing merchandise to his shop in Maybole from all districts of Ayrshire, it is probable Burns arranged his visit to fit in with a delivery of goods from the Mauchline district. The hired horse must have been past its best as Burns later described it as a beast that could only "hoyte and hobble and wintle like a Sawmont cobble." At that time (and for decades afterwards) it was a common practice for the Maybole men to say farewell to their visitors by walking with them to the milestone near the top of the Lovers' Lane and Niven and some other members of the party of the previous night arranged among themselves to go to this milestone and wait on Burns as he rode to Ayr before saying their goodbyes. Between them they composed a doggerel about the previous night's carousel and when Burns appeared on the old horse they recited their poem which Burns listened to with great patience. He was not greatly enamoured with their effort, however, and when the long and lamentable farewell was finished he remarked it would only have been necessary to say:

"Here comes Burns on Rosinate
She's damned puir, but he's damned canty."

This is the last factual record of Burns visiting Maybole and on his returning to Mossgiel he wrote to his friend William Niven on 20th August, 1786, thanking him for the hospitality shown him and asking to be remembered to the people with whom he had spent the evening. He referred to "spunky young Tammy" (Thomas Piper, assistant to Dr. Hugh Logan in Maybole) also Mr. Dunn, a schoolmaster in the town, and particularly to "the two worthy old gentlemen I had the honour of being introduced to on Friday, although I am afraid the conduct you forced on me may make them see me in a light I would fondly think I do not deserve." In the letter he paid his respects to Mr. and Mrs. Niven who had been his hosts during his visit and stated that he had been so busy on his return to Mossgiel that he had not been able to fulfill a promise made to his school friend but asked William to remember the old proverb: "The break o' a day's no the break o' a bargain" and to have patience and the matter would be settled. What the promise was and if it was ever carried out is unfortunately unknown. Burns went on to write that every one of his Maybole friends was welcome to a copy of his songs but they were not to be "blazed among the million as I would abhor every prentice mouthing my poor performances in the street."

Although possibly the Poet would again visit Maybole from time to time (at least before he went to Dumfries which was a distant part in those days) there is no record of any such visits but it can be truly said that the old town has many associations with our national poet and the chance meeting of William Burnes of Alloway and Agnes Brown at the booth at the bottom of the

High Street in 1756 was the real beginning of the immortal story of Robert Burns.

Maybole can also claim connection with another Scottish poet. The parents of the famous William McGonagall, "the world's worst poet", lived in Maybole for many years and all their family, excepting William, were born there. They moved to Edinburgh and William was born three months after they left Maybole.

Chapter 25

ABBOT OF CROSSRAGUEL AND JOHN KNOX

MOST Minniebolers at some time or other boast of the fact that a famous debate between two of the greatest churchmen of the 16th century, Quintin, Abbot of Crossraguel and John Knox, the great Scottish Reformer, took place in their town, but few townspeople know much of the details of this event. They have a pride in the fact that their old town should have been chosen as the arena for the debate, but apart from this they have little knowledge of why it should have been held in Maybole or even what it was all about. Although most people know it was some dispute between Catholic and Protestant leaders of that age, the religious controversies of the sixteenth century merit little regard in the twentieth century and excite little, if any, interest. It was, however, a most interesting and historical occasion in the ancient Capital of Carrick and a brief summary of the event may show that Minniebolers have good reason to boast of the fact that the famous "Debate" took place in their old town.

The disputants were Quintin, Abbot of Crossraguel, and John Knox, the famous Scottish Reformer, and the dispute was on the question of the Doctrine of the Mass as celebrated in the Roman Church. Quintin Kennedy was the fourth son of Gilbert, the Second Earl of Cassillis (who was Ambassador to England in 1515-1516) and his wife, Isabella, the second daughter of Archibald, the second Earl of Argyll. They had seven sons and two daughters and Quintin, who became Abbot of Crossraguel, was the most famous of the family. He was described as a man of great piety and austerity of manners, of considerable learning and a zealous and ardent defender of the Church of Rome. He was well versed in all matters relating to his Church and wrote many tracts before his death in 1564 when it was believed, according to some authorities, he was canonised as a Saint. His canonization, however, is a mere fable and probably arose through confusing Quintin with St. Kinedus Eremita, whom Dempster connects with the Cassillis family, although he lived in the seventh century and the surname of Kennedy was not assumed until the thirteenth century. The Abbot was strong in his faith and, under the protection of his nephew, Gilbert, the Third Earl of Cassillis, who was the ruling power in Carrick at that time, he continued as Abbot of Crossraguel until his death in 1564 although the Roman Church had been disestablished in Scotland four years previously and the practice of mass banned by law under penalty of death. Quintin was the last Ecclesiastical Abbot of Crossraguel and he was succeeded by a layman Commendator, Allan Stuart, who was the principal figure in the event which became known as "The Roasting of the Abbot" which is another story in the long chain of interesting events in Carrick history.

The other principal in the Debate was the sombre and fearless John Knox, the noted Reformer, who preached Calvinism throughout Scotland and fiercely attacked the Catholic faith of our young Mary, the tall and three times married Queen of Scots. Born in Haddington, John Knox was educated as a priest and was apostolic notary for the Church of Rome in the Haddington area until 1543 but by 1545 he was tutor to sons of the Protestant families of Langniddry and Ormiston. He has been described as a small stern and unbending man, sallow complexioned, with a long nose and full lips, heavy lidded eyes and a long black beard streaked with grey. He denounced his Catholic

Queen for her gayness and youthful follies and was unrelenting in his fight for Scottish Protestanism. After the murder of Cardinal Beaton at St. Andrews in 1545, John Knox joined the assassins who took refuge within the old Castle of St. Andrews. The castle was successfully attacked by the Regent Arran who captured the murderers and their supporters, and John Knox was sent to France and made a galley slave for nineteen months on a French ship. He was eventually released and on his return to Scotland continued his fight for the Protestant cause and overthrow of the Church of Rome.

It is strange that such a man should, in his later days, cast aside his usual sombre garb and after his second marriage, appear in rich garments with his "bands of taffeta" fastened with gold rings and precious stones. John Knox's first wife was a Berwick woman, Marjory Bowes, grand-daughter of Sir Ralph Bowes and she died in 1560 shortly after Parliament abolished the Roman Church in Scotland. In 1564 when he was fifty nine he married for the second time, his bride being a sixteen year old girl, Lady Margaret Stewart, the daughter of the Earl of Ochiltree and she bore him three daughters. Before his second marriage he paid court to Lady Barbara Hamilton, daughter of the Duke of Chatelherault but did not meet with favour with her and he transferred his attention to the Earl of Ochiltree's daughter where he was more successful. His second wife came of royal blood, being a descendant of the Duke of Albany, younger son of King Robert II and at the time it was said that Knox was hopeful his future sons might one day ascend the throne of Scotland. Although he always professed to be poor he was really quite a wealthy man which is often forgotten by many who picture him as a stern forbidding figure with no thought for material things in life. He died in Edinburgh in 1572 after a full and varied life and a small plaque with the initials "J.K." and the date 1572 set in the roadway in Parliament Square marks the approximate site of his grave. It is surprising that a man who made such a mark in the religious life of Scotland should rest in a grave where people walk over it daily and are entirely unconscious of doing so.

Those were the two men who made history in the old town of Maybole in 1562 when they met to settle their differences of religious principles, and three days later parted without coming to any agreement or decision, each convinced that he was right and the other wrong, as is now so often the case four hundred years later.

The Debate arose because of a sermon preached in the old Church in Kirkoswald by Quintin, Abbot of Crossraguel on 30th August, 1562, when he defended transubstantiation, or the doctrine that in the Mass, or Communion, the bread and wine used are actually changed into the body and blood of Christ. This of course was heresy to John Knox who heard of the sermon when he was at Ochiltree paying court to Margaret Stewart, his second wife, and on Sunday, 6th September, 1562, he attended church in Kirkoswald hoping to challenge the Abbot but on that day the Abbot did not preach in the village. (This visit by John Knox to Kirkoswald is commemorated in the name Knoxhill given to a hill behind the village).

Abbot Quintin on hearing of Knox's visit to Kirkoswald sent him a letter challenging him to a public debate on the Doctrine of the Mass and the challenge was readily accepted by John Knox who suggested the meeting should take place in Ayr. The Abbot, however, held out strongly for the old Capital of Carrick to be the meeting place and finally John Knox agreed to meet him on 28th September, 1562, at 8 o'clock in the morning at the house of Andrew Gray, the Provost (or Principal) of the Old Collegium, in Back Vennal, Mayboill (Knox's spelling of the name of the town). This house stood halfway down the hill then known as Back Vennal, later called Red Lion Brae and now known as John Knox Street. A house called John Knox's House stood for many years in this street, until it was demolished in 1967, bearing a tablet stating it was the house in which the debate took place, but this was hardly correct as experts from the Ministry of Works placed the date of the building much later than the 16th century. This house may have been built on or near the site of the house in which the debate was held and may have incorporated some of the original stonework in it, but it certainly was not the building. For some time it was an inn known as the "Red Lion" (giving rise to the name "Red Lion Brae") but it latterly became a private house. In 1870 it had a thatched roof with an outside open stair between the lower and upper storeys but about that date the roof was slated and the outside stair closed in. When it is taken into account that each contestant was to have forty supporters present at the debate, together with "as many more as the house might hold" it is clear to all that the house known to the townspeople in the 20th century as John Knox's House could not possibly have been the original place of the debate.

The disputants, with their forty supporters on each side and scribes to keep notes of the proceedings, duly met on the date and at the time agreed and the proceedings were opened by a prayer by Knox of which the Abbot commented: "By my faith, it is weill said." The Abbot then put forward his case for transubstantiation and based most of his argument on the contention that when Melchizedec took bread and wine to Abraham he was performing Mass or Communion. This was entirely irrelevant to the argument and Knox would have none of it and strenuously denied the Abbot's reasoning. The Abbot asked the Reformer to prove it was not so and naturally Knox pointed out he could not be expected to prove a negative. The Abbot, shifting his position, then asked what Melchizedec's action did mean and John Knox presumed it was merely an act of hospitality. Quintin argued that Melchizedec could not possibly, by himself show hospitality to such an army as Abraham had and Knox argued he would have helpers to give assistance in serving. The Abbot pled that Abraham's army were laden with the spoils of Sodom and the Reformer countered by arguing such spoils would not include food. It took three days of continuous argument to reach this stage and as the debaters simply indulged in cross talk without reasoned argument it was decided no good could come of further discussion and the meeting broke up with neither party giving way. The whole account of the debate was revised by Knox himself and is to be seen in a *"Black Letter"* reprint published in 1828 by the Auchenleck Library but it makes dry and, to present day readers, rather senseless reading.

To the "forty supporters" on each side the whole debate was wearisome and uninteresting and both parties wanted nothing more than to finish the matter and go home. The supporters of the Reformer especially were embittered at what they considered was the poor treatment given them by the townspeople and during the discussion one of them remarked that if anybody brought bread and wine he would gladly accept it and care naught what it meant. The townspeople were not in favour of the debate from the beginning, most of them being anti-papist, and when the disputants and their followers left after the third day's debate the Minniebolers collected all the books brought by the Abbot for reference purposes and publicly burned them on the Ballgreen. It is believed there were many Reformers in the town at that period even although the Abbot and the Church of Rome still ruled at Crossraguel only two miles south of the town.

It is surprising that so learned a man as the Abbot should have introduced Melchizedec's action into the discussion and that so able a contestant as Knox did not damn the irrelevancy from the start, as surely the giving of bread and wine by Melchizedec to Abraham has no bearing on the doctrine of the Mass nor does it prove or disprove transubstantiation and the Reformer should have held his opponent to the real issue. Four hundred years after the event it is now impossible to give the true reason as to why the Abbot introduced such an irrelevant point but from all accounts he was an astute and able man, well able to judge character and perhaps he played on the fact that

John Knox was known to be an impossible man to argue with, having the complete conviction that he was personally infallible in all things relating to his religious beliefs.

Such is a brief description of the event which is remembered in Maybole to this day as "The Debate". If it had been logically disputed it may have been that Maybole would have been the scene of a great theological decision but this was not to be and the small town in Carrick takes its place with Marburg, where the more famous debate between Luther and Zwingli took place with the same indecisive result.

Chapter 26

THE COUNTESS AND THE GYPSY

ALL old towns have local legends which are handed down from generation to generation until in time they become accepted as factual and Maybole is no different from other towns in this respect. Every Minnieboler is reared to believe that the King of the Gypsies eloped with a Countess of Cassillis and after the enraged Earl caught up with the elopers he hanged the gypsy and his followers on the Dule Tree at Cassillis and imprisoned his errant spouse in the old castle at the foot of the High Street for the rest of her life and the room with the oriel window facing up the street is pointed out to this day as the "Countess's Room".

Chambers, in his *"Picture of Scotland* gives at length his version of the escapade and the following extract from his book is perhaps the best way to recount the story which has been told in Maybole for generations. According to Chambers the story of the elopement is as follows:

"John, the sixth Earl of Cassillis, a stern Covenanter, and of whom it is recorded by Bishop Burnet, that he never would permit his language to be understood but in its direct sense, obtained to wife Lady Jean Hamilton, a daughter of Thomas, first Earl of Haddington, a man of singular genius, who had raised himself from the Scottish bar to a peerage and the best fortune of his time. The match, as is probable from the character of the parties, seems to have been one dictated by policy; for Lord Haddington was anxious to connect himself with the older peers, and Lord Cassillis might have some such anxiety to be allied to his father-in-law's good estates; the religion and the politics of the parties, moreover, were the same. It is therefore not very likely that Lady Jean herself had much to say in the bargain. On the contrary, says report, her affections were shamefully violated. She had been previously beloved by a gallant young knight, a Sir John Faa of Dunbar, who had perhaps seen her at her father's seat of Tynningham, which is not more than three miles from the town. When several years were spent and gone, and Lady Cassillis had brought her husband three children, this passion led to a dreadful catastrophe. Her youthful lover, seizing an opportunity when the Earl was attending the Assembly of Divines at Westminster, came to Cassillis Castle, a massive old tower on the banks of the Doon, four miles from Maybole, then the principal residence of the family, and which is still to be seen in its original state. He was disguised as a gipsy and attended by a band of these desperate outcasts. In the words of the ballad,

"They cuist the glaumourye ower her."

But love has a glaumourye for the eyes much more powerful than that supposed of old to be practised by wandering gypsies, and which must have been the only magic used on this occasion. The Countess condescended to elope with her lover. Most unfortunately ere they had proceeded very far, the Earl came home, and, learning the fact, immediately set out in pursuit. Accompanied by a band which put resistance out of the question, he overtook them, and captured the whole party, at a ford over the Doon, still called the Gypsies' Steps, a few miles from the castle. He brought them back to Cassillis, and there hanged all the gypsies, including the hapless Sir John, upon "the Dule Tree", a splendid and most umbrageous plane, which yet flourishes on a mound in front of the Castle Gate, and which was his gallows-in-ordinary, as the name testifies. As for the

Countess, whose indiscretion occasioned all this waste of human life, she was taken by her husband to a window in front of the Castle, and there, by a refinement of cruelty, compelled to survey the dreadful scene—to see, one after another, fifteen gallant men put to death, and at last to witness the dying agonies of him who had first been dear to her, and who had imperiled all that men esteem in her behalf. The particular room in the stately old house where the unhappy lady endured this horrible torture, is still called "the Countess's Room". After undergoing a short confinement in that apartment, the house belonging to the family at Maybole was fitted for her reception, by the addition of a fine projecting staircase, upon which were carved heads representing those of her lover and his band; and she was removed thither and confined for the rest of her life—the Earl in the meantime marrying another wife. One of her daughters, Lady Margaret, was afterwards married to the celebrated Gilbert Burnet. While confined to Maybole Castle, she is said to have wrought a prodigious quantity of tapestry, so as to have completely covered the walls of her prison; but no vestige of it is now to be seen, the house having been repaired (otherwise ruined) a few years ago, when size-paint had become a more fashionable thing in Maybole than tapestry. The effigies of the gypsies are very minute, being subservient to the decoration of a fine triple window at the top of the staircase, and stuck upon the tops and bottoms of a series of little pilasters, which adorn that part of the building. The head of Johnnie Faa himself is distinct from the rest, larger, and more lachrymose in the expression of the features. Some windows in the upper part of Cassillis Castle are similarly adorned; but regarding them tradition is silent."

Such is the legend of the love-lorn lady and her gallant gypsy which all MinnieboUers swear to be true, but "facts are chiels that winna ding" and the truth is there is no truth in the story. It is impossible to know what authority Chambers had for identifying the lady in the case with Jean, sixth Countess of

Cassillis, and documents in existence to this day prove him wrong in every point.

John, sixth Earl of Cassillis, and husband of the much maligned lady was a person of great virtue and a zealous Presbyterian, being one of the three elders sent to the Westminster Assembly of Divine in 1643. In 1621 he married as his first wife, Jean, daughter of Thomas first Earl of Haddington and they had one son and two daughters. All records show they lived a happy life together for twenty odd years until Lady Jean died in December 1642. On her death Lord Cassillis wrote the following letter to Lord Eglinton inviting him to the funeral of his Countess:

"My noble lord. It hath pleaseit the Almightie to tak my deir bedfellow frome this valley of teares to hir home (as hir Best in hir last wordis called it). There remaines now the last duetie to be done to that pairt of hir left with ws, qch I intend to pforme vpoun the ffyft of Januar nixt. This I intreat may be honoured with yor. Lo. presence, heir at Cassillis, yt. day, at Ten in the morning, and from this to our buriall place at Mayboille, qch shal be taken as a mark of yor. Lo. affection to

yor. Lo. humble servant,
CASSILLIS.

Cassillis the 15th Dcr., 1642".

If, as Chambers states, the Earl had imprisoned his erring wife in Maybole Castle and bigamously married another woman it is strange that a devout member of the Assembly of Divines should be so hypocritical as to refer to "my deir bedfellow" when inviting Lord Eglinton to attend her funeral. While the sixth Earl did in fact marry again it was not until February, 1644, more than a year after the death of Lady Jean, that he married Margaret, only daughter of William, tenth Earl of Errol and widow of the eldest son of the first Duke of Roxburgh. It was by this marriage that the heir to the title, John, seventh Earl of

Cassillis was born, as the son born to Lady Jean died during the sixth Earl's lifetime.

Surely these facts alone entirely disprove Chambers' story of the elopement but there are other errors in his description of the affair. He speaks of a room being added to Maybole Castle with an oriel window with carved heads representing Johnnie Faa and his men and would seem to indicate this was built to house the Countess during her imprisonment but this staircase and room was in existence long before Lady Jean's day. He also adds she was imprisoned for the rest of her life in Maybole Castle whereas there is proof she died at Cassillis in December, 1642. Chambers is also wrong in placing the "Gypsies' Steps" over the River Doon as "a few miles from the Castle" as they are only a few hundred yards below Cassillis House.

When fact is placed against fiction in this case, as always, fact must conquer and whilst the story of Johnny Faa and the Countess will, it is hoped, continue to be handed down to future Minniebolers, the truth must be remembered and the character of the much maligned and "wanton lady" redeemed.

There may be some grounds for believing that the story is founded upon a reality, however, and that the main features of the tragedy are based on some incident in history long before Lady Jean's time as there is a well-known old ballad of "Johnnie Faa" with many versions which tells the story of a noble knight who loved a lady before she married another and who disguised himself as a gypsy and captured his lady love when her husband was away from his castle. This ballad was sung all over Scotland at one time but differed slightly from district to district. Some versions start "The gypsie's cam' to our gude lord's yett," others "The gypsie's cam' to the Castle yett" and the version most common in Ayrshire "The gypsie's cam' tae Cassillis yett". It is therefore natural to associate the ballad with Cassillis and an easy step to link the name of Lady Jean with Johnnie Faa who was by no means an imaginary character. He was in fact the head of the Egyptians, or Gypsies, in Scotland and he was granted a letter under the Privy Seal from James V, dated 15th February 1540, establishing his authority over all the gypsies in Scotland and calling on all sheriffs in the country to "assist him in executione of justice upoun his company and folkis."

Tradition has it that Johnnie Faa and his men did from time to time stay in the district and is said he had a camp near Culroy—"the glen of the king." (An interesting old local story tells of a member of the Faa clan, Roy by name, quarrelling with his wife, Minnie, when she lifted a knife and ran at her man. Their son stepped in between them and cried "Na, na, Minnie shant kill Roy," and thus arose the names of the two villages Minishant and Culroy). Taking the fact that Johnnie Faa did at sometime live near Culroy, within a mile or two of Cassillis, it is understandable that the ballad of "Johnnie Faa" should be linked with the name of a lady of that house.

Chapter 27

MISCELLANY

WHEN the civic heads of the town "process" through the streets they are led by the Town Officer who carries a red and white staff. This has been the practice for hundreds of years and the right to carry the staff is based on an Act of Parliament passed by James I in 1432 which stated: "Ane officer of Regality must gae furth before his folk carrying ane rod or staff, three quarters of a yaird lang, tane pairt coloured reid and tother pairt coloured quhite." For generations a plain red and white rod was carried before the councillors but it was lost in the middle of last century and for about a hundred years the Town Officer did not display this badge of office. In 1945 Mrs. Chesney presented a new staff to the Council in memory of her father, Mr. James Miller, who had been Provost from 1912 to 1921. The new staff was made from a piece of the old Dule Tree of Cassillis, gifted by Frances, Marchioness of Ailsa, and Mr. James Jeff, the Kirkcudbright artist, carved a dolphin on one end of it and a burghal coronet on the other, painted it red and white as laid down in the statute of 1432, and now the councillors can march in order as their predecessors did.

A note in the Town Records about the end of the eighteenth century refers to the "toun flag" being in need of repair but no further reference is made to it and it must have lain until it rotted away. Mrs. Chesney again generously stepped in to bring back the old traditions which had been forgotten and in 1952 she presented the burgh with a new "toun flag". The flag has a yellow background, the red chevron of Carrick and the rampant blue lions of Bruce and is flown in the Town Green every year on the 14th November to commemorate the granting of the town's Charter in 1516 and on other noteworthy occasions.

The curfew was tolled from the town steeple for centuries until it was stopped during the Second World War and the Council decided not to continue it after the cessation of hostilities much to the regret of the older generation who were reared to the sound of the curfew each night. In days gone by the bell was rung each night at 8 p.m. when all douce Minniebolers were expected to be in their own homes. Last century the Council decided to ring the bell each morning at 6 a.m. to get the townspeople out of bed to start work and put back the nightly curfew from 8 p.m. to 10 p.m. After the first World War the morning rising bell was discontinued but the evening curfew was rung and many householders checked their clocks with the "ten o'clock bell". It is a pity the old custom of ringing the curfew was not renewed after the war as Maybole was one of the few towns in Scotland which had kept up the practice for hundreds of years.

The people of Maybole were mainly staunch Protestants and the town was a noted centre of the Covenanters and many are the tales told of local "preachings" in the hills around the town in these troublesome times. In 1678 the largest conventicle ever held in Scotland took place at Craigdow Hill when over 7,000 people gathered to listen to Peden and Cargil and other preachers, and 600 armed men were posted round the hill to guard the worshippers from attack by the government force stationed in the district to quell the Covenanters. Peden and Cargil were frequent visitors to the district as is evidenced by the local names of "Peden's Thorn" at Cultizeoun, "Cargil's Stone" on the Cross Roads, "Peden's Cave" at the Nick o' the Balloch and many other places. The original National Covenant, which is exhibited in the Antiquarian Museum in Edinburgh contains the signatures of many Maybole men and at the November Fair in the town in 1677 so many swords were sold to known Covenanters from the swordmakers' booths that a special report on this strange and sudden desire for arms was sent to the government.

One of the most noted covenanters in the district was John McLymont of Auchalton Farm near Crosshill. He was persecuted for years and his home was burned down and he and his family had to hide on Glenalla moor where the soldiers searched for them for days but fortunately were unable to find them. For years he could not return to his farm but finally, when the troublesome times were over, he and his wife returned to Auchalton where he lived until his death at the age of 69 on 1st November, 1714. He is buried in the old cemetery at Kirkport under a large "thruch" stone which is near the entrance gate and on which the following interesting inscription is engraved:

> "Under this neighbouring monument lies
> The Golden dust of man and wife,
> Of pious line, both soon shall rise,
> To long expected, glorious life.
> They for their constancy and zeal,
> Still to the back, did prove good steel
> For our Lord's royal truths and laws
> The ancient covenanted cause
> Of Scotland's famous Reformation,
> Declining laws of usurpation."

Many years after his death an old sword was found hidden in the thatched roof of Auchalton farmhouse and it was believed to belong to the staunch covenanter who may have bought it at Maybole Fair in 1677.

During the covenanting times Grier of Lagg was stationed in the district with troops to quell the local people and it is said he made his headquarters in the Dunnering Inn which was a famous hostelry in Weaver Vennal for many generations.

One of the most famous family feuds in Scotland raged for years around the old town of Maybole when the Bargany and Cassillis factions of the Kennedy family were at each others' throats. The feud started through the Earl of Cassillis persuading Allan Stewart, Commendater of Crossraguel Abbey, to sign over the lands of Crossraguel to the Earl and the story of this persuasion has been handed down, and greatly embellished, throughout the years. The Commendater (not the Abbot as so many wrongly state when they speak of the "Roasting of the Abbot") was loath to sign over the property to the Earl and he was taken to Dunure Castle and there toasted over a fire in the "black vault of Dunure" until he finally succumbed to pressure and signed the necessary documents. Allan Stewart naturally complained of his treatment at the hands of the Earl who was summoned by the Privy Council to appear personally before the Regent and the Secret Council, but they, with all the facts before them, treated the Earl extremely leniently, which tends to prove the incident was not so drastic as it seems now when related four hundred years after the event. The Laird of Bargany, however, who was the brother-in-law of Allan Stewart did not accept the Regent's findings on the case and chose to be his own judge and executioner by bitterly attacking the Cassillis branch of his family and this was the start of one of the most deadly and disastrous feuds in the country which was finally ended by the death of young Bargany at Ladycross in 1601.

Part of the feud which was centred around the old town of Maybole culminated in the trial of the Mures of Auchendrane which is said to be one of the most remarkable in the whole range of the criminal annals of this, or any other, country. On 3rd January, 1597, John Mure of Auchendrane with a party of followers came to Maybole and attempted to murder Sir Thomas Kennedy of Culzean who was then residing at his home in the town (where the Union Bank now stands) but the attempt failed and Sir Thomas managed to escape by hiding in the old kirkyard at the bottom of the hill below his home. Sir Thomas prosecuted Mure for the assault and attempted murder, but finally the parties became seemingly friendly when Mure apologised and, to seal the friendship between the two families, Mure's son married the daughter of Sir Thomas. Mure was then related to both the powerful Kennedy factions as his wife was a daughter of Bargany and his son the husband of a daughter of the Culzean family and he was in a position where he could perhaps have worked to put a stop to the feud. He was a false and treacherous man, however, and could not bury his enmity against the Casillis branch and it was he who really influenced young Bargany against the Earl of Cassillis and in the end brought about the death of the young man. Sir Thomas Kennedy of Culzean, although tutor and guardian of his nephew, the young Earl of Cassillis, kept apart from the quarrel, considering his connection as father-in-law to young Auchendrane to be too strong to be broken, even to assist his nephew. Unfortunately the Mures of Auchendrane were of a different stamp and they nursed their hatred to all connected with the House of Cassillis. Sir Thomas had to visit Edinburgh on business and sent word of his proposed visit to the Capital to Mure, offering to attend to any business which Mure might wish carried out while Sir Thomas was in the city. The message regarding the visit was carried to Mure by a schoolboy from Maybole named Dalrymple, who was nicknamed "Johnny Glegfoot", and when he received it Mure told the schoolboy to take it back to Maybole and say he had not been able to deliver it as Mure was away from home. Mure then gathered some of his followers together and waited on Sir Thomas on his journey to Edinburgh at a place called Duppil, a little to the west of the town of Ayr, and when Sir Thomas rode past they set on him and murdered him, and stole his money, rings and gold buttons from his coat. To prevent "Johnny Glegfoot" from betraying them the Mures sent him out of the district but he returned and was also murdered on the instructions of Mure. The murderers were apprehended and their trial dragged on until finally both father and son were found guilty and were beheaded in 1611 after one of the most famous trials in Scottish history. Sir Walter Scott based his "Tragedy of Auchendrane" on this incident of local history and the story should be read by all Minniebolers who would find it of great interest.

Many townspeople are often confused when mention is made of the "Auld Kirk" at Kirkport and are apt to think of the "Auld College" as the building in question but the two churches, although near each other were entirely separate buildings. The Old Collegium was a Roman Catholic church and originally stood in its own grounds, which were quite extensive, and had its own burial plot around it, entirely apart from what is now called the "Old Cemetery". Part of the burial ground of the Old College was east of where the Lorne Tannery formerly stood and where the council houses are now in Manse Street and for a time the area was used as a fairground, and locally known as "Aggie Henderson's Field". Some tombstones were uncovered when building was carried out on the site but they were mostly so defaced it was impossible to trace the dates on them but they must have been very old. The Parish Church was built adjacent to the "Old College" and a new "God's Acre" formed round it at the foot of Kirkwynd and was there until the new church was built in New Yards in 1808. Traces of the "Auld Kirk" may still be found near the present entrance to the old cemetery.

The oldest tombstone in the old town cemetery is beside the west wall and it is inscribed "Heir lyis ane honest man, Moreis Makmorrie, and his spouse, quha deceist in ye last of October 1618". There must have been older tombstones as the cemetery was in use in the 16th century but they probably crumbled away and would be removed. It has been said the cemetery was actually in use from the 13th century but this is only conjecture as no trace can be found of any burials so early as has been suggested and it is improbable that the small town required two cemeteries as the burial ground of the Old College would be sufficient for all interments, especially as all townsfolk were Roman Catholics until the 16th century. Although the new cemetery at Tunnoch was opened in 1851 interments took place quite often in the old one up until the second decade of the present century. For many years the old burial ground was allowed to lie rather derelict but recently old houses have been removed from around it and the boundary walls have been rebuilt in attractive stonework and the old God's Acre is now trim and neat. It is well worthy of a visit by townspeople interested in the history of the town, as many of the people whose names are household words in Maybole are buried there and some of their tombstones have interesting inscriptions. The tombstone of the famous Bailie Niven and his wife is situated in the centre of the site of the old church, a stone near the gate marks the grave of David Dunn, a well-known schoolmaster who spent a night carousing in the Kings Arms with Robert Burns in 1786, and many of the old stones are engraved with the usual skulls, crossbones, hourglasses, etc., while one has no inscription whatsoever, and, from the appearance of it, never was inscribed, which seems strange as the old generations were always keen on long and fulsome epitaphs. Many of the present Minniebolers could trace their forefathers back for generations by spending an odd hour browsing among the monuments in the "Auld Cemetery".

Although most of the Maybole men were staunch Covenanters and strict sabbatarians some were also hard headed farmers who considered the reaping of their hard won crops was of primary importance and this is illustrated by a curious little story of the early 19th century. At a Sunday morning service in September, 1807, the Rev. James Wright intimated from his pulpit that, as the day was good and ideal for harvesting the crops, those who wished to do so could work in their fields lest there be a change in the weather and the crops ruined, and they could do so without violating the Sabbath. Such an intimation was tantamout to heresy to many of the congregation (probably all the non farmers) and it caused such an uproar that it was taken to the Presbytery and an enquiry was set up and finally the matter was taken to the Synod in October, 1808. The Synod ruled that all members of the church "must be sensible as to the sanctification of the Sabbath" and to "beware how far they allowed cases of necessity which may form a stumbling block to any of the parishioners". It seemed that while Synod had to damn the Rev. Wright's practical advice to make hay while the sun shone they were not averse "to cases of necessity", in this instance the reaping of the crops. Perhaps they had in the back of their minds that the stipends came from the crops and a ruined harvest meant less stipend. The Town Council supported the Rev. Wright's action in advising the farmers "to make full use of suitable weather, irrespective of the day", and sent a petition to the Synod stating that in their opinion there was no need for any enquiry. They pointed out that although the Minister had advised those with crops to secure to get on with it he had also intimated there would be an afternoon service in church for those who did not need to work.

On Saturday, 30th May, 1953, a historical pageant was held in the town to commemorate the coronation of Queen Elizabeth which was to take place on 2nd June, 1953. This pageant was undoubtedly the greatest event held in the old town for very many years and every organization from Boy Scouts to Church Guilds took part in providing actors to show the town's history from its earliest days up to the coronation year. The "Pageant of Maybole" was written and produced by Raymond Lewis who was a teacher in Carrick Academy and he faithfully reproduced for the townspeople all the interesting events which had occurred in the old township over hundreds of years. The procession started at Carrick Academy and, led by the Town Band, "processed" to the Sheep Park where there were tableaux showing a conventicle, the roasting of the Commendater of Crossraguel, Marjory, mother of Robert the Bruce hawking at Turnberry, smugglers with their brandy kegs, knights in armour, and many other scenes from local history. The procession included people representing Robert the Bruce, Robert Burns, John Loudon McAdam, Sir Gilbert Blane, James Rodger and many other notables connected with the town including General Eisenhower the town's first freeman. Fortunately it was a beautiful summer day and for the thousands who came from far and near the "Pageant of Maybole" was a wonderful living spectacle of the town's history. Once again the friendly and couthy atmosphere of the old town was emphasised by the harmony in which the people worked together to make "their" pageant something worthwhile and their efforts were greatly appreciated and will be long remembered.

It is unfortunate that such an old town has not a small museum where old pictures of places and people could be shown along with a weaver's loom and a cobbling bench which were the tools of the trades which made Maybole a thriving town in the past. There must be many articles of interest in the town which could be gathered together and put on display so that those interested in old Maybole could see how their forefathers lived, and maybe such a museum will be formed. Meantime the Council Chamber is the only place where some items of local interest can be seen and on its walls there are pictures showing the visit of Queen Elizabeth and Prince Phillip, the freedom ceremony for General Eisenhower and a copy of the Town Charter of 1516. The Town Staff and the old town bell are also on view in the Council Chamber and the photographs of all provosts of the burgh since 1882. These are:

Charles Tennant	1882-84
James Gray	1884-85
John Marshall	1885-94
James Ramsay	1894-1905
William McKellar	1905-12
James Miller	1912-21
Hugh Fairlie	1921-24

John Crawford	1924-27
John McCubbin	1927-36
James McCulloch	1936-42
John Gibson	1942-44
Thomas Hicks	1944-47
Alexander Burns	1947-51
James T. Gray	1951-54
Thomas Murray	1954-57
John Dunlop	1957-60
Mrs. Sarah Dunn	1960-63
John McDowall	1963-66
James Macrae	1966-69
William Cuthbert	1969-

The photographs are in a frame in chronological order and show that the provosts had no chain of office until the time of Provost McCubbin who was first to wear it. This provost's chain was presented by Mr. John Edgar, who was a member of the Council for many years and it is a beautifully designed silver gilt collarette with a large pendant with the burgh coat of arms in enamel. The links are in the shape of the initial "M" and are engraved with the names and dates of the provosts since the time of Provost McCubbin. The photograph of Provost Thomas Murray is the first to show the robes of office which were purchased by the Council during his term of provostship. In 1952 the Bailies' badges were presented to the Council by some local people who subscribed to a fund raised to purchase them and the Senior Bailie's badge shows the seal of the burgh and the Junior Bailie's the Town Crest. These originally were fitted with lovely silk collarettes in the town's colours but are now suspended on small gilt chains which are not so decorative as the silk collarettes. When Scotland is "regionalised", as is now proposed and Town Councils, as such, are swept away, it is to be hoped these badges of office will be preserved in some manner and not be stored away and lost as has happened in the past.

It can be truly said that the power behind the Provost's chair in most small towns is the Town Clerk and Maybole has indeed been fortunate in the men who have filled this office. Since the days of Provost Tennant there have been only four Town Clerks, the first being James Gibson, the second James M. Gibson (son of previous clerk), David Briggs and the present clerk, John Boyd. Indeed it can be said that only two of these men have really directed the councillors in matters of law, etc., during the past eighty odd years as James Gibson was clerk for nearly fifty years, his son, James M. Gibson was clerk for less than a year and David Briggs was in office for over thirty years, retiring about seven years ago to be succeeded by his business partner, John Boyd. This is a record of long service which few towns can equal and another point regarding the town clerks which, it is believed, few other burghs can claim, is the fact that all these men were born and bred in the town. It would seem that the old custom of hundreds of years still persists and Minniebolers feel they are fit to govern their own affairs with their ain folks as they did when they ignored the laws of the country at the time of the Reformation and on many other occasions.

There have been many changes in the old town over the past sixty years and those who emigrated to Canada and elsewhere around 1909 would find it difficult to reconcile their memories of the place with present day facts. At the beginning of this century the High Street was cobbled and the traffic consisted of farm carts and an occasional high wheeled gig drawn by a high stepping pony and invariably followed by a covey of boys anxious to "haud yer horse, mister" should it stop at "Cowan's" or the Kings Arms or some of the shops. Nowadays the street is asphalted, "no waiting" is the rule and the endless stream of cars and lorries makes it a perilous journey indeed to cross from one pavement to another. Sixty years ago everyone stopped to admire, and wonder, at the first car in the district which was owned by the Marquess of Ailsa (registered number SD1) and it was a great event when His Lordship appeared in town in it.

It had solid, rubber tyred wheels, was steered by a pole like a boat's rudder, and the occupants sat facing each other in a box-like contraption at the back while the chauffeur sat perched on a high seat in front and grimly drove along at the terrific speed of about 15 miles per hour. Nowadays Rolls Royces, Rovers, M.G's, etc., race down the old High Street (often at speeds well over the permitted 30 m.p.h.) and no one turns their head to look at them, but all stop to stare if a tinker's pony and float spanks along the New Yards with a lurcher dog gliding along below the axle.

An old inhabitant would also find great changes in the shops and would miss many of the kenspeckle tradespeople and the manner of displaying their merchandise. No longer do the long carts from "Castlehill" and "Balchriston" unload barrels of newly dug early "Ayrshires", topped with green shaws, at the grocers, to be displayed on the pavement at the shop doors, invariably flanked by a keg of salt herrings. The townspeople could always be assured of a cheap and wholesome dinner of tasty "new tatties and greentails" with herrings fried in oatmeal, as Johnny McClure from Maidens would fill a housewife's apron with silver herring for a sixpence. Nowadays the potatoes are hygienically packed in polythene bags, (and invariably taste of inferior soap) while the herrings seems to have shrunk in size and grown in price. The merchants then displayed many of their wares on the pavements at the shop doors, or hung them on the walls, and it was often difficult to walk up the pavements for barrels of potatoes, kegs of herrings, glass cases displaying large tins of biscuits, with brushes, pots and pans hanging round the doors. If one had to step off the pavement to get round such merchandise it really did not matter much as the most one could fear was a horse breathing down one's neck. Nowadays the pavements are all bare of such impediments but one has to walk warily on the narrow pavements lest a large lorry rushing past should be too close to the kerb and spin one on to the street with the swish of its passing.

Sixty years ago there were many grocers in the town but "Gibbie", "Haddy", "Soda", "P.A.", "Hungry Archie", "Wattie" and many others have all passed away and now the housewives depend mainly on "The Store" and "Templetons" for their groceries with "R.A.O.'s" as the last stronghold of the private grocers. Many shops are closed and it is unlikely they will reopen as most of the townspeople do their shopping in Ayr. This has naturally harmed traders in the town and it has affected the drapers most of all as only McClymonts is left of the great number of drapers and tailors such as Wright, Jackson, McCreath, McCubbin, Murray, Miller, Wallace, Curran and others who clothed the folks of the town and district in the old days before the first World War.

The foot of the High Street would not be recognisable now to any old Minniebolers who left the town at the time of the great "exodus". The grand new Post Office stands where "Tup" Dobbie's yard used to be, "Doctor" Reid the chemist and "Willie" Burns the cycle agent, are now nearly forgotten, with the small windows to their shops, and the large bottles of blue and pink coloured water in "Doctor" Reid's windows and a Raleigh bicycle hanging from ropes above "Willie" Burns's door. "Haddy" Maltman's and McGhee's, the fruiterers is now a coffee room and bakers shop, while "Davie" Adam's, Scott the chemists and "Bob" Neil's stationers shop is now one large plate glass and chromium fronted showroom. The shop of "Cree" the baker, famous for his ashet pies, has been displaced by a cafe; "Amos" has passed away although his business is still carried on (one cannot get a plate of delicious hot peas with lashings of "brae" now, however); "Almonds" chip shop has disappeared and the boys of the present day will never relish "a plate of chips and a bottle of Vimto" in the back shop with the green lino covered tables and the sawdust on the floor. "Paraffin Oil" Bone, "Nellie McCulloch's" and Thomson the plumber, are now only memories and the site of their shops is now covered by a grand new Supermarket. The "Hen's Castle", Whitefords,

Battison's, McTaggarts, etc., are now only half remembered names to the older people and entirely unknown to the younger generation, but before the first Word War these were all tradespeople who supplied the townsfolk with all their needs from silver teaspoons to paraffin oil and "sweeties for the wean".

The shops at the top of the High Street are also all changed and "Cheenie" McClymont's, the "Spooncreel", the Buttercup and Eastmans, etc., are now all gone and unknown to the younger generation but nostalgically remembered by the older folks. To a returning wanderer the School Vennal would indeed be strange as there is no "Daisy" Kennedy's to slake one's thirst, no Miss Dinning to supply a fancy box of chocolates for the girl friend and no window full of hazel nuts for the old black cat to snooze on in "Maggie Rubbish's". The old Post Vennal is also greatly changed and there is no longer "Granny" Allan to dispense treacle yill or herb beer or "Francie" to buy old clothes and rabbit skins, etc.

One of the saddest changes to a Maybole man revisiting his hometown would be the complete disappearance of "Dents" tobacco shop in the old Spooncreel. No boy who puffed at his first Woodbine under the iron steps of Buchty Brig can ever forget "Dents". When the shop door was opened the sharp "ting" of the bell above it always made one falter for a moment and then one stepped out of a mundane world into a shrine to Lady Nicotine. Every possible brand of snuff, cigarettes, cigars and tobaccos lined the shop shelves and the indescribable aroma of tobacco pervaded the whole shop. Everything seemed a hopeless mixter maxter but when asked for any brand of cigarettes from Woodbines to Passing Cloud, any cigar from the finest Corona to the strongest Cheroot, or any tobacco from the heavy Bogey Roll to the finest cut Havana the "Old Man" (who never seemed to take his hat off) could unerringly put his hand straight to the brand wanted. The shop was small (two customers completely filled it) and, in memory, always dim, as the small window admitted little light and the half-glass door none whatever, but the small mahogany counter was so highly polished it gleamed like a pool of rich brown ale. The counter was always covered with all manner of pipes from the common clays to the magnificent meerchaums in their read velvet lined cases, with their bowls like bows of graceful yachts. Lucky indeed was the man who could afford one of these, to treasure and nurture it until it turned the colour of clear run honey and became the envy of his fellow men. The showpiece on the counter was the brass scales, so fragile in appearance and so symbolical of a tobacconist's shop. The small brass trays were polished until they gleamed with a lustre and depth far superior to gold and the little brass round weights were ever carefully marshalled and graded like soldiers in their little holes along the front of the mahogany base of the scales. This was a true tobacconists where the scent of the raw tobacco was much more titillating than the actually smoking of it. Today a tobacconists is as bright and sterile as a dairy, with the tobacco in hermetically sealed tins or polythene packaging. This may be more hygienic and a sign of progress but the lads of today can never experience the thrill of standing in the "Spooncreel" with noses twitching at the erotic scents which somehow seemed to give added value to the penny packet of Woodbines which was all a youth of a few decades past could afford to spend. "Dents" was not just an ordinary shop to Maybole smokers, it was an institution and it deserves more than a mere paragraph, but if ever its story is to be written it can only be by the proprietor's son, Alan, who left his hometown many years ago to cross the Border and became another famous Minnieboler who has made his mark in the literary world.

To the older generation the most striking change in the town must be the emptiness of the High Street on a Saturday night. Fifty or sixty years ago it was thronged every Saturday night up to about 10 or 11 p.m. and "Saunders" and the other message boys with their big baskets could hardly press through the crowds to make their last deliveries of the weekend's messages. The "message boys" are now practically unknown in the town but fifty years ago they were employed by all traders who prided themselves on giving every service to their customers and messages were delivered to homes by those boys. They were a cheerful lot and could invariably whistle like linties and every new song was soon popularised by the whistling message boys who could unerringly pick out the favourite tunes in a manner which would make modern "Disc Jockeys" turn green with envy. Although usually small in stature the boys could carry huge baskets of messages on their heads, with a round leather "scone" to protect their shaggy pates, and these "scones" were grand missiles to throw at other message boys from rival shops. While motor vans may deliver messages more efficiently today the whistling and happy youths are much missed by the older folks.

On a summer evening everyone promenaded the High Street and had time to chat with neighbours on the week's events, watch "Smillie" with his jacket off challenging all and sundry at the Pump, marvel at the dancing bear jigging round a pole at the head of the Kirkwynd or listen to the German bands, which often played in the town. At the foot of the street one could always count on seeing the white pony from Abbeymill waiting patiently on its master returning from his Saturday night's outing, while Inspector Barbour, resplendent in his uniform, would benignly watch the "drouths" winding home and instruct his constables to see they got safely home to their spouses who would deal with them much more firmly than any Bailie at court on Monday morning.

Nowadays Maybole is a "ghost town" on a Saturday night, and one could fire the proverbial shotgun up the High Street without endangering life. The miniskirted girls and long haired boys are off to "the dancing" in Ayr or somewhere else, the younger married people are away in their cars around the country, many of the older women (and some men) are glued to their bingo cards, and the remainder are staring at television or sitting in hotel lounges, and the old High Street, which rang with laughter years ago, is now empty and desolate. To the men and women who left Maybole half a century ago this would be the greatest of all changes in their hometown and no doubt if they returned they would miss the couthy country atmosphere, when time was of little importance, and friends could gather to "ca' the crack" on a Saturday evening when the week's work was over, and the husbands and wives would "daun'er" up the street for the household messages and glean the news of events in the district over the past week. Progress is not necessarily advancement in all things and certainly progress in transport, roads, etc., has brought the happy and friendly life in most small country towns to a standstill. The population of the burgh has steadily decreased since the beginning of the century and in 1969 the figures given by the Registrar General showed there were only 4,548 inhabitants, but it is hoped the new trades will bring strangers to the old town and that they, in time, will be proud to become true "Minniebolers".

There are many other interesting facts and traditions relating to the old Capital of Carrick which unfortunately must be omitted from these tales of the town but it is impossible to deal with them all in one book. The history of over eight hundred years cannot be condensed without many stories of fact and fiction being left out, not because they are uninteresting, but from lack of space. No book on Maybole has been published for over eighty years and indeed it is practically impossible to obtain any of the old books written by the Rev. R. Lawson and his predecessors as they are all out of print and it is hoped the foregoing notes on events and people will be of interest to those who claim to be Minniebolers, whether born or adopted.